—MEETING—
GOD'S PEOPLE

ISBN: 9798866947195

Published by:
The Jenkins Institute
thejenkinsinstitute.com

Professional Editing:
Renee Crawford

Logo & Cover Design:
Andrew Jenkins

Interior Layout:
Joey Sparks

Order additional copies of this resource at:

thejenkinsinstitute.com/shop

or

tji@thejenkinsinstitute.com

We dedicate Meeting God's People *to God's People everywhere around the world. To those, like you, who read His Word and strive to do His Will. Thank you for your example of faith, love, commitment, and persistence. You inspire many and pass on The Faith through your example.*

Table of Contents

With Thanks .... *xiii*

How to Use .... *xv*

Foreword .... David Shannon .... *xvii*

Week 1 - **Adam & Eve** .... Steve Bailey *1*

Week 2 - **Cain & Abel** .... Rick Brumback *7*

Week 3 - **Noah** .... Wayne Burger *13*

Week 4 - **Abraham** .... Doug Burleson *19*

Week 5 - **Isaac & Jacob** ..... Ferman Carpenter *25*

Week 6 - **Joseph** .... Evan Butler *31*

Week 7 - **Moses** .... Bill Watkins *37*

Week 8 - **Deborah** .... Sam Dilbeck *43*

Week 9 - **Gideon** .... Lance Cordle *49*

Week 10 - **Samson** .... Kirk Brothers *55*

Week 11 - **Eli** .... Russ Crosswhite *61*

Week 12 - **Samuel** .... Don Delukie *67*

Week 13 - **Saul** .... Cary Gillis *73*

Week 14 - **David** .... Justin Rogers *79*

Week 15 - **Mephibosheth** .... Dale Jenkins *85*

Week 16 - *Solomon* ....Ralph Gilmore...*91*

Week 17 - *Jeroboam & Rehoboam* ....Dick Sztanyo...................*97*

Week 18 - *Elijah* ....Zack Martin *103*

Week 19 - *Elisha* ....George Hulett...*109*

Week 20 - *Isaiah* ....John McMath *115*

Week 21 - *Josiah* ....Barry Grider *121*

Week 22 - *Jeremiah* ....Chuck Monan *127*

Week 23 - *Daniel* ....John Moore..*133*

Week 24 - *Shadrach, Meshach, & Abednego* ....David Duncan.........*139*

Week 25 - *Ezra* ....Justin Guin..*145*

Week 26 - *Nehemiah* ....James Hayes *151*

Week 27 - *Esther* ....Dale Hubbert...*157*

Week 28 - *Job* ....Wayne Jones...*163*

Week 29 - *Micah* ....Neal Pollard..*169*

Week 30 - *Habbakuk* ....Jeff Jenkins *175*

Week 31 - *Haggai* ....Sonny Owens *181*

Week 32 - *Malachi* ....Paul Shero...*187*

Week 33 - *Zechariah* ....Billy Smith..*193*

Week 34 - *Joseph & Mary* ....Chris Pressnell *199*

Week 35 - *John the Baptist* ....Scott Harp *205*

Week 36 - *Peter* ....Jay Lockhart...*211*

Week 37 - *Andrew* ....Keith Harris *217*

Week 38 - *James* ....Steve Loyd................................*223*

Week 39 - *John* ....Denny Petrillo............................*229*

Week 40 - *Philip* ....Chris Miller...............................*235*

Week 41 - *Matthew* ....Matthew Sokoloski *241*

Week 42 - *Mark* ....Travis Bookout............................*247*

Week 43 - *Judas* ....Anthony Warnes..........................*253*

Week 44 - *Lazarus, Mary, & Martha* ....Bart Warren *259*

Week 45 - *Mary Magdalene* ....Joey Sparks..........................*265*

Week 46 - *Luke* ....David Salisbury...........................*271*

Week 47 - *Paul* ....Jim Gardner...............................*277*

Week 48 - *Timothy* ....Larry Acuff................................*283*

Week 49 - *Titus* ....Mike Vestal...............................*289*

Week 50 - *Dorcas* ....David Sproule *295*

Week 51 - *Barnabas* ....Van Vansandt.............................*301*

Week 52 - *Aquilla & Priscilla* ....Kerry Williams............................*307*

Additional TJI Titles Available...*313*

With Thanks

A project on this size takes a lot of humble servants. Over 100 ministers helped in making this material come to life. We are thankful for them all. We hope you'll write notes of appreciation to some of them as the material blesses your life.

We are thankful for our friend, Joey Sparks. He sees our projects through to the end and puts up with our (Dale's) constant irritation about when it will all be done. He handles our formatting, helps with editing, and does it all while tracking yards per play by Alabama.

Our thanks to Renee Crawford who carefully and cheerfully edited over 50 different writers' material for this book.

We are thankful to congregations who purchase copies of this book to aid their members in their growth and for individuals who gift this book to others.

We're thankful for you and pray this book blesses your life.

Most of all, we thank the Lord who loves imperfect people and reveals his faithfulness to them. All glory and praise for this work goes to Him.

How to Use This Book

In 2016, a small group of preachers organized a weekly devotional and study guide, resulting in *One Word*. TJI has been honored to continue publishing similar editions. Gratefully, *Meeting God's People* is now the sixth weekly devotional guide we have published.

There are a number of ways to use this devotional guide. You might just read it a section a day each weekday for the year. It might be that each member of the church will have a copy and you all will be reading and growing together. It might be a book you'll use for a class, a small group, or some other Bible study group. With each lesson, there is a related Scripture reference and a fitting action prompt. We encourage you to make the most of these in order to apply these sacred truths.

There is also a Digital version you can have if you would rather read it on a device. In some churches the preacher will use the sermon companion that goes with this devotional guide and preach his lessons around the theme for this year.

All materials can be ordered at *TheJenkinsInstitute.com*.

Foreword

Who would be your top 10 people in the Bible? One online site published "Our Top 10 Favorite Bible Characters" in reverse order, Ruth, David, John, Daniel, Moses, Job, Abraham, Paul, Joseph, and Peter. Who would make your list? You would likely choose your favorites based on your knowledge of their lives and their impact on your life. One of the blessings of reading scripture is getting to know other people who lived for God.

God's people on earth today are one of our greatest blessings! They have led us to the Lord, nurtured our faith, and walked with us through seasons and situations. They have been our best friends, and they make up the congregations we love. But it isn't just God's people today that impact our lives.

Scripture is full of God's people who have influenced us. What have you learned from them? In Hebrews 11, the writer told stories about 16 men and women to strengthen our faith. Paul closed Romans and Colossians by mentioning almost 40 inspiring people. Others in scripture serve as a warning.

In 1 Corinthians 10, Paul says he does not want them to be unaware of what the Israelites did, recalls some of their sinful choices and summarizes by saying their examples "were written down for our instruction." You will meet every key person and several lesser-known persons in scripture through this devotional study. I hope your goal will be to make more good friends by *Meeting God's People*. One day, you can approach them in Heaven and say, "I've been wanting to meet you!"

Thank you, Jeff and Dale Jenkins of The Jenkins Institute, for providing this resource. Your leadership and each writer will no doubt draw us closer to our ultimate Friend. We are thankful to God, who does not leave us alone, but provides His presence and often, the presence of His people. Let's meet them!

David Shannon
President
Freed-Hardeman University
Henderson, TN

WEEK #1

Adam & Eve

STEVE BAILEY

Adam: The First Man

Today's Scripture: Genesis 1:27; Genesis 2:4-7; Genesis 3:17-19

When God created the world and everything in the world, all was made perfect. God even said His creation was GOOD! If God created something, we should know that it was certainly GOOD.

God blessed His creation; then He created man. That first man was not named until we read his name for the first time in Genesis 2:20. We also learn that after creating man, all other creatures that God made had mates. Man, however, was alone. Adam had no mate.

What did Adam do all day? How was his time filled? Did Adam ever "pine away" his hours longing for some other human and wishing for a mate? Did Adam have a hobby? How was his everyday relationship with God as he walked in the Garden of Eden? Did Adam have deep meaningful conversations with God as he made his way throughout the garden? Was Adam ever "blue" in spirit or depressed? Did Adam look at all of God's creation and simply smile all of the time? The Bible does not tell us the answers to these questions.

We do know that Adam was the first human, and God created him. The Bible records in Genesis 2:7-9, "Then the LORD God formed the man of dust from the ground and breathed into his nostrils the breath of life, and there he put the man whom he had formed. And the LORD God planted a garden, in Eden, in the east, in Eden; and there He placed the man whom He had formed. And out of the ground the LORD God made to spring up every tree that is pleasant to the sight and good for food. The tree of life was in the midst of the garden, and the tree of the knowledge of good and evil." Adam was the first man.

All was perfect with Adam in the Garden...for a while.

Today, I will...pray to God and be thankful that He created mankind.

Eve: The First Woman

Today's Scripture: Genesis 2:21-22

After he was created by God, Adam was alone in the Garden without a mate. Although both Adam and the animals were created from the ground, no suitable helper for Adam was found among the animals. It was impressed upon Adam that in every case there were two animals—a male and a female. He was the only creature without a corresponding person. Although all things were created good, it was not good for Adam to be alone. A need for a companion was created in Adam. We are simply not told exactly how God took a rib and made the first woman. It is often said that woman was not made from man's head for him to lord over her, neither was she made from the feet of man so that he could trample over her. She was made from his side so they could share their life experiences together. The couple was one unit.

It is certainly interesting that Eve received life from Adam. Life in Adam and in Eve only came through life. Life creates life, and God is the Original Life-giver. There is no evolution in the biblical account of Eve's creation. God had a marvelous plan. Male and female He created them.

It was not long, however, until Eve gave in to the devil and his temptations. "Then the LORD God said to the woman, 'What is this that you have done?' The woman said, 'The serpent deceived me, and I ate.' The LORD God said to the serpent, 'Because you have done this, Cursed are you above all livestock and above all beasts of the field!'" (Genesis 3:13-14). Sin had entered the world. Mankind was now separated from God because of sin.

Today, I will...pray to God and be thankful that God created woman. I will also reflect on how sin entered the world.

Cain: The First Son of Adam & Eve

Today's Scripture: Genesis 4:1

When the first husband and wife were blessed with a child, it must have been a happy time. We do not know all of what happened as this young man grew up physically and spiritually, but we do know some things. He was taught by parents that knew right from wrong. He was taught to honor God with sacrifices as was the command in the Old Testament. Cain was a man who was a tiller of the ground and grew crops. God was not pleased with his sacrifice. Something went wrong. God had no regard for Cain's sacrifice (Genesis 4:5). Cain wanted to worship and honor God, but that sacrifice was rejected. Oh, how very important it is today for every Christian to have a heart that offers God sacrifices of praise in ways that are scriptural and pleasing to God.

The tragedy in this biblical account is that Cain ended up killing his brother Abel. For killing Abel, God set a mark upon him—the so-called "Mark of Cain"—which ensured that if anyone took vengeance into their own hands and killed him, they would have God's vengeance delivered upon them seven times worse. We do not know what this "mark" was on Cain. He went to live in the land called Nod. The word *nod* means "wander."

Today, I will...thank God for my parents and my siblings, and pray that I never fall into such fits of jealousy and rage that will forever disgrace our God. I will also reflect on how "sin has a long reach."

Abel: The Second Son of Adam & Eve

Today's Scripture: Genesis 4:1

Abel was the second son born to Adam and Eve. His name means to "breath" or "vapor." Again, we do not know much about this younger brother to Cain. We can assume that he grew up like his brother, in a home with a dad and a mom who wanted the best for them both.

There are a few things to remember about Abel. One, it is important to offer God the correct components of worship. In the Old Testament, God required the very best in people as they worshiped, particularly in their sacrifices. Two, God required each person to give their "first fruits" to Him by way of sacrifice. Third, it must have taken a great deal of faith to give the best, whether a lamb, a goat, or other animal, to God. Fourth, God expected worshipers to give their very best. In like fashion, it is now important for every Christian to offer God our sacrifice of praise in ways that are scriptural and pleasing to God.

The tragedy in this biblical account is that Cain was angry and ended up killing his brother Abel over his sacrifice of praise to God. One form of worship was accepted, one was not. How very tragic that the first family had so many problems. First, they were removed from the perfection of the Garden of Eden; second, it resulted in the first murder. This was not a good beginning for the first family.

Today, I will...remind my family how important it to worship God as He commands and that examples are laid out in the Scriptures. I will do everything possible to be at peace with the members of my family. I will pray for them daily.

God's Church Is Perfect; The Family Is Not Perfect

Today's Scripture: Ephesians 5-6

The first man recorded in the Bible was named Adam. Then Eve was created from life given to her in the form of Adam's rib, which God fashioned to design as his wife. Life was created though the union of man and woman bringing forth a son, Cain, followed by another son, Abel, to form the first family.

The score card for the first family looks like this:
- Adam and Eve were deceived by satan.
- Eve and Adam were removed from their perfect garden first home to a place where Adam tilled and was cursed.
- Because of sin, Eve was made to bear her children with pain in childbirth, as has every woman since that time.
- Two sons were born into the first marriage. (Notice marriage was between a man and a woman and parenting was by a husband and a wife, just as God intended)
- The first murder was one brother, Cain, killing his brother, Abel.

Score Card Total: Not a good beginning for the first family

Adam's family continued to grow with another son, Seth.

Many families were godly in their service and devotion to God. Some were better than others, and some "stood out like stars in the night!" There have been good parents raising good kids. However, none have been perfect, but they have tried their best. Paul told the church members in Ephesians 5 and 6 how the Christian family should look. Children are to obey their parents by honoring them. Parents are not to provoke their sons and daughters to anger. Fathers and mothers are admonished to bring their children up in the discipline and instruction of the Lord. These are vital to the family unit.

Today, I will...remind myself how I love my family. I will remember how God designed the family. I will thank Him for each member of my family. I will do my best to be at peace with the members of my family. I will pray for their daily needs. I will ask God for help to never fall into fits of jealousy and rage like those that ravaged the first family. I will look forward to being with my forever family in heaven for all eternity.

WEEK #2

Cain & Abel

RICK BRUMBACK

A Chance to Honor God

Today's Scripture: Genesis 4:3-4

The mythical Narcissus worshipped himself, sitting by the pool gazing at his own image until he passed away. There are persons so centered on self that they are known as "narcissists." Some have worshiped imaginary deities associated with nature, like the water god, Poseidon, or Ceres, goddess of agriculture. But humanity truly is called to worship the God of Abraham, Isaac, and Jacob. As Jesus affirmed, quoting Deuteronomy 6:13, "You shall worship the Lord your God and him only shall you serve" (Matthew 4:10).

Worship makes a declaration. It announces whom we worship, the honor or worth we ascribe to the one whom we worship, and what we do to extend this worship. Our worship says something about God and about us. Are we teachable? Do we so adore the Lord that our love compels us to worship as He directs?

We know how the Israelites were directed to worship because the Law of Moses provided clear guidance (such as in the book of Leviticus). But we are not sure exactly what Adam and Eve, Cain and Abel, Enoch and Noah were told to do in offering homage to the Lord. Despite this, however, we know they were instructed to worship.

Isn't it noteworthy that, although we know very little about their lives overall, what we are shown about Abel and Cain are details stemming from their adoration? Cain was a farmer, Abel was a shepherd (Genesis 4:2), and they brought their offerings to the Lord. However, only Abel's was accepted. We do not know exactly what their worship guidelines were, but the fact that they had some indicates the Lord had a way He wished to be honored. And as Hebrews 11:4 says, Abel's offering was more acceptable than Cain's.

The recipient of our devotion is none other than the Creator Himself, the One who has given to us the very breath of life. Truly, the message of the entire Bible is contained in this thought: worship God.

Today, I will...truly reverence the Lord by worshiping as He directs.

TUESDAY
Measuring Ourselves by Others
Today's Scripture: Genesis 4:3-5

On the sidelines, the jubilant players looked directly into the camera, held up their index fingers, and shouted, "We're number one! We're number one!" Ah, to celebrate victory and a big win. Sports teams and competitors invest energy and sweat to excel and reach the pinnacle in their game. Similarly, we strive to receive a promotion or achieve some distinction at work, all of which seems very reasonable. But is there a way in which people measure themselves by others that is *unreasonable* or inappropriate?

When Abel and Cain brought their offerings to the Lord, there must have been some prior indication of what God sought in these offerings, information that the two brothers should have acted upon. Whatever the instructions and reasons, the Bible indicates that God respected Abel's offering but not Cain's. As Hebrews 11:4 reveals, "Abel offered to God a more acceptable sacrifice than Cain." He must have heeded the Lord's instructions, whereas Cain did not.

Cain, looking at how Abel's offering was received well when his own was not, became incensed. Rather than correct his own activity and faithfully adhere to God's instructions, he would ultimately murder his own sibling! Rather than judging his own actions by the guidance the Lord gave, he measured himself and his work against his brother. As John the apostle wrote, "We should not be like Cain, who was of the evil one and murdered his brother. And why did he murder him? Because his own deeds were evil and his brother's righteous" (1 John 3:12).

It's refreshing to see people take responsibility for their actions, hold themselves answerable to expectations, and not try to make excuses for failure by comparing themselves with others. Heaven's counsel is intended to *provide* what we need and to *protect* us from harm. "For this is the love of God, that we keep His commandments. And His commandments are not burdensome" (1 John 5:3). He blesses us while we show our love for Him by following what He says.

Today, I will...show my love for God by choosing to do what is right!

9

Controlling Our Behavior

Today's Scripture: Genesis 4:5-7

The bumper sticker says, "Never... shake a baby." Who could possibly be guilty of injuring a child in a fit of anger? You could. I could. A data breach at a major retail chain was found to be the work of skilled hackers. Who could commit such a crime? You could. I could. The elected official was found guilty of taking bribes. Who could do that? You could. I could. It's not that we *would* do such things, but we *could* commit such sins if we allowed ourselves. Each of us is capable of amazing deeds, but we can also do reprehensible acts if we do not control ourselves and rule over sin.

Cain was angry because his offering was not accepted while Abel's was. Did he feel envy? Frustration? Jealousy? Anger? The key lies in God's statement of Genesis 4:7: "If you do well, will you not be accepted? And if you do not do well, sin is crouching at the door. Its desire is contrary to you, but you must rule over it."

We are *expected* to follow heaven's teachings and hold ourselves to these standards for behavior. This is what Cain was told. However, too many, knowing what is right, yield and allow themselves to be influenced by fear, peer pressure, or selfishness. This is what Cain did.

What is the difference between ourselves and many people who are behind prison bars, or in whose lives are disrupted by sin? In many instances the difference is a matter of self-control, allowing principle to win out over temptation and impulse.

We don't want to be one of those about whom others say, "I can't believe he did that!" God said, "Sin is crouching at the door. Its desire is contrary to you, but you must rule over it." Alone, we will struggle and lose to evil and sin. But when at God's side, with the blood of Jesus to cleanse us (1 John 1:7), sin can be resisted and conquered.

Today, I will...submit myself to God and resist the devil (James 4:7)!

The Lord Knows Our Record

Today's Scripture: Genesis 4:9-16

In the late nineteenth century, Adolf Beck was twice wrongly convicted for check fraud in England. In these two related cases of mistaken identity, Beck spent more than five years in prison. When he was finally exonerated, he was compensated for his wrongful conviction, and a Criminal Court of Appeals was instituted in the United Kingdom to prevent such miscarriages in the future (forejustice.org).

No one would want to be falsely accused of wrongdoing. We want a fair and accurate accounting of our actions. And certainly, God is able to ensure this. Bible passages in both the Old and New Testaments affirm accurate and impartial judgment by the Lord (Ecclesiastes 12:13-14; 2 Corinthians 5:10). But this also means there will be no hiding our actions from heaven. When Cain slew Abel in the field, surely he would have tried to hide the deed from potential witnesses. But the one being he could not hide from was Jehovah. The Lord confronted Cain for his execrable act and pronounced his punishment. There was no hiding from the Creator, and we still read about Cain's deeds thousands of years later. He was even listed as the progenitor of an evil habit of life when Jude spoke of those who walk "in the way of Cain" (Jude v. 11). What ignominy to have one's name used to denote a category of evil action!

But we must not forget Abel, whose life is also remembered by God. Hebrews 11:4 states, "By faith Abel offered to God a more acceptable sacrifice than Cain, through which he was commended as righteous, God commending him by accepting his gifts. And through his faith, though he died, he still speaks." Jesus Himself recalled Abel's spilt blood, calling him "righteous Abel" (Matthew 23:35).

This horrible event between these brothers, and subsequent biblical commentary, reminds us that God sees what we do, whether righteous like Abel or wicked like Cain. And the Judge will deal with us according to how we live.

Today, I will...strive to walk uprightly and be pleasing in God's sight!

Christ Can Redeem Our Worst Moments

Today's Scripture: Genesis 4:10-15

"The saying is trustworthy and deserving of full acceptance, that Christ Jesus came into the world to save sinners, of whom I am the foremost" (1 Timothy 1:15).

When the Lord pronounced the punishment on Cain, the latter cried out, "My punishment is greater than I can bear" (Genesis 4:13). He envisioned his life as that of a fugitive and expected to be murdered himself. (It's ironic that he feared being the victim of violence, the very thing he had enacted against his brother?) So, the Lord gave Cain some type of mark or designation intended to safe his life.

Despite Cain's solicitude for his own life, the Bible relates no indication of remorse for his murder of Abel. Sadly. But what if, unknown to us, in later years he admitted to himself and to the Lord that he had sinned greatly against Abel. Could he be forgiven?

With a certain twist on his words, we could say Cain was right. His punishment was too great to bear...alone. Could he have been forgiven had he turned to the Lord and admitted his fault? David found forgiveness after his adultery with Bathsheba and murder of her husband Uriah (Psalm 51). By his own admission, Paul had committed violence against early Christians due to his hatred of the faith: he breathed "threats and murder against the disciples of the Lord" (Acts 9:1); he "persecuted the church of God violently and tried to destroy it" (Galatians 1:13); and he "was a blasphemer, persecutor, and insolent opponent" (1 Timothy 1:13). It is impossible for us to know how many figures he terrorized and harmed, yet he was still able to find mercy and forgiveness with Christ.

What wrong have you committed that is so extreme that the mercy-bearing blood of Jesus cannot cover it? The answer is "nothing." We might think that it easy to forgive only our youthful peccadilloes, but we can rejoice that there is forgiveness for *all* our wrongs through Jesus.

Today, I will...be honest about my behavior, repent, and allow Christ's blood to cleanse me.

WEEK #3

Noah

WAYNE BURGER

The Loneliness of Righteousness

Today's Scripture: Genesis 6:5-13; 7:1

Living a righteous life in a world of wickedness is lonely. Loneliness is not just experienced by being alone. One may feel the hurt of loneliness when in a crowd. Noah must have felt that way because

> the LORD saw that the wickedness of man was great in the earth, and that every intention of the thoughts of his heart was only evil continually. And the LORD regretted that he had made man on the earth, and it grieved him to his heart....Now the earth was corrupt in God's sight, and the earth was filled with violence. And God saw the earth, and behold, it was corrupt, for all flesh had corrupted their way on the earth. And God said to Noah, "I have determined to make an end of all flesh, for the earth is filled with violence through them." Then the LORD said to Noah, "Go into the ark, you and all your household, for I have seen that you are righteous before me in this generation." (Genesis 6:5-6, 11-13; 7:1)

How corrupt our country is compared to the country of Noah's day, no one knows, but we live in a very corrupt and violent society. No doubt it also grieves God's heart, and at some time in the future, He will destroy this earth and all its wickedness (2 Peter 3). How do we maintain a righteous life living in a wicked society?

First, we can be encouraged to know that when we live righteously, we find favor with God as Noah did (Genesis 6:8).

Second, we must strive to be completely obedient to God as Noah was (Genesis 6:22).

Third, we must stay closely connected to our righteous family whether it is our church family, our physical family, or both.

Fourth, we must realize that our righteousness shines brighter, the darker the society (Philippians 2:15-16).

Today, I will...strive to live a righteous life to show the wicked the way to God.

TUESDAY

Believing the Unbelievable

Today's Scripture: Hebrews 11:7

The Hebrew writer summed up Noah and the flood recorded in Genesis 6-9 with these words, "By faith Noah, being warned by God concerning events as yet unseen, in reverent fear constructed an ark for the saving of his household. By this he condemned the world and became an heir of the righteousness that comes by faith" (11:7).

Think about the phrase events as yet unseen. What events had not been seen by the millions who lived at that time? The words rain and"flood were not in their vocabulary, because until the flood there had not been rain and therefore there had been no flood (Genesis 2:5-6). What do you suppose Noah thought when God used the words rain (Genesis 7:4) and flood (Genesis 7:10)?

What do you suppose the reaction was when Noah preached about the coming rain and flood? He probably looked foolish building a boat that was 450 feet long, 75 feet wide, and 45 feet tall (Genesis 6:15). Even though Noah had never seen rain or a flood, "by faith" and "reverent fear" he constructed the ark. Speaking of endurance, Noah continued to build the ark for 120 years (Genesis 6:3). It would have been easy to have given up with the attitude, "it hasn't happened yet, maybe it will never happen." What a great example for us!

How do we face what we have never seen before or at least have never gone through before? How do we handle the unknown?

First, we trust God, no matter how much of life is unknown, nor how long it lasts. Someone has said, "Never doubt in the darkness what you have learned in the light." Solomon taught us, "Trust in the LORD with all your heart, and do not lean on your own understanding. In all your ways acknowledge him, and he will make straight your paths" (Proverbs 3:5-6).

Second, in reverent fear, we work to prove that we have faith.

The results will be that we prove to the world that we are righteous, and we become an heir of righteousness.

Today, I will...face the unknown by trusting God and being obedient to Him.

15

The Olive Branch of Peace
Today's Scripture: Genesis 8:11

It is interesting that for centuries the olive branch and the dove have been symbols of peace. Some have traced the olive branch back to Greek mythology. Others have stated that the symbol even goes back to the days of Noah and the flood.

Near the end of the year that Noah's family lived in the ark, he sent out a dove, "and the dove came back to him in the evening, and behold, in her mouth was a freshly plucked olive leaf" (Genesis 8:11). (Nehemiah 8:15 shows that Hebrew word for leaf can be translated "branch"). Why did inspiration name the specific kind of leaf (branch) the dove possessed? Is there a message?

How about the fact that it was a dove which brought the branch? Like the olive branch, doves are also the universal symbol of peace and love. Is there a message?

Noah, being obedient to God, had escaped a wicked world that was at odds with God. Noah and his family were about to land on an earth that had been cleansed of wickedness and was now at peace with God. The price had been paid: The world was once again at peace with God. What a wonderful condition if our world could once again be at peace with God so that there was no wickedness and violence!

Today we sometimes hear the phrase "extend an olive branch." What does that mean? It is used when one wants to end a conflict or confrontation with someone or wants to come to some peaceful solution to a conflict. We will never bring the total world to a total peace with God, but we can do it on a personal level. Is there some conflict between you and another person where you need to "extend an olive branch" to be at peace again?

Today, I will...extend an olive branch to someone with whom we are in conflict.

The Altar of Thanksgiving

Today's Scripture: Genesis 8:20-21

The year that Noah and his family spent in the ark probably gave them a lot of time for reflection about all that they had gone through. The world they left was so contaminated with sin that "the LORD saw that the wickedness of man was great in the earth, and that every intention of the thoughts of his heart was only evil continually" (Genesis 6:5). Of the millions of people who lived on the earth at that time, only Noah, his wife, their three sons, and their son's wives were saved. No doubt they could remember the struggle of building the ark, maybe of the ridicule they received as they built a boat when the world had not even seen rain or a flood (Genesis 2:5-6). They may have remembered all of the friends who perished in the flood. By following God's instructions, as strange as those instructions might have seemed at the time, they were saved.

With all of their thoughts about the wickedness of the world and God's grace to save them, it is no wonder that the first thing they did when they got out of the ark was to build an altar to offer thanks to God. The text says, "Then Noah built an altar to the LORD and took some of every clean animal and some of every clean bird and offered burnt offerings on the altar" (Genesis 8:20).

From what kind of trouble has God delivered you recently? Did you think to thank Him? We get so busy living life that we often forget to offer thanks to God, especially if things are going well for us. God does not want us to offer animal sacrifices to express our thanks to Him, but the Holy Spirit exhorts, "give thanks in all circumstances; for this is the will of God in Christ Jesus for you" (I Thessalonians 5:18). To help us not forget what God has done for us, Christ established His church and wants His people to assemble to praise and remember Him (Hebrews 10:25).

Today, I will...remember to give thanks to God for all that He does for me.

FRIDAY

Noah and Jesus

Today's Scripture: Genesis 5:29

In Genesis 5 the inspired writer lists the genealogy of Seth, whose lineage was more righteous than that of Cain listed in chapter 4. In this list, Lamech is said to be the father of Noah. Lamech "called his name Noah, saying, 'Out of the ground that the LORD has cursed, this one shall bring us relief from our work and from the painful toil of our hands'" (5:29). What did he mean?

Lamech mentioned that the ground had been cursed because of the sin of Adam and Eve (Genesis 3:17). He also said that Noah would bring relief. Maybe he only meant that this son would bring relief by helping the work of farming. Maybe, by inspiration, Lamech was hinting at what Noah would do. The world continued to get more sinful (Genesis 6:5) until God decided to destroy it by the world-wide flood (Genesis 6-9). Noah did bring relief, because he led his family by his righteous life so that they were saved from destruction. Thus, when the ark came to rest, they were in a world that had been delivered from wickedness and had the opportunity to find spiritual relief.

As Noah brought a temporary relief from sin, so Jesus Christ brings an eternal relief from sin. Jesus said, "Come to me, all who labor and are heavy laden, and I will give you rest. Take my yoke upon you, and learn from me, for I am gentle and lowly in heart, and you will find rest for your souls. For my yoke is easy, and my burden is light" (Matthew 11:28-30). But there is also the promise which says, "And I heard a voice from heaven saying, 'Write this: Blessed are the dead who die in the Lord from now on.' 'Blessed indeed,' says the Spirit, 'that they may rest from their labors, for their deeds follow them'" (Revelation 14:13)!

Today, I will...express appreciation for the earthly and eternal rest Jesus gives.

WEEK #4

Abraham

DOUG BURLESON

Abraham Walked by Faith

Today's Scripture: Acts 7:5; Hebrews 11:8

Abraham is mentioned in sixteen Old Testament books and eleven New Testament books. God is sometimes even referred to as "the God of Abraham" (Genesis 24:42, 48; 26:24; Exodus 3:6, 15-16; 4:5; Psalm 47:9). In Genesis 12, God chose Abram and his family to bless generations. Abraham's example would impact the whole human race through both the Old and New Testaments. When Abram was ninety-nine God changed his name to Abraham, meaning a "father of a multitude of nations" (Genesis 17:5), and even in old age his faith was still steady.

Abraham's faith propelled him to leave his homeland (Genesis 12:1-10) and to compassionately deal with Lot (Genesis 18:22-33). At seventy-five Abraham packed up and left his extended family, not knowing where the Lord was leading him (Genesis 12:1-9; Acts 7:2-3). The Hebrews writer says Abraham "obeyed when he was called to go out to a place that he was to receive as an inheritance. And he went out, not knowing where he was going" (11:8). Amidst war, family dissension, famine, and his and Sarah's struggle with infertility, Abraham pressed on. Abraham trusted God even when his nephew Lot was separated from him and threatened because of the city in which Lot lived. Abraham was a peacemaker who in his wealth tried to bless and care for others.

Like Jesus, Abraham went to a foreign land full of dangers (Hebrews 11:8). He left his homeland and traveled to a place full of unknowns: people, languages, temptations, and trials. Jesus likewise went on a journey when He came to earth in the flesh (Philippians 2:5-11). He emptied himself and suffered despite the choice He could have made to avoid suffering. Jesus is the "founder and perfecter of our faith," who did the Father's will with joy (Hebrews 12:2).

Today, I will...have the faith to go where God wants me to go and do what God wants me to do. I will not allow the fear of the unknown to prevent me from walking by faith.

Abraham Didn't Have a Perfect Family

Today's Scripture: Genesis 12:14-20; 20:1-18

Abraham lied. Twice. About the same thing. But why?

Pharaoh took notice of the fact that Sarah was beautiful (Genesis 12:14-15). So, while in Egypt, Abraham asked her to lie about being his wife. After being plagued, Pharaoh rebuked Abraham and kicked them out of the country (Genesis 12:18-20). Later, Abraham would try the same trick with Abimelech, king of Gerar. The pagan king took Sarah as his wife until he was warned in a dream and prevented from touching her (Genesis 20:1-7). It appears that Abraham, "the father of faith," did not believe that God would deliver him from these difficult situations.

In addition to being liars, Abraham and Sarah were doubters. They both laughed at the promise of a son in their old age (Genesis 17:17; 18:9-15). Isaac would eventually come as God promised after they preempted His plan by allowing Abraham to have a son with Hagar. This decision had a huge impact on the remainder of their story and on much of the conflict that still exists today.

By this point in the story of Genesis, God had already made a covenant with Abraham (Genesis 15:18; 17:1-5). Later, it would be declared about Abraham, "You found his heart faithful before you, and made with him the covenant to give to his offspring the land of the Canaanite" (Nehemiah 9:8), but Abraham was a sinner with an imperfect wife. His family was not perfect. Yet, how did God use his imperfect service? How was his faith counted as righteousness? Even imperfect people through imperfect service can be counted as righteous by the goodness of God.

A God who was able to raise up children of Abraham from stones (Matthew 3:9) sent His perfect Son and because of that we have hope. Abraham wasn't perfect. The Lamb of God is our hope.

Today, I will...acknowledge my imperfections and repent of sin for the purpose of striving to have a deeper faith that will honor the Lord more today than I did yesterday.

Abraham Offered His Unique Son

Today's Scripture: Genesis 22:1-19; Hebrews 11:17

Abraham and Sarah waited seventeen years for their promised son (Genesis 15:4; 21:1-8). Through their trials with Hagar and Ishmael and the testing of time, God's instruction to Abraham in Genesis 22:2 had to have come as a shock. "Take your son, your only son Isaac, whom you love, and go to the land of Moriah, and offer him there as a burnt offering." The text does not give us the impression that there was hesitation as he "rose early in the morning" and went (22:3).

As he made the journey, prepared the sacrifice, and tied Isaac on the altar, Abraham passed the sacrifice test. The Hebrews writer says "when he was tested, offered up Isaac, and he who had received the promises was in the act of offering up his only son" adding that Abraham believed God would be able to raise the dead (Hebrews 11:17-19). What parent could imagine doing what Abraham did? Abraham obeyed God, even laying him on the altar with plans to kill him. Abraham's faith was credited to him as righteousness as he selflessly offered his son (James 2:21-23).

As Abraham raised the knife to kill his unique son, God stayed the hand of the executioner. Years later, God's unique Son would not be spared as He with wood tied to His back walked to the place of sacrifice. Though He was precious and innocent, God would allow His only begotten to be killed to offer salvation to the world. What can be said about a God who is willing to make this kind of sacrifice on our behalf? Isaac's ram has now been superseded by God's Lamb. God's offer of His unique Son has opened the door of opportunity for us to all be saved by grace through faith (Ephesians 2:8).

Today, I will...specifically thank God for the sacrifice He made at the cross on my behalf. I will think about the burdens that my Savior bore so that I through His sacrifice might be made whole.

22

Abraham Believed God

Today's Scripture: Genesis 15:6; Romans 4:1-3, 9; Galatians 3:6-9, 29

Before we help people understand what they need to do to be saved, let's help them understand what God's already done.

For Paul and other writers, Abraham's faith could be contrasted from the Jewish believers who were boasting about their own religious accomplishments. But why? While many of Paul's opponents wanted to talk about Moses, Paul spoke of Abraham's simple trust in God in Romans 4:3, 9, 22; and Galatians 3:6. In these passages, as we first read in Genesis 15:6, Abraham "believed the LORD, and he counted it to him as righteousness." In a setting where many of his contemporaries were wanting to point to their circumcisions or other meritorious works as reasons for their good standing with God, Paul reminded them that the "works of the law" could not justify them (Galatians 3:2, 5, 10), while citing Abraham as an example of justification by faith. Abraham was the one with whom God established the covenant of circumcision (Genesis 17:7-14), but even Abraham wasn't justified in this manner! While faith requires action in repentance, confession, and baptism, even these responses in faith cannot be cited as meritorious reasons for one to earn salvation.

Like Abraham, we cannot boast as if we were justified by our works (Romans 4:2). Instead, we long to experience the blessing of Abraham through Christ, even as those who are Gentiles by race (Galatians 3:14). God made a promise to Abraham that has been fulfilled in Jesus (Galatians 3:16-18). The Law helped to prepare God's people for the reality of Jesus' coming in which we could all participate in Christ, the One who justifies us by faith. By faith we all are sons and daughters of Abraham, children of promise, who have been justified by faith.

Today, I will...seek to avoid boasting about any works or meritorious actions that I believe have earned God's favor. Instead, I will give thanks to the God who has saved those who are in Christ by His grace through faith.

One Greater Than Abraham Is Here

Today's Scripture: John 8:51-59

As a kid I thought the song "Father Abraham" just provided an opportunity to dance around during Vacation Bible School, but there is a message that get lost in the shuffle (pun intended). We are sons and daughters of Abraham.

Jesus was a son of Abraham. As Jesus's ancestor, Abraham is highlighted as a key figure, along with David, in Jesus' lineage (Matthew 1:1-2, 17; Luke 3:34). Yet when pressed by His opponents, Jesus was once asked, "Are you greater than our father Abraham, who died?" (John 8:53). Note carefully what Jesus said, "before Abraham was, I am;" and how Abraham rejoiced to see His day (John 8:56-58). Jesus' hearers picked up stones to throw at Jesus because they didn't think it was possible for anyone in their day to be greater than Abraham, but they were wrong. They were listening as One greater than Abraham spoke.

Sometimes Jesus encountered people who trusted more in their family history than they did in God. Jesus said that God was able to raise up children of Abraham from rocks (Matthew 3:9; Luke 3:8). Some of Abraham's descendants failed to have the faith of their ancestor. Abraham was created, but Christ was not created. Christ was before Abraham and is more important. When some think of Abraham, perhaps they see the head of a great nation, who inherited great land, had many descendants, and had a great faith. But what about Jesus? He is even greater. He established a greater nation (the church), has greater "descendants" (Christians), and shows greater faith (at the cross). By sons and daughters of Abraham, we are in Christ. I am one of them, and so are you, so let's all praise the Lord!

Today, I will...allow the example of Abraham to help me be even more thankful for Jesus. I will commit to making sure that any character study from Scripture I engage in will ultimately take me back to Jesus and help me to love Him even more.

WEEK #5

Isaac & Jacob

FERMAN CARPENTER

Faithful Fathers

Today's Scripture: Genesis 18:19

It is doubtful that Abraham would have acquired the designation "father of the faithful" had he failed as a father. Before Abraham became a father, he was first a man of God. He had an unparalleled faith that had a hold on Jehovah God few people ever experienced. His background of experience enabled him to convey his faith and abiding loyalty to his son Isaac and grandson Jacob.

Fathers today who have a strong faith and trust in God can be successful in helping their children clasp the hand of our Heavenly Father. If Abraham had failed at parenting, it would have kept the designation "the God of Abraham, Isaac, and Jacob" from ever becoming a meaningful expression. For Abraham, it was essential that he lead his first and second generations to Jehovah. Abraham was blessed to be the father of Isaac for seventy-five years. Isaac's son Jacob was fifteen when his grandfather died. These must have been rich and rewarding years for Isaac and Jacob as they enjoyed firsthand the beautiful fruits of Abraham's faithfulness.

In Genesis 18:19 (NKJV), God said about Abraham, "For I have known him, in order that he may command his children and his household after him, that they keep the way of the LORD, to do righteousness and justice, that the LORD may bring to Abraham what He has spoken to him."

When we have more modern-day Abrahams leading their families to Christ, we will have more faithful children growing and living surrendered lives to the Savior.

The faithfulness of Abraham led Isaac and Jacob to be faithful men of God. What kind of confidence can our Heavenly Father place in us regarding our success in bringing our children up in the training and admonition of the Lord (Ephesians 6:4).

Today, I will...pray for all parents to live surrendered lives before God and diligently bring up their children to "fear God and keep His commandments" (Ecclesiastes 12:13 NKJV).

Faith Greater than Fear

Today's Scripture: Genesis 22:1-19

Maybe the most interesting part of the life of Isaac is when he was about to be killed by his father and offered as a burnt sacrifice. When we read Genesis 22:1-19 (NKJV), it is so easy to focus our minds on Abraham. Nevertheless, have you ever thought about what could have been running through the mind of Isaac when he realized that he was about to be the burnt sacrifice?

As they approached the place where the offering would be made, Isaac asked Abraham where the lamb was. Abraham answered Isaac, "My son, God will provide for Himself the lamb for a burnt offering" (v. 8 NKJV).

The next scene could have been the most frightening situation for Isaac. "Then they came to the place of which God had told him. And Abraham built an altar there and placed the wood in order; and he bound Isaac his son and laid him on the altar, upon the wood" (v. 9 NKJV).

The Bible does not say if Isaac reacted, but we can assume there was no struggle. By this time, Isaac could have been a teenager or older. He could have been old enough to resist, but he willingly let his father bind and offer him.

As Christians, Jesus tells us to "be faithful unto death" (Revelation 2:10 NKJV). Isaac was indeed a faithful man, even during his youth. There is no doubt that the thought of being killed and burned sent a flood of fear through Isaac's mind. As he lay down there and watched his father raise a big knife to drive through his body, he did not resist but lay still. We can see that his faith was greater than his fear. Isaac was courageous and believed his father when he said, "God will provide for Himself the lamb." Isaac was willing to be faithful even to the point of death.

In the same manner, Christians are expected to sacrifice their lives in the service of God. In the new covenant with God, we are not expected to kill a lamb and lay it as an offering. On the contrary, God wants us to do a greater sacrifice. "I beseech you therefore, brethren, by the mercies of God, that you present your bodies a living sacrifice, holy, acceptable to God, which is your reasonable service" (Romans 12:1 NKJV). God expects us to surrender our lives to Him without holding anything back. We must present our lives as living sacrifices to Him, sacrifices that are holy and acceptable. It is only through living our lives for God that we will surely find fulfillment in this life.

Today, I will...pray that no matter how dark and uncertain our future may be that we will boldly say: "The Lord is my helper; I will not fear. What can man do to me?" (Hebrews 13:6 NKJV).

WEDNESDAY
Faith Holds On
Today's Scripture: Genesis 32:22-32

Jacob is popularly known as the man who wrestled with God. The Bible said that a "Man wrestled with him until the breaking of day" (Genesis 32:24 NKJV). We know this Man will later be known as God.

Of course, God could have easily won the match. However, the point of the whole wrestling match was not about who would win, but to test the faith of Jacob. At this point in time, Jacob recognized that he couldn't continue relying on his own ability and wit to acquire blessings. He knew that it was only God who would be able to give him genuine blessings.

God wanted to know how badly Jacob wanted the blessing. He wanted to see how far his perseverance would take him and see his limit. To further test Jacob, God "touched the socket of his hip; and the socket of Jacob's hip was out of joint as He wrestled with him" (v. 25). So, in pain and tears, Jacob wrestled with God (Hosea 12:3-4).

Finally, when the day was dawning, God told to Jacob to let Him go. Jacob responded, "I will not let You go unless You bless me!" This is where Jacob finally obtained God's blessings. His "name shall no longer be called Jacob, but Israel."

It is true that following God and keeping His commandments are not always easy. As a matter of fact, "We must through many tribulations enter the kingdom of God" (Acts 14:22 NKJV). However, this must not discourage us, but rather inspire us. We know that something is worth it when it is difficult.

The Christian race is not a sprint, but a marathon. We must keep going. The price is never found in the beginning, but at the end! The road to eternal life is not an easy path to take. There are a lot of challenges and obstacles. But we can be assured that it will be all worth it when we have already finished our Christian race. For it is written; "Eye has not seen, nor ear heard, nor have entered into the heart of man the things which God has prepared for those who love Him" (1 Corinthians 2:9 NKJV).

Today, I will...pray that no matter how long and hard our struggles may be that we hold on to what Paul said, "be steadfast, immovable, always abounding in the work of the Lord, knowing that your labor is not in vain in the Lord" (1 Corinthians 15:58 NKJV).

Seek God's Will

Today's Scripture: Genesis 25:20-34; 27:1-40

It was obvious that Isaac favored his son Esau more than Jacob. He was more than willing to give the double portion of his inheritance to Esau. It was the custom of the land—the elder brother must receive more inheritance than his younger siblings. But this did not happen in the case of Esau and Jacob.

Before Esau and Jacob were born, the Lord said to Rebekah: "Two nations are in your womb, two peoples shall be separated from your body; one people shall be stronger than the other, and the older shall serve the younger" (Genesis 25:23 NKJV).

Isaac might have also known about this prophecy, if Rebekah had told him. This was the will of God from the very beginning. However, it is important to note that God was not playing favorites here as well, because Esau possessed the wrong attitude. Esau did not put enough importance on his birthright. As a matter of fact, he sold it to Jacob for bread and a bowl of stew (Genesis 25:33). The Genesis account further added, "Thus Esau despised his birthright" (v. 34 NKJV).

When the time finally came to give the blessing to Esau, Isaac was deceived and blessed Jacob instead. When Isaac realized that he had blessed the wrong person, he "trembled exceedingly" and wept (Genesis 27:33 NKJV). At that point in time, Isaac recognized that it was really the will of God. He knew that what had transpired was contrary to the tradition of the land. He could have withdrawn the blessing he had given to Jacob since it was done in deceit. Nevertheless, Isaac submitted to the will of God and said to Esau, "Indeed I have made him your master, and all his brethren I have given to him as servants; with grain and wine I have sustained him" (Genesis 27:37 NKJV). For this reason, we read in Hebrews 11:20 (NKJV): "By faith, Isaac blessed Jacob and Esau concerning things to come."

Like Isaac, we might have our own plans and wants for our lives. However, we must align our will to God's will if we really want to live lives pleasing to Him. If there is something that we want to happen in our lives, we must seek the will of God.

God's will is perfect and we can never improve something that is already perfect. We can always have the confidence that God's plan is way better than our plans, far more than what we can imagine. Yes, it is undeniable that sometimes life is often unfair, but God is always fair, just, and merciful. When our plans fail, we can take comfort from this beautiful passage: "For I know the thoughts that I think toward you, says the LORD, thoughts of peace and not of evil, to give you a future and a hope" (Jeremiah 29:11 NKJV).

Today, I will...pray that I humble myself in the sight of the Lord and seek His will and not my own.

They Finished Well

Today's Scripture: Hebrews 11:20-21

The expression "They Finished Well" could certainly be said of Isaac and Jacob. Their names are mentioned no less than 480 times throughout the inspired, infallible, and everlasting Word of God, and no less than 40 times in the New Testament. Not because they were perfect, but because they finished well. The Bible reveals to us their lives as they really were—the good, the bad, and the ugly.

We can profit and learn from the study of Isaac's and Jacob's lives, not only in studying their good points but also their weak points. If we choose to look at only the good part of their lives, we would assume that their characters were impeccable, without flaws or blemish. On the other hand, by only examining Isaac and Jacob when they stumbled, they would appear to be weak, frail, faulty, and completely unusable in serving the Heavenly Father. However, one's life is not one huge sentence. One's life, like Isaac's and Jacob's, is broken up into verses, punctuated sometimes very strangely and surprisingly. To pick out any one sentence from a chapter and say, "This is who they are," is a cruel and great injustice. Certainly, one event can alter our life, but it does not reveal our whole story. Rather, one's life is the sum total of all those events that cast our characters and mold our lives. "By faith Isaac blessed Jacob and Esau, even regarding things to come. By faith Jacob, as he was dying, blessed each of the sons of Joseph, and worshiped, leaning on the top of his staff." (Hebrews 11:20-21 NASB 1995).

One of the greatest lessons of Isaac was his submission to his father. Isaac willingly laid down his life, submitting to his Abraham (Genesis 22:9). Jesus submitted to His Father's will and laid down His life for our sins (Luke 22:42, Romans 5:8). One of the greatest lessons of Jacob was his change. The life of Jacob was not perfect. There was a lot of family drama, deception, and confusion. But in the end, Jacob changed, becoming a faithful patriarch.

The story of Isaac and Jacob in many ways parallels and foreshadows Christ's life and points directly to the Savior's lineage. This proves that no matter how we start off in life, God can change us for the better. Isaac and Jacob valued their past and heritage. If we fail to embrace and value our Christian heritage, we will have no future blessing. In Christ, we have a good heritage. We must value the commitment and cost of His sacrificial life, and the faithfulness of previous generations who would not compromise their faith in God. They too had to look to God's Word to pass along truth to us. If we do not value God's Word, we will lose the distinction of being the Lord's church, and future generations will be in jeopardy on our watch.

Isaac and Jacob's names were the last in the string of those beloved names as God revealed Himself to be "the God of Abraham, Isaac, and Jacob." May we be the generation that reveals Him in our day. May we, like Isaac and Jacob, value the blessings and birthright offered to us through Scripture and rejoice in the faithfulness of our God by trusting and obeying His word and "finish well."

Today, I will...pray that for the rest of my life I will trust in the LORD with all my heart and lean not on my own understanding, and in all my ways I will acknowledge HIM, and HE will direct my path (Proverbs 3:5-6).

WEEK #6

Joseph

EVAN BUTLER

Joseph and Partiality
Today's Scripture: Genesis 37:1-28

Jesus loves the little children, All the children of the world,
Red and yellow, black and white, They are precious in His sight,
Jesus loves the little children of the world.

These are words to a familiar song with a lesson that is easily understood. However, showing partiality or favoritism to one individual over another is an ongoing topic of discussion in the world today. We learn from Israel that troubles arise when we show respect of one over others. "Now Israel loved Joseph more than any other of his sons, because he was the son of his old age. And he made him a robe of many colors. But when his brothers saw that their father loved him more than all his brothers, they hated him and could not speak peacefully to him" (Genesis 37:3-4).

Partiality can lead to envy and jealousy on the part of those who feel neglected (Genesis 37:11). Jealousy fueled Joseph's brothers' actions. "They saw him from afar, and before he came near to them they conspired against him to kill him" (Genesis 37:18). Consider their thoughts. They stripped him of his coat of many colors and cast him into a pit. They ended up selling Joseph to travelers for twenty shekels of silver.

Men tend to show favoritism. James teaches us to think differently. "My brothers, show no partiality as you hold the faith in our Lord Jesus Christ, the Lord of glory....But if you show partiality, you are committing sin and are convicted by the law as transgressors" (James 2:1, 9). While men may look upon appearance, skin color, and social standing, the Bible teaches us to not dishonor one over another. The words of Peter to Cornelius teach us a better way. "So Peter opened his mouth and said: 'Truly I understand that God shows no partiality, but in every nation anyone who fears him and does what is right is acceptable to him'" (Acts 10:34-35).

Today, I will...strive to treat all men with the proper respect they deserve being created in the image of God.

Joseph and Peculiarity

Today's Scripture: Genesis 37:1-11

Which one is different? This may be the way that a test question is worded. To answer correctly, you must choose the answer that doesn't belong with the rest.

Joseph was different. He was one of many sons, but he was unique. Even his father recognized it. Do you recall the dreams of Joseph? Joseph told of the brothers binding sheaves in the field. He said that his sheaf arose and stood upright. To his brothers he said, "Your sheaves gathered around it and bowed down to my sheaf" (Genesis 37:7). Then he had another dream. This time, the sun, the moon, and the eleven stars bowed down to Joseph. Eventually, these dreams would prove to be true.

In 1 Peter 2:9, God's people are called to be peculiar people—a people that belong to God. How are we to be peculiar? In what sense are we to be different? In our thinking. Joseph thought about things in a peculiar way. His brothers looked to do him harm, but Joseph recognized the good that came from his life's experiences (Genesis 50:20). Are we thinking on things that will draw us closer to God? "Finally, brothers, whatever is true, whatever is honorable, whatever is just, whatever is pure, whatever is lovely, what is commendable, if there is any excellence, if there is anything worthy of praise, think about these things" (Philippians 4:8).

We are to be different in our pursuits in life. Joseph could have used his various positions to pursue selfish ambitions. But he spent his life thinking about others. How he could help others. How he could feed others. How he could spare the lives of others. He went about doing good.

May we be different from the world for the right reasons. "In the same way, let your light shine before others, so that they may see your good works and give glory to your Father who is in heaven" (Matthew 5:16).

Today, I will...strive to be different from the world in having good thoughts and pursuing what is good for others.

Joseph and Purity

Today's Scripture: Genesis 39:1-20

What is pure? You may think of a child who is free from sin as being pure. What about the snow that falls from the sky? Is it possible for gold to be refined to the point that it is pure gold? Scripture says, "Blessed are the pure in heart, for they shall see God" (Matthew 5:8). Paul wrote that we are to think about things that are pure (Philippians 4:8). John described the holy city as being pure gold (Revelation 21:18).

In Genesis 39, Joseph showed us how to practice purity in our lives. Somewhere between the ages of seventeen and thirty years old, Joseph was bought by Potiphar, an Egyptian officer under Pharaoh. He found favor in the eyes of his master (Genesis 39:6).

Joseph was willing to abstain from temptation. Potiphar's wife desired him, but Joseph refused. We must learn to reject the advances of evil that come our way. The devil is looking to catch us in any transgression. The word of encouragement is to keep watch on yourself unless you too be tempted (Galatians 6:1).

What did Joseph do? He had an answer for the wickedness. He said, "How then can I do this great wickedness and sin against God?" (Genesis 39:9). Seeing sin as God sees sin will guide our actions away from evil and towards acts of righteousness. When we sin, we ultimately sin against God. This is not where it ended for Joseph. The Bible says Potiphar's wife spoke to Joseph day by day. It also says he did not listen to her (Genesis 39:10). Sin sets us up for trouble, and we should follow the example of Joseph and run from evil.

Remember, there is a price to pay for doing right. Joseph ended up being put in prison unlawfully. He was charged with that which he never did or intended to do.

Today, I will...strive to live a pure life and pay the necessary price for doing so.

Joseph Is a Servant of the Lord

Today's Scripture: Genesis 40; 41:9-13

"It shall not be so among you. But whoever would be great among you must be your servant, and whoever would be first among you must be your slave, even as the Son of Man came not to be served but to serve, and to give his life as a ransom for many" (Matthew 20:26-28). Christ left us an example that we should follow. We also see that Joseph was willing to be a servant. When his father sent him to check on his brothers in the field, he said, "Here I am"(Genesis 37:13).

Who will serve the Lord? Who is willing to serve their fellow man? First, there must be a willingness to serve. Do you recall Isaiah's call to service and his response? "And I heard the voice of the Lord saying, 'Whom shall I send, and who will go for us?' Then I said, 'Here am I! Send me'" (Isaiah 6:8). May we develop the desire and willingness of Joseph and Isaiah.

May we never forget that our service is to the Lord. Sometimes, like Joseph, we might find ourselves in unexpected roles of service. Do you think Joseph planned on being a servant of Potiphar, the cupbearer, the baker, or Pharaoh? However, he was seeking to accomplish a greater good. He even served while in prison. "And Pharaoh was angry with his two officers, the chief cupbearer and the chief baker, and he put them in custody in the house of the captain of the guard, in the prison where Joseph was confined. The captain of the guard appointed Joseph to be with them, and he attended them. They continued for some time in custody" (Genesis 40:2-4). Later, the chief cupbearer remembered Joseph while talking with Pharaoh and referred to him as a servant (Genesis 41:12).

As we look to Christ, let us also look to the example of Joseph in learning how to become a better servant.

Today, I will...have the desire to serve and never forget that my service is to the Lord.

Joseph Purposes to Do Good

Today's Scripture: Genesis 50:18-21

First Corinthians 13:5 tells us love is not resentful. That is, it keeps no record of wrongs. How easy it is to keep a record of the times that we have been wronged. Some people allow this to direct their lives. Joseph could have been such an individual because of everything he had suffered at the hands of others.

Joseph told of the coming of a famine. The famine struck. and Joseph's brothers came to Egypt to buy grain. They bowed down before Joseph. Remember the circumstances that led to this. First, they had sold their brother to a traveling caravan. Some of them wanted to kill him. Later, they were at his feet, saying "We are all sons of one man. We are honest men. Your servants have never been spies" (Genesis 42:11).

What did Joseph do? What would you do? Joseph showed them kindness and gave them grain to carry back to their family. Joseph did this same thing a second time filling their sacks with food and returning their money to them.

Joseph purposed to do good time and time again. He provided for his family. This one who was hated by his own would not allow their prior actions to dictate his practice later. He told his brothers, "There I will provide for you, for there are yet five years of famine to come, so that you and your household, and all that you have, do not come to poverty" (Genesis 45:11).

Do not live waiting for the opportunity to "get even" for all of the times that others have wronged you. It will be a miserable existence. After the death of Jacob, Joseph's brothers wanted to make sure that Joseph would not do them harm. Joseph said, "'So do not fear; I will provide for you and your little ones.' Thus he comforted them and spoke kindly to them" (Genesis 50:21).

Today, I will...strive not to keep record of the times I have been wronged, and I will purpose to do good.

WEEK #7

Moses

BILL WATKINS

The Need for Courageous Parents

Today's Scripture: Hebrews 11:23

Four hundred years had passed since Joseph brought his family to Egypt. During that time, Joseph was forgotten, his people increased greatly, and the Egyptians had enslaved them. To stop the population growth of the Israelites, Pharaoh had decreed that all newborn Israelite males be killed (Exodus 1:22).

Amram and Jochebed bore Moses and hid him for as long as they could, but it was clear after three months that they had to do something more. So, they made a basket of bulrushes, put him in it, and placed it in the river. His sister, Miriam, was told to watch the baby and see what would happen.

As you probably know, Moses was found by Pharaoh's daughter and raised as a part of the royal family. His own mother became his nurse.

Their reason for hiding the child was not because of their fear of Pharaoh. It was because of their love for God and for the child.

There is a principle here that holds true in all ages. The more we fear God, the less we fear people—even powerful people.

The world we live in today is just as hostile towards the people of God as it was in the days of Moses. The tactics are different, but the hostility remains. Today, the world uses peer pressure, shame, and the allure of popularity, wealth, and power.

As Moses' parents protected him, today's parents must protect their children as well. Godly parents must be people of the courage that comes from the love and fear of God. If we hope to raise courageous children, we must be courageous ourselves. Our times call for it, our children deserve it, and our God demands it!

Today, I will...put my faith in God rather that the things of the world that are passing. I will look to the day with courage and the determination not to let go of God in the face of pressure, criticism, shame, or difficulties. I will live and speak in such a way that people will see that this is God's world, made for God's glory, and for God's purpose.

The Value of Faithful Teaching

Today's Scripture: Exodus 2:5-10; Hebrews 11:24-25; Romans 10:17

How was it that Moses knew that he was a part of the Israelite nation and destiny? Hebrews 11:24 says that he knew and chose "by faith." Romans 10:17 tells us that faith comes from hearing God's Word. Who taught him these things? It seems quite clear that he was taught these things by his mother when he was young.

In a world where the role and influence of parents is often ridiculed and minimized, there is still no relationship more powerful than that of a parent to a child. Because of the teaching of his parents, Moses knew who he was and to whom he belonged. Our children need to know these things as well.

Today, I will...live in a way and speak in a way that will help others discover who they are, where they come from, to whom they belong, and the destiny God has planned for them. I will not be intimidated because I am one voice among billions. I will be God's voice, and He is more than a majority.

Human Wisdom Is Not Enough—But God Is

Today's Scripture: Exodus 2:11-15; Acts 7:23-25

God's timing and our timing are almost never the same. Moses knew that he was not an Egyptian. He knew that he was an Israelite. He knew that God's people were oppressed, and he knew that he was in a position to do something about it. So, Moses sought to begin to do something about it.

But his timing was not God's timing.

If Moses had succeeded in bringing about an insurrection, how many Israelite lives would have been lost? God had a better plan, but Moses didn't know that yet. He acted on his own wisdom, but human wisdom is never enough. Moses' actions make sense from a human point of view, but real wisdom does not come from human wisdom, or ingenuity, or insight—it comes from God.

Moses would become the great leader and deliverer of Israel, but it would be in God's own time and God's own way.

"They who wait for the LORD shall renew their strength; they shall mount up with wings like eagles; they shall run and not be weary; they shall walk and not faint" (Isaiah 40:31).

Today, I will...pray for God to give me patience while He unfolds His plan for my life. I will not be anxious to do everything on my own. I will remember that I am not alone and that I am in the hands of the One who made the worlds.

When You Feel You Are Not Enough

Today's Scripture: Exodus 3:10-12; 4:1-2, 10-11

Earlier in his life, Moses believed that God would deliver Israel out of slavery through him. Time and disillusionment convinced him that he was not that person. When God commissioned him to bring His people out of Egypt, Moses felt inadequate to the task.

He says, "Who am I that I should go to Pharaoh and bring the children of Israel out of Egypt?" (Exodus 3:11). God's answer is stunning. He did not say, "Moses, your training and position in Egypt make you the ideal person." Instead, He said, "I will be with you" (v. 12) God's call on our life is not dependent on our ability or insight. When we are not enough—God is! "If God is for us, who can be against us?" (Romans 8:31).

When Moses said, "They will not listen to me" God asked, "What is that in your hand?" (Exodus 4:2). God does not ask us to use what we do not have. He takes our hands and what is in our hands and uses them to accomplish His purpose. It may be as insignificant as a staff, but God can use it to do great things. When God calls you, what you have in your hand is enough.

God was patient with Moses and his doubts. But when Moses said, "Send someone else," God got angry. When God calls you, He accepts no substitutes. Trust Him. God knows what He is doing. If He calls you, He supplies everything you need to fulfill the task. "My God will supply every need of yours according to his riches in glory in Christ Jesus" (Philippians 4:19).

Today, I will...trust that God knows everything I need and remember that He has put me in this place in my life for a purpose.

FRIDAY
A Prophet Like Me
Today's Scripture: Deuteronomy 18:15-19

Moses was an amazing prophet of God. He had a unique relationship with God. Exodus 33:11 says that "The LORD used to speak to Moses face to face, as a man speaks to his friend." The Scriptures do not say that of any other prophet in the Old Testament.

But God revealed to Moses that there would one day be Another with whom God would have such a relationship. You know His name—Jesus. And you know that He is more than a prophet—He is the Son of God, our Savior, our Lord, our King, our Brother. He sits at the right hand of God and makes intercession for us. He is our Redeemer, and one day He will be our Judge.

I find it fascinating that God used the greatest prophet of the Old Testament to point us to One who is even greater. Moses, like all the Old Testament, let's us know that the story of his life was not simply given to entertain us with history, valor, or struggle. All of this was given so that we can see the threads of history being woven together by God to create His great tapestry of life. And the pattern on the tapestry is the face of Christ!

Today, I will...thank God that history—even my history—has a purpose and a place in the great tapestry of God. I will believe that all of my life—both the bright and the dark experiences—are a part of the glorious work of God. And I will believe that one day it will all become clear to me. Until that day, I will trust that God knows what He is doing—with the world and with me.

WEEK #8

Deborah

SAM DILBECK

Leading with Wisdom

Today's Scripture: Judges 4:1-5

At a time when the children of Israel were caught in a vicious cycle between faithfulness and faithlessness, God employed judges to lead them back from dereliction and out of persecution. Deborah was one of those storied judges. Deborah was the only woman to serve as a judge of God's people, and as only one of a handful of women to reach a position of power in ancient Israel.

In her own words, she "arose as a mother of Israel" (Judges 5:7). What quality elevated Deborah above her contemporaries? Her leadership. She led the people against superior enemies: Jabin, the king of Canaan, and Sisera, the commander of his armies.

Deborah's wisdom made her a great leader. While "the people of Israel again did what was evil in the sight of the Lord" (Judges 4:1), Deborah "was judging Israel at that time" (Judges 4:4). She spoke the word of God to the people who came to her for her judgments (Judges 4:5). Before an army was raised or a plan of action devised, she was already acting as a leader for God.

Wisdom stands out in a crowd. It elevated Deborah, aided Solomon, and it indwelled Jesus. Wise people usually lead people. They use their knowledge to make good decisions and offer sound advice. Others naturally gravitate towards their influence and grow from the relationship.

To be good leaders, we need to seek wisdom and understanding. James spoke of two kinds of wisdom: the wisdom from above and the wisdom from below (James 3:13-18). Paul referred to them as the wisdom of God and the wisdom of the world (1 Corinthians 1:18-31). We get the wisdom from above through prayer (James 1:5) and study (2 Timothy 2:15). By using God's wisdom, we can make good decisions in every sphere of life—salvation, home, church, work, relationships, etc.

Today, I will...pray for wisdom because God wants to use me to change my part of the world.

Leading by Example

Today's Scripture: Judges 4:6-10

The "do as I say, not as I do" approach to parenting or leadership seems unfair. As we get older, we understand better the roles of children and adults, but we still see a disconnect when leaders dictate instead of demonstrate.

Deborah was a mighty leader of the Israelites. Her leadership was born out of her character. When the people were oppressed by the Canaanites, she summoned Barak and gave him God's instructions (Judges 4:6-7). Barak was to gather an army of 10,000 to Mount Tabor, then engage the Canaanite army at the Kishon River where God would deliver victory to Israel.

Barak was understandably hesitant. The Canaanites outnumbered the Israelites and were better equipped, commanding 900 chariots of iron (Judges 4:3, 13). He told Deborah, "If you will go with me, I will go, but if you will not go with me, I will not go" (Judges 4:8). The task seemed too daunting. Despite her other duties, she bravely agreed to go with the army into battle.

Great leaders take the time to lead by example. They get in the trenches and demonstrate by their actions. Whether it is joining the widget assembly line or loading goods on a truck, workers and lower-level members of an organization appreciate leaders who know the job. In their book, *Primal Leadership*, Goleman, Boyatzis, and McKee call this "resonant leadership" because it resonates with people.

When good leaders need to deliver bad news or to push people out of their comfort zones, they do it in person. Deborah was with the army when it was time to attack and said, "Up! For this is the day in which the LORD has given Sisera into your hand" (Judges 4:14). The initial push into battle is frightful, but Deborah was there to help avert some of those fears and steel the hearts of the warriors. That's leading by example.

Today, I will...set the example of righteousness I want others to follow.

Leading through Motivation

Today's Scripture: Judges 5:1-23

The Pareto Principle, often called the "80/20 Rule", states that 80 percent of the outcome results from 20 percent of the input. In the church, it is often interpreted as 80 percent of the work is done by 20 percent of the people. This ratio is often questioned, but what is not questioned is the need to get Christians involved in the church's mission.

Good leaders motivate people to do the hard work. History is filled with coaches, generals, and CEOs who have been instrumental in motivating their people to overcome insurmountable odds. Deborah was one such leader. As the only female judge of Israel, she was able to motivate many to get involved in a fight that seemed unwinnable. How did she motivate them?

First, she reminded them their calling was from God: "Has not the LORD, the God of Israel, commanded you" (Judges 4:6). Appealing to a higher authority can motivate people.

Second, she addressed concerns and objections. When Barak refused to go unless she accompanied him, Deborah replied, "I will surely go with you" (Judges 4:9). Quelling fears helps motivate people.

Third, she celebrated those who did the work. Specifically, she praised the army for going into battle: "the people offered themselves willingly, bless the LORD!" (Judges 5:2). She also praised the commanders of the army: "My heart goes out to the commanders of Israel who offered themselves willingly" (Judges 5:9). Celebrating victories motivates people to seek more victories.

Fourth, she held those who refused to engage accountable for their lack of action. She rebuked the people of Reuben, "Why did you sit still among the sheepfolds, to hear the whistling for the flocks?" (Judges 5:16). Deborah made similar statements about Gilead, Dan, Asher, and Meroz (Judges 5:17, 23). Holding people accountable for failure and inaction can motivate people to get involved.

Finally, Deborah accompanied the people in battle (Judges 4:9-10). Seeing a leader leading from the front instead of pushing from behind helps motivate people.

Today, I will...motivate those around me to seek a deeper relationship with God and to do hard things.

THURSDAY

Leading with Direction

Today's Scripture: Judges 4:12-16

As a child, I was grounded for bad behavior on a particular occasion. Unfortunately, I did not understand the concept of being grounded or restricted. The next day, I went to play with some friends a couple of blocks away. When my dad found me, my punishment escalated. If I had more instruction when I first got into trouble, I might not have received a "whooping" later!

How important are good directions? Most of us would agree directions are essential to success. Whether it is a task at work or maneuvers in war, we need clear, concise directions to accomplish our goals.

Deborah was called to be a judge and deliverer of Israel. She called upon Barak to muster a small militia to fight against King Jabin and the Canaanites. In her charge to Barak, she gave him specific directions. She told him how many warriors to gather, where to assemble, what tribes to call upon, whom to engage in battle, and where to fight the battle (Judges 4:6-7). When Deborah finished giving directions, Barak had a clear understanding of his mission.

Barak went to Mount Tabor and mustered an army of 10,000 soldiers from Zebulun and Naphtali. When Sisera, the opposing general, heard of Barak's army, he marched against him with 900 chariots of iron. The two armies clashed at the Kishon River. There, God destroyed the Canaanites with Barak's forces and a flash flood (Judges 4:15; 5:4-5).

Good leaders do not leave their people guessing on what comes next or how to accomplish their assigned tasks. They give clear directions to their teams that will lead them to success. If we leave people guessing, they will begin second-guessing our leadership.

Today, I will...focus on the outcomes I expect and develop step-by-step directions on how to accomplish those outcomes.

Leading with Trust

Today's Scripture: Psalm 23; 1 John 4:4

As individuals, we may feel small and inadequate for the challenges we face. Maybe we do not have the skills or knowledge to be successful. Maybe we lack strength or fortitude. For whatever reason, we all face those moments of uncertainty and doubt.

Barak certainly felt that when Deborah called him to battle, but Deborah herself seemed confident, brave, and assured. What gave her a sense of competence? Trust. The Bible called her a prophetess, meaning she was a spokeswoman for God. It was not her position that gave her confidence— it was her trust in God. Deborah could not defeat the Canaanites by herself. The under-equipped Israelites could not gain the victory alone. Deborah did not put her trust in Barak, the army, or herself. Her trust was in God and God only.

This same kind of trust was exemplified by Jesus during His ministry. Speaking of Himself, Jesus said, "I can do nothing on my own. As I hear, I judge, and my judgment is just, because I seek not my own will but the will of him who sent me" (John 5:30). When He was in the garden, Jesus prayed, "My Father, if it be possible, let this cup pass from me; nevertheless, not as I will, but as you will" (Matthew 26:39). Whatever doubt or uncertainty Jesus had was lost in His complete trust in God.

Deborah and Jesus had the confidence to face the unknown because they trusted that God walked beside them. Whatever battles we face, we can be assured God walks with us—even if it is through the "valley of the shadow of death" (Psalm 23:4). We can endure conflict, insult, rejection, hate, abuse, and anything else because "he who is in you is greater than he who is in the world" (1 John 4:4).

Today, I will...face whatever the devil and the world throw at me with confidence, because God walks with me.

WEEK #9

Gideon

LANCE CORDLE

Gideon Receives a Message from God

Today's Scripture: Judges 6:11-16

Times were bad for Israel. Their enemies, the Midianites took control and invaded the land repeatedly. They were "like locusts in number." When crops were planted, the Midianites swept in and consumed the produce. The land was "laid waste." Conditions were so bad that the Israelites were living in caves within their own land (Judges 6:2-5). The people cried out to God and, as He had so often done, He sent a prophet to remind them of His mighty works of the past and His deliverance. God did not promise deliverance in this instance, however.

In one of the strangest scenes in the Bible, the angel of the Lord appeared to a man named Gideon as he was threshing wheat. However, because of the oppressive Midianites, he was not threshing that wheat on an open plain, or high hill (as common sense and practice would dictate). Rather, he was down in a wine press, probably a vat. As he was going about this arduous task, a man appeared, sat, and watched him. The man spoke, "The LORD is with you, O mighty man of valor!" A smile comes to my face as I picture Gideon: tired, scared, astonished, looking around to see who this person was addressing. Though the messenger (the angel of the LORD) was referring to Gideon, it is also clear that Gideon was going to have to be convinced that God was with him. Gideon asked how he could save Israel because he was from the weakest clan of his people, and he was the least among his relatives (Judges 6:6-17).

The follower of God knows that God can work powerfully through anyone (Othniel, Ehud, Deborah, Shamgar). We need to also know that God sees us, not only as we are, but as we can be, with Him (John 1:42; Romans 8:31).

Today, I will...try to see myself as God sees me—with my weaknesses, but also as I can be, with Him as my helper.

50

TUESDAY

Sin and Suffering

Today's Scripture: Judges 6:1-10

When Gideon was called by God, he was in the midst of a national and personal crisis. The people of Israel were being oppressed by the Midianites, and Gideon was living in fear. So, it is not a surprise to know that when Gideon was visited by the messenger of God, he reacted by saying, "Please, my lord, if the LORD is with us, why then has all this happened to us?" (Judges 6:13).

It is a question that has reverberated through the ages and still haunts the followers of God. Why do people suffer? Why do good people suffer? There are some logical, even "cold" answers that begin to answer that question.

The people of Gideon's day were not following God and were suffering because of it (Judges 6:1). Sometimes people suffer because they violate God's physical laws. If a person walks off a cliff, the law of gravity brings about consequences. Sometimes they violate God's spiritual laws. Adam and Eve were expelled from the Garden of Eden and their problems were multiplied because of their sin (Genesis 3).

Sometimes people suffer because of the sins of others. Clearly, there were righteous people in the time of the judges (Ruth, Naomi). However, when the oppression from other nations came, it affected the righteous people along with the wicked. Even so, today, a person is not murdered or raped because they murdered or raped, but because someone else has decided to sin. The righteous suffer because of the sins of someone else.

Sometimes people suffer because we live in a fallen world. Disease and natural disasters come about because the pristine environment of Genesis 1 was violated by the sinful actions of Adam and Eve.

Gideon and his people were suffering because of their choices, either their own or those of their family and friends.

Today, I will...look around our world and ponder the devastating effects of sin.

Life Is Hard

Today's Scripture: Judges 6:13-14; Proverbs 3:5-6

When Gideon was told that God was with him, he responded with a question of why the suffering was occurring.

Sometimes people suffer for reasons other than their sin or those of anyone else. The disciples of Jesus were observing a blind man and were wondering, philosophically, why he was born blind. "Rabbi," they said, "who sinned, this man or his parents, that he was born blind?" (John 9:2). There was no apparent reason for the man's condition. We mortals are curious. We want a logical explanation for circumstances. Having a sense of oughtness within us, we want something on which to place blame for those circumstances. However, when a person is born with, or develops a disease, it is not necessarily anyone's fault.

When Job was tested, he was not told of the conversations between God and Satan (Job 1, 2). Even though Job was described twice as "blameless and upright" (Job 1:1, 8), he, like all human beings, sinned (Romans 3:23). Job's friends tried to explain the things that were happening to him by using their wisdom and experience, and Job did the same. The difference, however, was that Job knew he was innocent of sins that would bring about such horrific suffering (Job 31). Job was later blessed again and commended by God for his "steadfastness" (Job 42:10-17; James 5:11).

Life is hard (Job 14:1), and suffering comes upon all people, both those who are good and those who are wicked. Followers of God know that sin brings consequences. However, they should also know that God loves them and disciplines them (Hebrews 12:5-8). If we suffer, we must not jump to the conclusion that we have committed a terrible sin or that God hates us. Instead, we must trust Him (Proverbs 3:5-6).

Today, I will...carefully assess the suffering that comes to those around me and be careful in assigning blame for those conditions.

THURSDAY
Strength from the Lord
Today's Scripture: Judges 6:17-40

Most people who have heard of Gideon may think first about his great victory over thousands of Midianites while he commanded just three hundred Israelites. They may also believe that Gideon had great faith from the beginning of his discussions with the angel of God. From the beginning of Judges 6, it is clear that Gideon's trust in God grew as the relationship grew.

Early in his dealings with God, Gideon asserted that he was from a weak clan of the Israelites. However, God still wanted to use him. Gideon must have had a genuine desire to walk with God, because God did not reject him.

As the conversation continued, the angel of God allowed Gideon to request proofs of the messages being delivered. Gideon set out food and the angel consumed it by fire (Judges 6:17-23). After a mission to break down the altars to Baal in his hometown, Gideon set out a fleece of wool and asked God to first keep the ground dry overnight while the fleece would be wet. Then he asked that the fleece remain dry, and the ground be wet (Judges 6:36-40). There is no indication that Gideon had a stubborn or rebellious heart. He just needed to grow in faith.

Amazingly, Gideon later amassed a great army of 32,000 men. However, in God's plan that was too many. After having his army pared down to the meager amount of three hundred, Gideon and a companion were sent to the camp of the Midianites, where they heard the recounting of a dream that foretold the great victory of God through Gideon (Judges 7:9-14).

Do you believe in God (Hebrews 11:6)? Do you trust Him (Proverbs 3:5-6)? Our strength is not of ourselves, but of God (Ephesians 6:10). Allow yourself to grow.

Today, I will...trust God, even when my faith feels weak, and pray that He will strengthen me as I follow Him.

Jesus, the True Deliverer

Today's Scripture: Hebrews 12:1-3

Gideon lived in a time when the culture around him was much like ours. The Bible says, "In those days there was no king in Israel. Everyone did what was right in his own eyes" (Judges 21:25). How Gideon must have been inwardly challenged when the angel of God told him to "save Israel from the hand of Midian" (Judges 6:14)!

We must be careful in ascribing too much honor and power to Gideon or any other biblical hero. First, he was a mere human being. Gideon obeyed God and defeated the Midianites. He even refused to become a king (Judges 8:23). However, Gideon later made an ephod of gold, and the people worshiped it (Judges 8:24-27). Though we are not told the details of this object, we do know that it was displeasing to God. The events following the death of Gideon and the wickedness of his son, Abimelech are also evidence of his frailty.

Second, the judges of Israel were deliverers. They were raised by God to deliver Israel. Cycle after cycle, time after time in those days, God raised up a "savior," but they were woefully inadequate. They could only do what they did with the power of God.

In contrast, we have a powerful Savior. The Bible tells us that Jesus is greater than the angels of God (Hebrews 1:4), and even Moses (Hebrews 3:3). Further, we are told He is one "who in every respect has been tempted as we are, yet without sin" (Hebrews 4:15). What's more, Jesus "became the source of eternal salvation to all who obey him" (Hebrews 5:9).

The men and women profiled in Hebrews 11 serve as examples of those who walked by faith, and Gideon is in their number (Hebrews 11:32-34). However, they could not and cannot save us from our sins. Only Jesus has done that (Hebrews 9:11–12).

I am to look to (trust and obey), "Jesus, the founder and perfector of our faith" (Hebrews 12:2).

Today, I will...read Hebrews 12:1-3 and run the race set before me, looking to Jesus, my Deliverer!

WEEK #10

Samson

KIRK BROTHERS

Where Have All the Heroes Gone?

Today's Scripture: Judges 21:23

"I am not a role model." Those words were stated by NBA legend, Charles Barkley, in a famous (or infamous) 1993 Nike commercial. Let me begin my focus on Samson by being completely transparent with you: I do not view Samson as a role model. "How can you say that?," you might ask, "He is one of the heroes of faith in Hebrews 11:32."

The theme verse for Judges is "In those days there was no king in Israel. Everyone did what was right in his own eyes" (21:25, cf. 17:23). Multiple times the book notes that there is no king in the land (18:1, 19:1, etc.). Yet, the problem is not so much that they do not have permanent leadership (a key difference between a king and a judge), as it is that the people did what was right in their own eyes and not what was right in God's eyes. There was a godly leadership vacuum and a failure to follow God. Here is the outline I use for the book:

I. The Cycle of Sin (1-3)
    a. Early Success
    b. Unfinished Business
    c. The Cycle of Summarized
II. The Judgements and the Judges (4-16)
    a. The Military Leaders
    b. The Civil Leaders
    c. The Lowest Leader (Samson)
III. The Depth of the Depravity (17-21)
    a. Israel's Idolatry: Micah and Dan
    b. Israel's Immorality: Concubine and Civil War

The book describes what a nation looks like when it does not follow God. Judges begins on a positive note with early military victories and the godly leadership of Caleb. It then spins into this downward spiral of rebellion, rebuke, repentance, and restoration until you hit rock bottom with Samson and the stories of Micah, Dan, the concubine and the Civil War. So, as we move forward, it is helpful to remember that the book of Judges is more about what not to do than it is about what we should do. That applies to the story of Samson as well.

Today, I will... do what is right in God's eyes, not my own.

TUESDAY
Samson Was a Beekeeper
Today's Scripture: Judges 14:8

I have already confessed that I do not view Samson as a great role model. Yet, one of the reasons I like to study him is not that he carried the gates of a city on his shoulders, or killed a thousand men with a donkey's jawbone, or that he brought down a building with his power. One reason I like to study him is that he was a beekeeper. Well, at least he built a beehive, sort of. Samson killed a young lion and then later found a bee colony living in the carcass. I started keeping bees a few years ago and have ten colonies as of this writing. I find this story to be interesting, so please humor me for a few devotionals as I explore it.

The lions in the region of Israel during this time were likely Asiatic lions. (They are no longer in this region today but are still found in India.) They are related to African lions but slightly smaller. Adult males weigh 350-450 pounds and adult females weigh 240-360 pounds. The lion in Judges 14 was a young lion, so it would have been on the smaller end of these scales.

Bee colonies swarm when they run out of space in their homes. The queen and 40-60 percent of the bees will leave to look for a new home, while the remaining bees raise a new queen. According to Dr. Thomas Seeley, swarming bees typically reject a cavity less than 10 liters (2.64 gallons) and larger than 100 liters (26.4 gallons). They prefer a cavity around 40 liters (10.57 gallons). What likely happened is that a colony ran out of room and part of it swarmed. The chest cavity of a young lion would fit within the parameters noted above. [1]

Swarming bees will double their body weight by carrying honey to their new home (a "to-go" lunch if you will). They will need that energy to start building wax comb for food and brood (baby bees) in this home. Building comb and storing food would have been of first priority for this colony after it moved. Thus, it would not have been surprising for Samson to find some honey soon after the colony relocates. I appreciate the fact that he shared the honey with his parents, but he did not tell them where it came from. I find myself wondering why. If I found a bee colony in the carcass of a lion, I would be excited to tell someone. Was he already plotting to use it for a riddle? Was he afraid his parents would spoil it and share the info with people? Did he feel that he could not trust them? These may seem like strange questions but when I study a passage I tend to wrestle with the emotions and motivations of the characters in the story. This process helps me to consider my own emotions and motivations.

Today, I will... share my blessings from God with others.

[1] Thomas Seeley, *Honeybee Democracy*.

WEDNESDAY

It Was from the Lord

Today's Scripture: Judges 14:4

Samson set his heart on a Philistine woman. In his journey to the hometown of his new bride-to-be, Samson encountered a young lion. Filled with the power of God, he tore the lion apart. When he returned to the area, he noticed a bee colony and honey in the carcass of the lion.

As I mentioned in the last devotional, about half of a bee colony will swarm to a new site when they run out of room in their previous home. The median size of a bee swarm in the US is 11,500 bees. The swarm will travel a short distance from the old home site and stop on a branch or something similar to let the queen rest (she has likely flown only one other time in her life). Scout bees will search for appropriate sites and report their findings back to the colony using waggle dances. Other scout bees will follow the waggle dance directions, visit the various sites, and report back to the colony until there is consensus among the scout bees on the best site. The whole swarm will then fly to their new home. Typical bees in the US would prefer a nesting site approximately 20 feet off the ground. Thus, choosing a lion's carcass on the ground would not be normal but by no means impossible. I have seen and heard of colonies making their homes in all kinds of places (including in the walls, eaves, and attics of people's homes). I once had a swarm move into a wooden box on my back porch. [1]

It is possible that the colony in Judges 14 moved into the carcass because there may not have been many good choices in the area. It also may simply be that God directed them there to fulfill His purpose of inciting Samson against the Philistines.

This whole story happens because Samson wanted to marry a Philistine woman. This concerned his parents, and rightfully so. In Judges 2:2, the Israelites were warned to "make no covenant with the inhabitants of this land." Deuteronomy 7:3-4 tells God's people not to marry women from idol-worshiping nations because they will turn Israel away from God. Samson's request violated God's commandments. Yet, Judges 14:4 states, "His father and mother did not know that it was from the LORD, for he was seeking an opportunity against the Philistines."

We are reminded here that the book of Judges represents a dark time in the history of Israel, a time when "everyone did what was right in his own eyes" (Judges 21:25). The book of Judges gives us more bad examples than good ones. God did not choose each of these judges because they were good. He chose to use them in spite of their sins and imperfections. God can even work in bad choices to fulfill His will.

Today, I will...seek to live in a way that honors the will of God.

[1] Thomas Seeley, *Honeybee Democracy*.

THURSDAY

Cheater, Cheater, Pumpkin Eater

Today's Scripture: Judges 14:18

Bee larvae need the protein in pollen to grow, and adult honeybees need the carbohydrates in nectar to have the energy to work. Workers prefer fresh nectar over honey. They make honey so they will have food when fresh pollen and nectar are not available. Honey is created by drying out the nectar to reduce the water content to 20 percent and by adding enzymes to the honey. This process allows honey to last longer without fermenting than nectar alone. "A typical nest in a bee tree contains some 100,000 cells arranged in eight or so combs whose total surface area is about two and half square meters (3 square yards)."1 It is estimated that it would take about 16 pounds of honey to build these combs. In the US, a typical hive will eat about three times that amount in an average winter.

The honey that is stored for hard times becomes a blessing to human beings. Strong honeybee colonies can store more honey than they need, and that extra honey can be a food source for us. In Judges 14, we learn that the presence of honey in the carcass of a lion leads to God's judgement against the Philistines. Judges reveals a sin cycle of rebellion by Israel, rebuke by God through enemy nations, repentance by Israel, and restoration by God. God uses the judges for this restoration (Judges 14:4).

Samson wanted to marry a Philistine woman. Judges 14:10 tells us that he was headed to the wedding feast when he saw the bees in the lion carcass. He decided to use a riddle to make a bet with his Philistine guests: "Out of the eater came something to eat. Out of the strong came something sweet" (Judges 14:14). The Philistines threatened Samson's new wife, in order to learn the secret to the riddle. Thus, we get one of the top quotes in the Old Testament: "If you had not plowed with my heifer, you would not have found out my riddle" (Judges 14:18). Though the story is in fact a sad one, I cannot help but smile when I read this quote. Samson responded by killing thirty Philistines and taking their clothing to pay off his debt. In spite of Samson's poor choices, bad influences, and betrayal by his wife, God was able to use these events to punish the Philistines for their sins against Israel.

Today, I will...be careful about allowing bad influences into my life.

1 Thomas Seeley, *Honeybee Democracy.*

One Shining Moment

Today's Scripture: Judges 16:28

How does a guy prone to anger, driven by a passion for idol worshiping women (a violation of God's commandment), and who has given in to peer pressure on multiple occasions (or at least wife pressure) end up in the Faith Hall of Fame in Hebrews 11:32? Though a man known for his strength, Samson also had great weaknesses. I think the primary reason he was a hero of faith is that in spite of his faults, he believed in God and knew that He was the source of his power. As Hebrews 11:6 says is necessary, Samson believed that God "exists and that he rewards those who seek him." This reality gives me hope because I am pretty weak myself. It is also important to realize that he led during a dark time in Israel's history. His faith in God was greater than most of his day.

I tend to believe that the primary reason Samson is listed as a hero of faith is that he ended well. Samson was brought from the prison to be paraded in front of the Philistine royalty. The humiliation of defeat, blindness, weakness, slavery, and mocking would have been bad enough, but he would also have heard them praising the false god Dagon and giving him credit for Samson's capture (Judges 16:24). This is in fact the saddest part of the story. When we make poor choices, evil is honored, and God is dishonored. We know that Dagon was worshiped in that part of the world as early as the third millennium B.C.[1]

They put Samson between two pillars in the building housing 3,000 Philistines. Archaeologists have unearthed at least two ancient Philistine temples. Temples of this period featured pillars, often made of wood and placed on stone pedestals, that supported the roof in a central hallway. The weight of the roof held the pillars in place, and it was not uncommon for part of the roof to be open aired. The *IVP Bible Background Commentary* observes that the term translated as "bowed" Judges 16:30 of the ESV can mean "to twist." The idea would be that Samson twisted the pillars off their bases and the release in pressure from the roof brought the house down. Two things stand out to me as I consider Samson words to God. First of all, he asked for God's help. He believed firmly in God and knew that God was the source of his strength. I also note that he said he wanted his strength back to avenge his two eyes. He did not say anything about doing it to honor God.

Samson ended well. I have seen many leaders who did not end well. I have seen leaders, for example, who undid much of the good they had done by staying two years too long in their positions. Leaders can become addicted to power and struggle to pass the torch when it is time. Other leaders let pride get the best of them as they get older and experience more success (forgetting that the success is all God-generated (1 Corinthians 3:6). Still other leaders make poor moral choices late in life (consider the story of David). In spite of his poor choices and all the pain he caused and experienced, Samson ended well. He literally went out with a bang!

Samson's character was nothing like that of Jesus. Yet, as I think of the words of Jesus on the cross, "It is finished," I am reminded that in the end, Samson also finished the job God gave him to complete. That makes him a hero of faith.

Today, I will...seek to be faithful until I draw my last breath

[1] *IVP Bible Background Commentary*

WEEK #11

Eli

RUSS CROSSWHITE

MONDAY
Eli, the Priest and Judge
Today's Scripture: 1 Samuel 1-4

The first few chapters of 1 Samuel are the closing period of the judges. Israel was still under Philistine repression after Samson's death as recorded in the book of Judges. Eli was a priest and judge. He was the fourteenth judge of Israel. We don't know much about his priesthood and judgeship except that it impacted the life of Samuel.

An unidentified man reminded Eli that it was a tremendous honor to be a priest of God.

> And there came a man of God to Eli and said to him, "Thus says the LORD, "Did I indeed reveal myself to the house of your father when they were in Egypt subject to the house of Pharaoh? Did I choose him out of all the tribes of Israel to be my priest, to go up to my altar, to burn incense, to wear an ephod before me? I gave to the house of your father all my offerings by fire from the people of Israel" (1 Samuel 2:27-28).

The priests were to offer sacrifices (Hebrews 5:1) and teach the law (Leviticus 10:11). A good summary is stated in Deuteronomy 33:10: "They shall teach Jacob your rules and Israel your law; they shall put incense before you and whole burnt offerings on your altar."

Eli must have forgotten the privileges that were his. He apparently forgot how thankful he should have been to serve as a priest of God. Note what the man of God said to Eli: "Why then do you scorn my sacrifices and my offerings that I commanded for my dwelling, and honor your sons above me by fattening yourselves on the choicest parts of every offering of my people Israel" (1 Samuel 2:29)?

Today, I will...be thankful for the privilege of being a priest of God under the new covenant. Every day I will present myself as a living sacrifice to God and teach others about the salvation found in Christ.

Honoring the Lord Above All

Today's Scripture: 1 Samuel 2:29

When the unknown man of God prophesied against Eli's household, he said, "Why then do you scorn my sacrifices and my offerings that I commanded for my dwelling, and honor your sons above me by fattening yourselves on the choicest parts of every offering of my people Israel" (1 Samuel 2:29)?

Eli failed to honor God properly. How did he do that? First, learning to honor God is a direct correlation from learning to honor our parents. When we know how to honor them, we can better learn how to honor God. Apparently, Eli did not discipline his sons like he should. They were given too much leeway. Because of that, they did not respect their earthly father, which probably led to no respect for God. Obedience is part of this honor. Children are to obey their parents (cf. Ephesians 6:1). We respect our parents' wishes. What about God? Doesn't He deserve more? Second, could it be that Eli served well externally as a priest, but his day-to-day life was not one totally devoted to God? His daily priorities were not what they should have been.

The following is taken from *Truth for Today* under the heading "A Father's Failings":

1. Do not take God's commands lightly (1 Samuel 2:27-29).
2. Do not honor children above the Lord; if they sin, do not allow excuses to justify them (1 Samuel 2:29).
3. Do not become party with a child's evil deeds (1 Samuel 2:29c).
4. Do not accept lightly your parenting role; the way your children are trained will have a drastic effect on many (1 Samuel 2:30-36).

Eli did well at "work," but he did not do so well at home. The strength of a nation, a community, and a local church is determined greatly by the strength of the homes found therein.

Today, I will...pray for strong homes and I will encourage fathers to sincerely live for the Lord daily so that their children will have an example to follow.

The Sins of Eli's Sons

Today's Scripture: 1 Samuel 2:12-26

When we look at Eli's sons, we learn where Eli failed in rearing his children. This is a lesson on what not to do. In spite of the fact that Eli did some good concerning Samuel, his sons hurt his overall influence with the nation.

First, Eli's sons were corrupt. "Now the sons of Eli were worthless men" (1 Samuel 2:12). They were crooks. Their integrity was almost non-existent. Installing honesty is a fundamental principal fathers must teach their children. Could it be that Eli did not show by example personal integrity? One cannot teach what he does not practice.

Second, Eli's sons did not know God. "They did not know the Lord" (1 Samuel 2:12). They did not respect God, nor did they honor Him. Could it be that they did not respect God because they did not respect their father? If children respect their earthly father, the chances of honoring their heavenly Father are greater. Fathers who strike the balance of not being too strict nor too easy will be respected by their children.

Third, Eli's sons were treating the offerings of the Lord with contempt. "Thus the sin of the young men was very great in the sight of the LORD, for the men treated the offering of the LORD with contempt" (1 Samuel 2:17; cf. verses 12-17). Because the sons did not respect or trust God, they did not follow His commands about the offering.

Fourth, Eli's sons were committing immoral acts with the women who served at the tabernacle. This is an example of sin's progression. Because Eli did not firmly put his foot down, his sons went deeper into sin. "He kept hearing all that his sons were doing to all Israel, and how they lay with the women who were serving at the entrance to the tent of meeting" (1 Samuel 2:22).

Today, I will...pray for fathers to strike the balance of a firm hand with a tender touch and to daily set the right example before their children.

THURSDAY

Growing Old

Today's Scripture: 1 Samuel 4:12-22

In life, we know that time moves on. As time passed, Eli grew old and feeble. "Now Eli was ninety-eight years old and his eyes were set so that he could not see" (1 Samuel 4:15). When I get to the end of my life, what will be the most important thing to me? Will it be how well known I was in the brotherhood, or will it be how my physical family has been taught and led to the Lord? Will it be the relationships I have in my spiritual family, the church? When we get to the end of our lives, we want them to be ones of great satisfaction and not ones of bitterness and sadness.

Eli apparently died a feeble and sad man. His two sons, Hophni and Phineas, were a great disappointment to God. Eli could not claim full innocence concerning his sons. He apparently did not teach them properly or set the right example before them, and he did not discipline them like he should. The following paragraph is adapted from the book by Ray Miller, *Bible Bad Boys*:

> Eli's two sons, who were priests, had every air of religiosity and piety about them, but "They did not know the LORD" (1 Samuel 2:12). What does this mean? It doesn't mean that they did not know about the Lord, or that they didn't know anything with regard to the Lord, or the Law of the Lord, or the Word of the Lord. They would be very familiar with all of these things. But they did not know the Lord personally or intimately. They did not maintain a close relationship with the Lord. How tragic it is to say that someone did not know the Lord. Eli had to say that about his sons.

Today, I will...do all I can to make sure my loved ones understand what it really means to "know the Lord." I want to make sure that the end of my life is one of joy and peace, and not one of regret.

65

Relating to Christ

Today's Scripture: 1 Samuel 2:35

In spite of the unfaithfulness of Eli and his sons, there is a Messianic prophecy of a faithful priest. "And I will raise up for myself a faithful priest, who shall do according to what is in my heart and in my mind. And I will build him a sure house, and he shall go in and out before my anointed forever" (1 Samuel 2:35). The man of God warned Eli of the consequences of his family's behavior. They would no longer serve as priests, and Eli's sons would die on the same day (1 Samuel 2:27-36).

Who is this "faithful priest" God will raise up? Some say this was initially fulfilled in Samuel or Zadok. Most conservative commentators believe it ultimately was a reference to Jesus Christ. In contrast to Eli, Jesus' priesthood did not fail. He fulfilled it perfectly and completely. "Although he was a son, he learned obedience through what he suffered. And being made perfect, he became the source of eternal salvation to all who obey him, being designated by God a high priest after the order of Melchizedek" (Hebrews 5:8-10).

Note the following from The Books of History by James E. Smith: "Who is the faithful priest of 1 Samuel 2:35? The prophecy is best interpreted messianically. The faithful priest is Jesus, God's anointed. For him God built an enduring house, the royal priesthood of 1 Peter 2:9. Before the Faithful Priest, a 'house' or priestly family would 'walk' or minister." Because Jesus was faithful to the Father's will, we can have confidence that His priesthood is sufficient. Instead of being condemned as in the case of Eli, we are blessed beyond our imagination through Jesus Christ. Thank God for the faithful High Priesthood of Jesus.

Today, I will...remind myself that Jesus never fails, but is aways victorious in accomplishing His purpose. Also, today I can have peace believing that.

WEEK #12

Samuel

DON DELUKIE

Special Things that Gave Samuel Advantage

Today's Scripture: 1 Samuel 1-2

We are losing so many young people. Can greater emphasis in their early days help?

Let us, through the story of Samuel, learn ways to give our children special advantage. His mother prayed for his conception. (1 Samuel 1:9-11). God heard and answered that prayer, (1 Samuel 1:19-20) She wasn't looking for a child to dress up. She wasn't looking to see how he turned out. Her intention was to thank God for her child's existence by offering him to the Lord's work. The priest at the time, Eli, did not offer much help. We can't expect religious people to take the responsibility of training up a child. Handing the youngster over to a man whose own sons were out of control must have been challenging to say the least. We must remember that perfection is never found in people, not even in those leading. She knew that God could guide her son. This incredible effort of unselfishness produced one of the great characters of God's Word.

Those in religious activities may not know the Lord. The sons of Eli did not. (1 Samuel 2:12). Think about all of the reasons we keep children out of churches, out of proximity to the Lord, because there may be some unsavory character in the mix. If we ground them in God, trust Him to guide them based on our fervent prayers, and give them first-hand experience from youth to serve Him, characters like Samuel can still be generated for the Lord's work. First Samuel 2:1-3:

And Hannah prayed and said,
"My heart exults in the LORD;
my horn is exalted in the LORD.
My mouth derides my enemies,
because I rejoice in your salvation.
There is none holy like the LORD:
for there is none besides you;
there is no rock like our God.
Talk no more so very proudly,
let not arrogance come from your mouth;
for the LORD is a God of knowledge,
and by him actions are weighed.

Today, I will...give my children training in the Lord like Samuel received.

Formulating Faith in Youth Under Difficulty

Today's Scripture: 1 Samuel 3-4

Samuel's mother, Hannah made pilgrimages to see Samuel and give him clothing, love, and instruction. Also, he had been committed to the care of the Lord—providentially, to protect him from evil and messages from God. Circumstances and weak people wear us. Samuel grew and was in favor with God and man (1 Samuel 2:26). The sons of the priest created havoc, made a mockery of things, stole offerings, and were immoral. God warned Eli that it would end with their death (1 Samuel 2:34). Eli the priest was very old and required assistance. What else bolstered this young man of God? First Samuel 3:1 (KJV) says the word of the Lord was "precious."

Samuel got his first message from God (1 Samuel 3:1-10). He told Eli the priest about the end of his priesthood. This judgment would come on Eli, because when his sons became vile, he made no move to restrain them (1 Samuel 3:13). In the mix, Samuel wasn't required to fix it, he was required to be faithful.

Enemies came and took away the ark of the covenant. The two sons of Eli were killed. When Eli heard the news, he fell over backward and broke his neck.

In all of this, Samuel proved himself a man. As Solomon suggested in Ecclesiastes 11:9; 12:1, "Rejoice, O young man, in your youth, and let your heart cheer you in the days of your youth....Remember also your Creator in the days of your youth, before the evil days come and the years draw near of which you will say, 'I have no pleasure in them."

Today, I will...pray that our children can be strong in the Lord, and that we will get involved in grounding them, as we fervently beseech God's help.

Samuel Grows from Youth to Maturity

Today's Scripture: 1 Samuel 7-8

What appears to be a meteoric rise to leadership is actually a condensed version of a long span of time. From his birth to his presentation to Eli, the priest, and the subsequent actions of Eli's sons and their final demise, to his stepping up as a new leader of God's people covers the life span of Samuel.

Servanthood respects God's timing, trial and error, and suffering through tough times. The aggravation of the soul awaiting the needed changes burns many out. Elders proclaim, "I never knew, etc."

Think of the times Samuel agonized over the evil all around him. Think of the times he could not do anything about it—separated from his family, daily viewing moral hypocrisy, embarrassment at things like the ark being taken, seeing leaders become ineffective and corrupt, and wondering, "When will my time come?"

When it did, Samuel stepped up to the challenge. Instead of wondering what to do, his years showed him the answer—God's way. He turned the hearts of the people to the Lord and His Word! First Samuel 7:3-5,

> And Samuel said to all the house of Israel, "If you are returning to the LORD with all your heart, then put away the foreign gods and the Ashtaroth from among you and direct your heart to the LORD and serve him only, and he will deliver you out of the hand of the Philistines." So the people of Israel put away the Baals and the Ashtaroth, and they served the LORD only. Then Samuel said, "Gather all Israel at Mizpah, and I will pray to the LORD for you."

The Lord, the Word of the Lord, and the power of prayer to God – this is spiritual leadership.

Today, I will...consider how Samuel's humble beginnings, deprivation, menial duties, repeated for years, and dedication led to victory for God's people.

THURSDAY

Samuel Increases in Excellence

Today's Scripture: 1 Samuel 8-9

In 1 Samuel 8, Samuel was aging, but his faith was getting stronger. Samuel spent time balancing his dealings with God's people. He recognized his age restrictions and sought to place his sons into more dominant roles. The people rejected this and clamored for a king instead. God explained that they were not rejecting Samuel but God Himself. He wanted Samuel to warn them of the consequences of a king. Samuel did this, but the people rejected his warning.

Following his spiritual character, Samuel always told the Lord the straight of what they were saying, and he never altered what God told him to say to the people. Samuel knew the Lord, he knew the people, and he knew another disaster was coming on them. Yet understanding God's methods, he complied.

Samuel sought Saul, selected him, honored him, fed him, anointed him, and introduced him to the people! After repeated confrontations with a rebellious people, he still prayed for them. We must learn to serve with excellence in the midst of all kinds of situations. Samuel always stood for what was right and instructed the people to do the same. First Samuel 12:20-23,

> Do not be afraid; you have done all this evil. Yet do not turn aside from following the LORD, but serve the LORD with all your heart. And do not turn aside after empty things that cannot profit or deliver, for they are empty. For the LORD will not forsake his people, for his great name's sake, because it has pleased the LORD to make you a people for himself. Moreover, as for me, far be it from me that I should sin against the LORD by ceasing to pray for you, and I will instruct you in the good and the right way.

Today, I will...consider God's servant Samuel and serve God no matter what the circumstance.

Samuel—Faithful unto Death
Today's Scripture: 1 Samuel 12

Who do you know that has left spiritual service? Do you know why? Did it have to do with "burnout"? Have they grown weary with repeated failure on the part of God's people? Have they "had it" with all the drama? Are they exhausted with the constant problems and disappointments? Are they past the point of enduring another hypocrite? Perhaps their contributions are getting little effect and even less appreciation? Could it be...you?

What a great example in Samuel! Due to his mother's actions, he had little choice to start with. He quickly accepted and adopted the ways of the Lord. He lived in the midst of weakness and strength. Positive and negative. Without expecting others to always comply, he served anyway. He never compromised his principles. Consider this passage from 1 Samuel 12:14-15, "If you will fear the LORD and serve him and obey his voice and not rebel against the commandment of the LORD, and if both you and the king who reigns over you will follow the LORD your God, it will be well. But if you will not obey the voice of the LORD, but rebel against the commandment of the LORD, then the hand of the LORD will be against you and your king."

One thing all of us who follow God will face is conflict. Conflict may cause the loss of relationships. A sad thing , but not as sad as those who allow others to sever their relationship with God. Samuel had to face King Saul alone, confront him, and denounce him. So great was his respect that Saul said, "I have sinned, for I have transgressed the commandment of the LORD and your words, because I feared the people and obeyed their voice" (1 Samuel 15:24).

Today, I will...love the Lord, serve the Lord, and determine to be unwavering in my faithfulness in the face of every scenario.

WEEK #13

Saul

CARY GILLIS

Little in My Own Eyes

Today's Scripture: 1 Samuel 15

The power of temptation is either fueled or extinguished by how much I elevate self. The ego and the flesh want to be elevated. This mindset is so championed by our culture that people's identities are being defined by their own feelings and sexual preferences. There has been such a push to validate and mainstream evil and perverted desires that shame has become shameful. Now, it is virtuous to take pride in fulfilling any and all desires. Evil is called good (Isaiah 5:20). This pride has become such a virtue that mental illness is being enabled. In reality, sin is ruling and ruining the lives of everyone who elevates self.

God selected the first king of Israel from the humble tribe of Benjamin. Saul, the chosen of God, was said to have stood head and shoulders above everyone. Despite his stature, he carried himself with humility at the beginning of his reign. Samuel described him as having been "little in [his] own eyes" (1 Samuel 15:17). When Saul started down the royal path, he was nothing, and he knew it. In fact, when Samuel first presented Saul to Israel as their new king, he was reluctant to take center stage. They had to look around and finally found him hidden among the baggage (1 Samuel 10:22).

The humble heart does not resist or compete with God's sovereignty. The humble heart has no aspirations of being first. Diotrephes' propensity for the preeminence led him to reject John's authority as an apostle of God (3 John 9). James described the meek heart as the heart that the word of God can penetrate and transform (James 1:21). Humility is the perfect starting place for being an instrument of God's work. It was at the moment of humble self-perception that God elevated Saul to be king. And with the loss of humility was a loss of Saul's divine elevation.

Today, I will...be little in my own eyes and elevate God in my heart.

Convincing Myself I'm Right

Today's Scripture: 1 Samuel 13

As children, our parents' rules didn't make much sense. Don't eat crayons. Don't jump off the roof. Don't play with matches. As we got older, we were told to be more mature, think through our decisions, and take ownership of our faith (if we had godly parents). One of the reasons the teen years are so hard is that we are told to grow up and take responsibility for ourselves, while simultaneously being expected to submit to our parents. We had rules about dressing modestly, who we could hang out with, regular church attendance, etc. We were also good at rationalizing why those rules didn't apply to us. Perhaps we underestimated sin and overestimated our ability to exercise self-control. The older we get, the more we understand the wisdom that guided our parents' decisions. If only we had trusted them...

On at least two occasions, King Saul rationalized disobeying God. In 1 Samuel 13, he takes it upon himself to make a sacrifice to God, rather than waiting for Samuel to do it. When Samuel arrived, he rebuked Saul's disobedience. Saul rationalized that he needed to seek the favor of the Lord because of the Philistine threat. Samuel told him that his kingdom would be taken away because of his disobedience. Similarly, in 1 Samuel 15, Saul was told to utterly destroy the Amalekites. In an act of presumption, he brought the king and the best of the livestock back alive, rationalizing that they would be sacrificed to the Lord. Though he had convinced himself that he was right, Samuel told Saul that his rejection of God's word meant the rejection of his kingdom, for God desires obedience rather than sacrifice (1 Samuel 15:22).

Paul warned us about the self-deception of thinking we are something when we are nothing (Galatians 6:3). John warned us not to be presumptuous and go beyond the teachings of Christ (2 John 9). God expects His children to trust that He knows better what is best for them.

Today, I will...fight the temptation to rationalize my disobedience and just trust God's wisdom.

But Goliath

Today's Scripture: 1 Samuel 17

Standing in confident defiance of Goliath, David proclaimed that "the LORD saves not with sword and spear. For the battle is the LORD's" (1 Samuel 17:47). When an unlikely participant prevails in a mismatched rivalry, sports commentators like to invoke "David and Goliath" language. Referencing this boy-versus-giant story misses the point that David clearly understood. David was not Goliath's opponent. Goliath's opponent was God. Victory was never in question.

The only reason that David was ever in that position to begin with was because King Saul led the people with the spiritually blind mindset that Goliath had to be defeated by another man. God chose Saul for the specific purpose of defeating the Philistines (1 Samuel 9:16). When Saul knew that he was supposed to be leading the people to victory, the thought "but Goliath" paralyzed him. "But Goliath stands so tall!" "But Goliath has such strength!" "But Goliath can tear us to shreds!" In the Valley of Elah, Saul beheld a terrifying giant, and he beheld himself. Saul was really thinking "but I." "But I am so small." "But I am so weak." "But what can I do against such an enemy?"

Saul saw Goliath and himself; but David saw Goliath and God. In Ephesians 2, Paul explained how our sin has brought us into a state of spiritual death. If it's just me and my sin on the battlefield, then death is my fate. Then Paul brought a cosmic clarity to what's really going on in that valley, when he said, "But God...made us alive" (Ephesians 2:4-5). Remember, Saul put his armor on David with hopes of bringing him some kind of advantage. Truly, if David went into that valley with a "but Goliath" mindset, Goliath would have fed him to the birds, regardless of any perceived advantage. But God was in that valley, which meant that David never thought "but Goliath" or "but I." He just let the Lord do what the Lord does... win.

Today, I will...do away with the "but I" mindset and see that it is the Lord who fights for me.

One Man

Today's Scripture: 1 Samuel 11:1-11

Beautiful is a swarm of people cooking, cleaning, being present, and consoling a family in a home visited by death. Powerful is that moment when shepherds rally around one of their sheep who has been chewed up by sin. God designed the church as a body in which the members are knit together with one another. If one part of a body is injured or under threat, every member of the body joins in unison for the health of the whole. There are no go-it-alone Christians, but only a unified front in God's plan for His people.

At the beginning of his tenure, King Saul received messengers from the city of Jabesh-Gilead who said that they were under attack by the Ammonites and needed reinforcements. It is recorded that the Spirit of God rushed upon Saul...and his anger was greatly kindled" (1 Samuel 11:6). Immediately, he cut a yoke of oxen into pieces and sent them throughout the kingdom with a warning that anyone who did not step up to aid their countrymen would have the same thing done to their oxen. This act so motivated the people that they are described as coming out "as one man" for battle (1 Samuel 11:7). Among his many missteps, Saul showed a great moment of leadership in being able to rally the troops for war as a unified front. When the enemy saw the solidarity of the Israelites, they raised the white flag.

If I am part of the Lord's army, I need to fully embrace two truths. First, God expects me to ask for help when I need help. It's His plan! Second, God expects me to be a part of that unified front that comes to defend, rescue, and heal those who find the enemy invading their lives. The church needs more of that meet-the-enemy-as-one-man intentionality. We are always better together, and never better alone.

Today, I will...open my eyes to how the enemy is attacking the body of Christ and be the one who rallies God's people for battle as one man.

Our Divine Purpose

Today's Scripture: Ephesians 1:4; 4:13

Throughout redemptive history, God has used the lives of Bible characters to paint an imperfect portrait of the perfect life and purpose His Son would later embody. The dark cloud over the latter half of King Saul's reign makes it easy to forget that God was with him, that he was anointed by God, that the Spirit of God was upon him, and that God gave him another heart (1 Samuel 10:1-10). In no uncertain terms, Saul was chosen with the specific purpose of being the king who would save God's people from their enemies.

Jesus was chosen by God to fulfill His eternal purpose of being King and Savior. Christ literally means "anointed one." His ultimate fulfillment of the Father's will is described in this way, "And being made perfect, he became the source of eternal salvation to all who obey him" (Hebrews 5:9). In this verse, the word perfect does not carry the full meaning of what is being conveyed. Elsewhere, this word is translated as "complete" or "mature." It carries the idea of embodying in your life who God has purposed you to be. Jesus embodied God's purpose for Him in His sacrifice. He completed the work that God sent Him to do. While the selection, elevation, and purpose of King Saul parallels Christ, his tragic end serves as a warning that even those who have been hand-selected by God can fail to fulfill their divine purpose.

In Christ, we are the chosen of God (Ephesians 1:4). We have the Spirit of Christ (Romans 8:9). We have the mind of Christ (1 Corinthians 2:16). God has purposed us to grow up into the image of Christ (Ephesians 4:13) We join with Him as heirs of His royal and priestly identity (Romans 8:17; 1 Peter 2:9). With one foot in the presence of God and one foot in a dying world, our divine purpose is to build a bridge between the lost and the Savior.

Today, I will...be that bridge-builder, and so embody God's purpose for my life.

WEEK #14

David

JUSTIN ROGERS

David and Samuel

Today's Scripture: 1 Samuel 16

We first met David as a teenager tending his father's flocks. Like Israel's greatest leader, Moses, he was called away from shepherding to lead God's people. To set the scene, Samuel went to the house of Jesse at God's command (1 Samuel 16:1). Samuel privately approved the appearance of the oldest, Eliab, concluding that he must be "the LORD's anointed" (v. 6), to which the Lord replied, "Do not look on his appearance or on the height of his stature, because I have rejected him. For the LORD sees not as man sees: man looks on the outward appearance, but the LORD looks on the heart" (v. 7). This is the biblical basis for the well-known statement that David was "a man after" God's own "heart" (Acts 13:22). After Jesse paraded each of his sons before the prophet, Samuel asked, "Are all your sons here?" (v. 11). David's family thought so little of him that Jesse refused to call him from the field.

After David was summoned, Samuel anointed him, "and the Spirit of the LORD rushed upon David from that day forward" (v. 13). The term Spirit of the LORD seems to be a reference to divine favor in 1 Samuel. We read immediately after that "the Spirit of the LORD departed from Saul, and a harmful spirit from the LORD tormented him" (v. 14). Saul lost his divine Spirit for an "evil spirit" (literally). David became who he was by the Spirit of God.

We can learn three lessons from this episode. First, God's approval is about the heart. Physical and intellectual gifts may impress people, but God seeks a pure heart (Matthew 5:8). Second, "the last will be first, and the first last," as Jesus said (Matthew 20:16). Others may think you are insignificant, but you can become great in the kingdom. Third, God's Spirit produces success.

Today, I will...pray for the strength to surrender self to make space for the power of God.

David and Goliath

Today's Scripture: 1 Samuel 17

We love to pull for the underdog. Perhaps that's why the story of David and Goliath captivates the imagination. However, in our enthusiasm for the underdog, sometimes we exaggerate the facts.

First, David was not a small child (as Bible class coloring books have it) but around seventeen years old (the term youth in verse 42 means "young man"). Second, Scripture does not say Saul's armor was too big, but that "he had not tested them" (v. 39). Speed was the most important element on the ancient battlefield, and Saul's armor hindered David's movement. Third, David was not Dennis the Menace with a slingshot. Slings were weapons of war, and ancient armies outfitted soldiers with them. God's providence may be responsible for bringing David and Goliath together, but David went to war with deadly weapons and practiced skill.

We can learn four lessons from this story. First, play to your strengths. David set aside Saul's armor because it made him worse. Don Clifton became well-known for contradicting the mantra, "Turn weakness into strength." Instead, he advised maximizing strengths (cf. the CliftonStrengths test). We should hone our strengths, not obsess over our weaknesses. Second, be courageous. "Courage," one of the four cardinal virtues in ancient philosophy, is rarely discussed today. Doing hard things makes you better. Have the courage to engage what scares you; God is on your side (vv. 45–47).

Third, be smart. David was victorious not because of superior strength or miraculous intervention, but because he was smarter. Swords, spears, and javelins (v. 45) are short-range weapons, but a smooth stone fired from an expert slinger has a kill range of several hundred feet. Goliath never had a chance.

Fourth, be consistent. David never wavered in his faith. He predicted the Lord's empowerment (v. 37) and stands face-to-face with the enemy (vv. 46–47). Some have a faith that rises and falls with their experiences; David maintained his faith consistently.

Today, I will...stand firm in the face of the enemy.

David and Saul

Today's Scripture: 1 Samuel 18-31

No matter how successful some people are, they cannot be content. Their insecurity provokes jealousy and prevents gratitude. They view everything as a competition and ascribe malicious motives to their opponents. Saul was one such person. David rose to prominence and became the subject of a popular song: "Saul has slain his thousands, and David his ten thousands" (1 Samuel 18:7; 21:11 NIV). The song is not malicious; it merely recognizes the greatness of both men. However, Saul could not share the credit.

Saul relentlessly pursued David, all the while further disqualifying himself as king. When Jonathan attempted to defend David's innocence, Saul tried to kill him (20:30–33). When the priests at Nob offered David provisions and the sword of Goliath (21:1–9), Saul had them executed (22:17–19). When Samuel died, Saul visited a forbidden necromancer to have his spirit conjured up (28:3–25).

By contrast, David had multiple opportunities to kill Saul. On one occasion at Engedi, Saul entered a cave alone. David's men were certain that God had delivered Saul to him (24:4), but David's response was respect for "the LORD's anointed" (v. 6), and Saul's life was spared. On another occasion, David sneaked into Saul's camp and took his spear and water jug, again foregoing the opportunity to take his life (26:6–12). Finally, the Lord sorted out the rivalry, taking the life of Saul and elevating David to his anointed position (31:3–6).

We learn three lessons from this account. First, don't give way to envy. There can be no love for others in a heart full of self. Second, respect the position if not the person. David refused to strike "the LORD's anointed" (24:6; 26:11) and executed the man who did not show similar restraint (2 Samuel 1:14-16). God has assigned authorities their positions; respect God (Romans 13:1–4). Third, be patient. For ten years David suffered fear, homelessness, loss, and betrayal. Yet, through all his suffering, God was working His glory (cf. Joshua 1:5; Romans 8:28).

Today, I will...surrender to the will of God, trusting His timing.

David and Bathsheba

Today's Scripture: 2 Samuel 11-12

David's life teaches that our mistakes need not define us in the eyes of God. Adultery and murder were capital crimes in ancient Israel (Leviticus 20:10; Deuteronomy 22:22), yet David was able to receive forgiveness for both (2 Samuel 12:13). Still, David suffered enormously for his sin. The account opens with David walking on his roof. Since the palace of David rested on the eastern mountain of Jerusalem, he had an excellent view. On this occasion, Bathsheba was bathing (2 Samuel 11:2-3). Nothing in the text indicates she was naked, and perhaps she was cleansing herself from menstrual impurity (v. 4; Leviticus 15:19–24). Her appearance was visually striking and, like Eve attracted by sight to the forbidden fruit (Genesis 3:6), David's passion was stirred (2 Samuel 11:3).

Although she was married, David ordered her taken (v. 4). Scripture does not claim he raped her, but neither does it suggest a willingness on her part. The indiscretion becomes worse when Bethsheba sent word of her pregnancy (v. 5). David doubled down, summoning the hero Uriah (2 Samuel 23:39) from the battlefield. After his plot failed, David had Uriah shamefully executed (2 Samuel 11:15–21). Finally, Nathan confronted David with his sin, provoking repentance (12:1–13).

We learn three lessons from this narrative. First, by passion fed is a person led. When we surrender to our emotions, we sacrifice our rationality and allow Satan to take the place of God in our hearts. Second, sin earns compound interest. David had an opportunity to repent at each stage, but only compounded his sinfulness. Third, forgiven does not mean forgotten. First Kings 15:5 declares, "David did what was right in the eyes of the LORD and did not turn aside from anything that he commanded him all the days of his life, except in the matter of Uriah the Hittite." The sin with Bathsheba remains the outstanding blemish on an otherwise exemplary life.

Today, I will...control my temptation and remember the consequences of sin.

David and Jesus

Today's Scripture: Isaiah 9:6-7

No Old Testament figure is more closely associated with Jesus than David. Matthew's gospel begins by describing "Jesus Christ" as "the son of David, the son of Abraham" (Matthew 1:1). The connection with David is important for at least four reasons. First, David was associated with the identity of the Messiah. David wrote of Israel's "Messiah" as the Son of God. Psalm 2 depicts God's "Anointed" (Hebrew: *meshiach*, v. 2) as the "Son" of God (vv. 7, 12). Second, David was associated with the location of the Messiah's birth. It was well-known that the Messiah would be from Bethlehem (John 7:42), as the Jewish authorities well understood (see Matthew 2:4-6 quoting Micah 5:2). Third, David was associated with the position of the Messiah. As "king" of the Jews, the Messiah occupied the role David played over the nation (Isaiah 9:7). This passage makes clear that the future king of Jerusalem would be no different from the first king of Jerusalem, with one important difference: the Christ would reign over an everlasting kingdom. Fourth, David was associated with the ingathering of the Gentiles (Isaiah 55:3–5). God planned centuries before the time of Jesus to use the Messiah (the new David) to unify the world under His Messiah.

We can learn three lessons from the Messianic background of Jesus. First, he is God's King. David was the ideal king (Ezekiel 37:24), who put God first and served as an example for all rulers (2 Kings 14:3; Zechariah 12:8). Second, Jesus has an eternal kingdom. This kingdom "will never be destroyed," as Daniel says (Daniel 2:44 NIV), and thus remains for us today (cf. Hebrews 12:28). Third, David wrote of Jesus' death. Psalm 22 is a virtual program of the crucifixion, beginning with those haunting words, "Eli, Eli lema sabachthani" (Matthew 27:46). Jesus appropriates David's words to connect the prophetic content of the chapter with His own saving death.

Today, I will...surrender to the Son of David who sacrificed Himself to sanctify me.

WEEK #15

Mephibosheth

DALE JENKINS

A Doomed Dynasty

Today's Scripture: 1 Samuel 29

We first meet Mephibosheth, in a subplot to the fall of King Saul's dynasty: "Jonathan, the son of Saul, had a son..."

First Samuel 29 tells the tragic tale of a doomed dynasty. King Saul had marched his army into a battle that he knew he would not win. Whether he had just resigned his deluded mind to his and his kingdom's death or maybe he thought God might just change His mind and give him one last victory. Saul was prone to bargaining with God (nevertheless, honor me this last time...1 Samuel 15:20).

It was not to be. In the miserable defeat that Israel suffered in the war, both their leader and each of his sons died that day (1 Samuel 31:1-6). There would be no son succeeding Saul, no dynasty to begin. The one who stood head and shoulders above them all would not live to enjoy the kingdom over which he was the first leader.

When the rest of the army on the other side of the valley saw their fallen leader and his sons, they fled and left cities and houses to be occupied by the enemy idol worshippers. It was a sad day.

It is not until you get to 2 Samuel 4 that you learn there was a remaining heir, but his story at that point is just as tragic. Here he is mentioned as not much more than a footnote: "Jonathan, the son of Saul, had a son who was crippled in his feet. He was five years old when the news about Saul and Jonathan came from Jezreel, and his nurse took him up and fled, and as she fled in her haste, he fell and became lame. And his name was Mephibosheth" (2 Samuel 4:4). But as his story unfolds we will find a story that teaches us rich lessons of grace.

Today, I will...pray for my family and examine my own faithfulness to the Lord in leading them.

Lost and Found
Today's Scripture: 1 Samuel 20:13-17

As we closed our study yesterday, we met Saul's only surviving grandson, Mephibosheth, who was lame in both his feet from a fall incurred with his nurse as they fed at the report of Saul, Jonathan, the Israelite army's defeat. As they fed, he fell, maybe on some hard stones, crushing his little legs. I imagine the child cried out in agony, but there was no time to set the badly broken bones. It was a day to survive.

The years that followed were not kind to the boy. Mephibosheth grew up crippled, poor, and in hiding. A terrible way for a child to grow up. The name of the place he lived was, "Lo-debar" (2 Samuel 9:4), which in the Hebrew language means "no pastureland."

For Israel, however, the next few years were a time of growth and prosperity. The new king, David, united all of the tribes in one glorious kingdom. Together they defeated every enemy, one by one, and became the premier power in the known world. David established Jerusalem as the new capital with his magnificent palace.

The last paragraph of 2 Samuel 8:15 tells us that finally "David reigned over all Israel." And in chapter 9, we find the ever warring, ever busy David at peace and in a moment of reflection. "And David said, 'Is there still anyone left of the house of Saul, that I may show him kindness for Jonathan's sake?'" (2 Samuel 9:1). David had made two promises: One to his best friend, Jonathan (1 Samuel 20:13-17) and the other to Jonathan's dad, King Saul (1 Samuel 24:20-22). He promised to spare their families. So, David sought and found Mephibosheth in Lo-debar through Ziba, a former servant of Saul's (2 Samuel 9:2-5).

Today, I will...remember someone who may need my prayers, texts, a visit, or a call, and reach out to them in love.

That Is Grace

Today's Scripture: Titus 2:11-14

David found Mephibosheth. It must have been a harrowing moment in the young boy's life as these emissaries from the most powerful man in the world show up at his door of exile in Lo-debar. Surely a thousand thoughts went through his mind. It was, and even today is, in many countries the practice of a new empire to kill all the descendants of the previous dynasty. Perhaps he thought, "Well, at least I made it this long."

The text unveils enough for us to see the awkward meeting. "Mephibosheth the son of Jonathan, son of Saul, came to David and fell on his face and paid homage. And David said, 'Mephibosheth!' And he answered, 'Behold, I am your servant'" (2 Samuel 9:6). A bow gone bad by the crippled lad, or perhaps groveling for his life. But instead of a cold blade across his neck, David's next words are deeply moving even today. Verse 7: "David said to him, 'Do not fear, for I will show you kindness for the sake of your father Jonathan, and I will restore to you all the land of Saul your father, and you shall eat at my table always.'" That last phrase will be repeated four times in these seven verses.

What's so moving here? A mighty king reaches down and adopts the grandson of the one who tried to kill him. A powerful and rich ruler bestows his wealth to one who was everything he was not for no worldly reason. A fierce warrior demonstrates a kind heart. A strong and famous king stoops down and reaches out to one who represents everything David was not! Most of all it is the story of grace. Perhaps one of the greatest stories of grace in the Old Testament. David gave Mephibosheth that which he did not deserve, could not earn, and which he was not obligated to give.

That is grace.

Today, I will...reflect on what my life was or would be without the Lord and pray a prayer of thanks for His grace.

A Dead Dog?

Today's Scripture: Revelation 22:17

In case you missed it. Just as David brought a crippled boy to his table, so God adopts us into His household. You and I are Mephibosheths, too. The similarities are too clear.

God knocks on the doorway of our lives, regardless of where you are or were in your life and invites us into His presence. Revelation 22:17 (NLT) says, "The Spirit and the bride say, 'Come.' Let anyone who hears this say, 'Come.' Let anyone who is thirsty come. Let anyone who desires drink freely from the water of life.'" That's grace.

He doesn't say, "Those who are worthy;" doesn't say, "Those who have lived a perfect life." He says, "anyone who desires." Hear God's servants knocking at your door, and respond. How awesome to think the King of the Universe invites us into His presence. That's grace.

Yet, we must come as Mephibosheth came before David, broken and bowing down in His presence. Proclaiming to all around watching, "I am your servant."

Notice Mephibosheth's response, "And he bowed himself, and said, 'What is thy servant, that thou shouldest look upon such a dead dog as I am?'" (2 Samuel 9:8 KJV). For Mephibosheth to call himself a "dead dog" was to compare himself to the nastiest, foulest thing he could think of. For a Jew it was a double slam. To them, a dog was one of the most repulsive animals imaginable. On top of that, anything dead was vile.

By the way, personal insults were nothing new to him. Mephibosheth wasn't even his real name. At birth he was name Meribaal, name of valor. But as time when on, he was given another name. Mephibosheth, which means, "a man of shame." But there, before the king, in his moment of greatest vulnerability, perhaps the name-calling of a lifetime came flooding over him. He felt worthless.

But the king did not treat him the way he often felt.

Today, I will... praise God and keep a godly outlook for His goodness to me.

A Place at His Table

Today's Scripture: Ephesians 2:4-9

Please forgive a little imagination here:

We can only image what it must have been like to have dinner at the king's house from that day forward. A beautiful table, royal linens, the finest foods, servants standing along the walls. Military officials. Suddenly they rise, for the king is coming. As he approaches the head of the table, they all sit down together. One of the younger boys grabs for the bread, but the king commands, "Wait! I don't think everyone is here yet." The room grows quiet. Then they hear a familiar noise echoing down the hallway: the sound of clumsy crutches beating the floors. A moment later, all heads turn. Standing in the doorway is Mephibosheth, the king's adopted son.

Perhaps, one night a visiting dignitary from a far country watches the scene with interest. He leans to a palace guard and whispers, "What's all the commotion over a crippled kid?" The guard responds, "That crippled kid was born an enemy of the king, but David has chosen to make the boy his son." Can't you hear the visitor, "But I don't understand." The guard just smiles and says, "Not many people do. Isn't he a great king?!"

Ponder your life in His kingdom for a moment. Why do you think the King of heaven keeps us at the family table? Is it because we deserve it? Is it because of our holiness or good works? Maybe it's because you're a first-round draft choice? Or do you think it's because He can't make it without you? Maybe it is our strong personality. Surely it is all your potential!

No! It is because He knows our Savior, Jesus the Christ. It is for His sake that the Father gives us back everything we lost. But even more, He invites us to sit at His table and refer to ourselves as one of His children. Ephesians 2:4-9 (NKJV),

But God, who is rich in mercy, because of His great love with which He loved us, even when we were dead in trespasses, made us alive together with Christ (by grace you have been saved), raised us up together, and made us sit together in the heavenly places in Christ Jesus, that in the ages to come He might show the exceeding riches of His grace in His kindness toward us in Christ Jesus. For by grace you have been saved through faith, and that not of yourselves; it is the gift of God, not of works, lest anyone should boast.

Today, I will...share with my children, grandchildren, or another how good God has been to me.

WEEK #16

Solomon

RALPH GILMORE

Solomon Received a Gift

Today's Scripture: 1 Kings 3:1-15

If you just had one wish, and it could not be for limitless wishes, what would it be? I guess "world peace" would be the stereotypical answer. However, Solomon's request from Yahweh was for wisdom and an understanding heart so that he could rule over Israel as he should. There are at least three factors that made his request for wisdom such a wise choice. First, Solomon had predecessors who had raised him in the right way. He was the son of David and Bathsheba. Solomon had watched his father rule over Israel, and he must have known how difficult and all-encompassing it was. Second, Solomon had purpose. As David had entrusted him, Solomon was to be strong, show himself a man, and keep God's statutes and commandments (1 Kings 2:1-4). Solomon knew that he was being charged with the greatest purpose on earth at the time and that he needed wisdom and understanding to fulfill this charge. Finally, Solomon had pure motives when he made this request. His heart's desire was to rule over Israel in such a way that all could see his wisdom in the way he ruled (I Kings 3:8-15).

Of these three (predecessors, purpose, and purity), two are not under our control. We cannot pick our ancestors. However, for many of us, our Christian families have already given us quite an honorable legacy because we were brought up in an environment favorable to the growing of faith (Ephesians 6:1-4). Many of us have seen Christ modeled in our homes. We had little to do with the family into which we were born. Also, we had nothing to do with God's instilling purpose into our lives, a purpose which we may or may not be living at the moment. Yet, we have everything to do with the purity of our hearts (Matthew 5:8). Purity of heart is having a heart with pure motives unmixed with worldly passions.

Today, I will...be thankful for God instilling purpose for me, for those who helped to form faith in me, and for the challenge to be pure in heart.

Solomon Used His Gift as a Judge, Writer, and Administrator

Today's Scripture: 1 Kings 4:20-34

How am I, and how are you, using the divine gifts we have? I guess, it depends on the day you ask. All Christians have gifts from God, beginning with our salvation (Romans 6:23; 12:6-8). Solomon was given the gift to be the wisest man on earth at the time (the wisdom of Jesus, of course, superseded the wisdom of everybody). Wisdom is the proper application of knowledge. Outside of his personal life, Solomon excelled in applying wisdom as a judge, a writer, and an administrator.

As a judge, Solomon's wisdom was revealed in the well-known case of the two women with two children, one of which died during the night (1 Kings 3:16-28). Solomon's wisdom allowed the real mother of the surviving baby to be identified. The news of his wisdom in ruling over Israel spread like wildfire through the ancient near east (1 Kings 4:20-21). As a writer, he spoke over 3,000 proverbs and wrote 1,005 songs (1 Kings 4:32). Solomon wrote most of the proverbs in the book of Proverbs with his name appearing in three sections (1:1, 10:1, and 25:1). As an administrator, he oversaw the 30,000 men who built the Lord's house (which his father did not get to build) and his own house. Even the queen of Sheba was so impressed with how efficiently everything ran in Solomon's massive kingdom that she admitted she had only heard about half of the grandeur and splendor of it (1 Kings 10:1-5). Personally, I never liked administration, although I have done some of it. Solomon was a master at it.

Today, I will...take an inventory of my own gifts and reflect on how they are being used. We should examine the quality and the quantity of them. We should examine the relationship between our gifts and our ministries in the church. Are we effective in ministering in areas that are suited to our gifts? Will you be willing to do the same?

Solomon Used His Gift to Build God's House

Today's Scripture: 1 Kings 6-7

In this lesson, we focus on the most important building project that Solomon undertook: to build God's own house, (i.e., the temple). In this brief lesson, four points about the building of the temple will be referenced.

First, David had purposed a permanent place for the temple. The tabernacle was a temporary dwelling, although moving it required many strenuous steps (Exodus 25-27).

Second, the temple was where the presence of God was. According to Exodus 20:24 and Deuteronomy 12:5, God wants us to worship Him where His name is recorded. It was first recorded at the altar (Genesis 8:20; 12:7; et al.), then the tabernacle (Numbers 9:15-22), then the temple (2 Chronicles 5:14). The temple was where God recorded His name.

Third, the temple was to accompany a time of peace. Most Christians know that King David was prohibited from building the temple because he had shed so much blood (1 Chronicles 22:7), and the builder of God's house should be a man of peace. Most of the blood on David's hands, it seems to me, was there because David was following the instructions of the Lord. However, David was restrained from building the temple, yet at this point in history he had already begun to stock a massive building supply list. It was to be David's successor to the throne who would build God's house.

Finally, the temple was a precursor to Christ's church in many ways. Peter compared the church-kingdom to the temple in 1 Peter 2:4-8. The Holy Spirit represents the presence of God both in the church corporate (1 Corinthians 3:16-17) and individual Christians (1 Corinthians 6:19-20). The golden laver in which priests washed their hands foreshadowed our entry into the kingdom of God by baptism (Romans 6:3-4; Acts 2:38; et al.). What a magnificent structure Solomon's temple must have been.

Today, I will...focus on the presence of God in your life. It is God's will that His name is no longer recorded on a building because now we are God's building, and His presence is surely in us.

Solomon Made Poor Life Choices and Lost the Gift

Today's Scripture: 1 Kings 11:1-8

How could Solomon, who was the wisest of the wise, become the most foolish of the fools? This is one of the most puzzling life reversals in all of Scripture. Early in his reign, Solomon raised a warning flag of a divided heart when we learn in 1 Kings 3:3 that "Solomon loved the LORD, walking in the statutes of David his father, only he sacrificed and made offerings at the high places." The phrase "high places" is a metaphor for pagan worship. Why would Solomon do this when it was a slap in King David's face? There is no doubt of Solomon's departure from the Lord when he was an older man (1 Kings 11:1-8). Moses issued a warning about the behavior of kings of Israel in Deuteronomy 17:16-17 (NIV), "The king, moreover, must not acquire great numbers of horses for himself or make the people return to Egypt to get more of them, for the LORD has told you, 'You are not to go back that way again.' He must not take many wives, or his heart will be led astray. He must not accumulate large amounts of silver and gold."

Solomon broke 3 out of 4 of God's laws: he acquired many horses (he had four thousand stalls for horses and chariots, and twelve thousand horses (2 Chronicles 9:25); he had 700 wives and 300 concubines; and he accumulated thousands of pounds of silver and gold (1 Kings 10:14-29). His wives turned away his heart (1 Kings 11:3). To illustrate, he set up places for worship of many pagan deities worshiped by his wives: Ashtoreth, Milcom, Chemosh, and Molech.

Yahweh will not settle for competition, because there is none. Pagan gods have no power, no breath, and no reality (1 Corinthians 8:4-6; Exodus 20:3). Why would Solomon endorse and advocate pagan worship? It seems that he had lost his mind. Solomon made poor life choices for which he paid a heavy penalty. Thus, his heart was turned to evil.

Today, I will...guard my heart to set apart in it the one true and living God. God always deserves first place and will settle for no other.

Solomon Echoed Jesus as Shepherd/King

Today's Scripture: Song of Solomon 1-8

Whether Christ is reflected in the Song of Solomon (afterwards known as "The Song"), is a matter of scholastic debate. However, John made allusions to The Song in the book of Revelation. For instance, Christ's knocking at the door in Revelation 3:20 may be one of several allusions to The Song in 5:2. Allusions to the Bride and Bridegroom, Virgins, and City/Temple/Dwelling Place personification run throughout both highly symbolic books. Was Shulamith (the woman in The Song) loved by two men—a lowly shepherd and a majestic king—or was she loved by one man playing two roles? I believe it is the latter. Solomon in The Song first appeared to Shulamith (6:3) as a shepherd (1:7-8). Later, he revealed himself as a king (3:6-11).

Whether there are allusions to The Song in Revelation, the theme of Jesus as the Shepherd-King from The Song is worthy of today's reflections. Jesus is the Great Shepherd of the flock (1 Peter 5:4), who loves each sheep (John 10:1-18). Once, He has you in His grasp when you obey Him (John 10:26-30), He will not let go. You can turn loose of Him, but He will always have your back. God's covenant love is reflected in the Song by the love shown to Shulamith. Jesus has this love for His church and all who are in it. Relative to His Kingship, He is the King of all kings and the Lord of all lords (1 Timothy 6:15). In Revelation 5:1-10, only Jesus is worthy of loosening the seven seals on the scroll before God's throne. When Jesus loosens the seals, the created inhabitants of heaven fall down and worship Jesus—as we should. One final allusion from The Song—the love between Solomon and his bride is pictured in the famous passage "Set me as a seal upon your heart" (Song 8:6-7). When you first came to the Lord through obedience and baptism, He sealed you with His Spirit (Ephesians 1:13).

Today, I will...rejoice, if I am in God's flock (the church), because He is my Bridegroom and I am His bride. I will take security in the fact that He is my Shepherd-King who holds me in His hand.

WEEK #17

Jeroboam & Rehoboam

DICK SZTANYO

A Kingdom Divided

Today's Scripture: 1 Kings 11:26-40

Jeroboam was an Ephraimite who was raised up as an adversary to Solomon. But, as he proved himself to be an industrious man, Solomon put him in charge of all the forced labor in the house of Joseph (1 Kings 11:26-28).

Solomon was blessed with remarkable wisdom; however, he also made many foolish mistakes. He had been warned against turning away from God, but the influences of others (especially his wives) and other things became his legacy. The Lord told him that, because he had turned away, "I will surely tear the kingdom from you and will give it to your servant" (1 Kings 11:11). Tear is a very descriptive word to show the seriousness of how his life was turning out. God then told Solomon that this would happen, not to him, but to his son Rehoboam. The prophet Ahijah informed Jeroboam, after dividing his cloak into twelve pieces and having Jeroboam take ten of them, that God would "tear the kingdom from the hand of Solomon and will give you ten tribes" (1 Kings 11:31). Rehoboam would retain Judah (Benjamin was small and thus combined with Judah to form one tribe) "for the sake of my servant David" and "for the sake of Jerusalem" (1 Kings 11:32). Jeroboam was plainly told, that so long as he remained faithful, God would be with him and "build . . . a sure house, as I built for David, and I will give Israel to you" (1 Kings 11:38). Solomon then sought to kill Jeroboam. So, Jeroboam fled to Egypt to escape. He stayed away until Solomon died (1 Kings 11:40).

It's difficult to understand how Jeroboam felt about all of this, but apparently, God saw some promise in Jeroboam as a leader because this was part of His plan for the "divided kingdom." God did not leave Jeroboam until Jeroboam first left God, which, of course, he did. He was explicitly warned of the consequences of apostasy (1 Kings 11:38-39), but he was also told that King Solomon's wives indeed turned his heart away and influenced him to worship their gods (1 Kings 11:2, 31-37). In other words, the "divided kingdom" was partially caused by Solomon's foolish mistakes.

Today, I will...celebrate God's plans for how He uses human authorities over people, in spite of the human tendency to sink into the depths of sin. "He changes times and seasons; he removes kings and sets up kings; he gives wisdom to the wise and knowledge to those who have understanding" (Daniel 2:21).

TUESDAY

Turning from Wisdom to Intimidation

Today's Scripture: 1 Kings 12:1-20

Rehoboam was an impetuous man with a very flawed character. To insure survival of the Davidic line that ultimately led to Christ and His church-kingdom, the Lord placed Rehoboam as the king of Judah. Actually, when Solomon died, Rehoboam reigned in his place.

The whole story of his inept leadership becomes clear when one reads of the foolish decisions he made. Rehoboam asked the elders who had served his father Solomon for advice in ruling Judah. This was a good start, and a wise move. But, Scripture plainly states: "he abandoned the counsel that the old men gave him and took counsel with the young men who had grown up with him and stood before him" (1 Kings 12:8). Instead of listening to the wise counsel of the old men (called elders in some versions), Rehoboam took the path of force and intimidation.Rehoboam

> spoke to them according to the counsel of the young men, saying, "My father made your yoke heavy; but I will add to your yoke. My father disciplined you with whips, but I will discipline you with scorpions." So the king did not listen to the people, for it was a turn of affairs brought about by the LORD that he might fulfill his word, which the LORD spoke by Ahijah the Shilonite to Jeroboam the son of Nebat (1 Kings 12:14-15).

Jeroboam and those who followed him were told to give three days to Rehoboam, in order for him to make his decision as to how he would rule over the people of Judah. When Jeroboam and the others returned, they received the message from Rehoboam, who flatly told them that he was going to rule "harshly, and forsaking the counsel that the old men had given him" (1 Kings 12:13). "And when all Israel saw that the king did not listen to them, the people answered the king, 'What portion do we have in David? We have no inheritance in the son of Jesse. To your tents, O Israel! Look now to your own house, David'" (1 Kings 12:16). The kingdom left to God's people following Solomon's reign was officially divided!

Today, I will...be able to see God's hand in preserving the Davidic line, in spite of the terrible arrogance of Rehoboam. Even though the kingdom was divided, the Lord was very much involved in the plan that fulfilled the "seed" promise made to Abraham, which culminated in the coming of and sacrifice of the Christ (Galatians 3:16).

99

The Fall of Jeroboam

Today's Scripture: 1 Kings 12:21-33; 14:1-16

After the terrible events that finally led to the "divided kingdom," both Jeroboam and Rehoboam sought to consolidate and solidify their respective kingdoms. Rehoboam was trying to get the ten tribes back by force, but God told him not to wage war against his relatives. So, Rehoboam listened to the Lord, and his followers returned home (1 Kings 12:21-24).

Meanwhile, Jeroboam was almost paranoid about the possibility of losing his domain. To prevent the people from going back to the house of David, in which case he thought that they would likely kill him, he came up with a sinful plan. "So the king took counsel and made two calves of gold. And he said to the people, 'You have gone up to Jerusalem long enough. Behold your gods, O Israel, who brought you up out of the land of Egypt.' And he set one in Bethel, and the other he put in Dan. Then this thing became a sin" (1 Kings 12:28-30). Jeroboam then set up temples on the high places and appointed priests who were not from the Levites. He also established a feast similar to the ones they had known in Jerusalem. This began a steep downward slide away from God for Jeroboam. In fact, the Lord said: "Because I exalted you from among the people and made you leader over my people Israel and tore the kingdom away from the house of David and gave it to you, and yet you have not been like my servant David, who kept my commandments and followed me with all his heart, doing only that which was right in my eyes, but you have done evil above all who were before you" (1 Kings 14:7-9). This sad beginning resulted in severe consequences for Jeroboam, and ultimately began to set the stage which would lead Israel into the Assyrian captivity in 722 B.C. from which they never fully recovered.

Jeroboam's good leadership qualities actually were put into the service of rebellion against God. The prophet Ahijah reported to Jeroboam's wife "the LORD will raise up for himself a king over Israel who shall cut off the house of Jeroboam today. And henceforth, the LORD will strike Israel as a reed is shaken in the water, and root up Israel out of this good land that he gave to their fathers....And he will give Israel up because of the sins of Jeroboam, which he sinned and made Israel to sin" (1 Kings 14:14-16).

Today, I will...remember that God will bring all who are guilty of sin apart from repentance under judgment. God will right all wrongs and make things the way they should be. In spite of how things sometimes look to us, we remember that our God is in control of the final outcome.

THURSDAY

Leading through Service

Today's Scripture: 1 Peter 5:1-3

We are curious creatures to say the least. One thing that has my curiosity level running at an all-time high is what would have happened if Rehoboam had actually followed the advice of the elders? These men had served King Solomon with distinction, and they had given good advice to Rehoboam. They said, in effect, that good leaders are servants, rather than domineering tyrants. Leaders always do better to serve their subjects, instead of intimidating them by force.

We get this same advice from Jesus as He was training His apostles. "You know that the rulers of the Gentiles lord it over them, and their great ones exercise authority over them. It shall not be so among you. But whoever would be great among you must be your servant, and whoever would be first among you must be your slave, even as the Son of Man came not to be served but to serve, and to give his life as a ransom for many" (Matthew 20:25-28). The Son of Man (Creator of the universe) came not TO BE SERVED but TO HIMSELF SERVE! Does this not speak volumes as to the leadership style that is best for all those in authority? Wouldn't it have been better than the dictator style of Hitler, Stalin, Lenin, Mussolini, and others?

Rehoboam took the more common approach which was to rule with an "iron fist"—to rule from a position of power. We may be told, "don't let your guard down; you'll come across as weak, and you will lose your edge." Many people who are placed in positions of authority have a difficult time believing that those who are their subjects will respond better to servant-leaders than to keep them in line with brute force.

Recall how the apostle Peter used the training he had received from our Lord for his own leadership style. "So I exhort the elders among you, as a fellow elder and a witness of the sufferings of Christ, as well as a partaker in the glory that is going to be revealed: shepherd the flock of God that is among you, exercising oversight, not under compulsion, but willingly, as God would have you; not for shameful gain, but eagerly, not domineering over those in your charge, but being examples to the flock" (1 Peter 5:1-3). And, "humble yourselves, therefore, under the mighty hand of God so that at the proper time he may exalt you" (1 Peter 5:6).

Today, I will...notice servant-leaders in the church, and I will pray for God to richly bless them. Additionally, I will gladly submit myself to those who are true servants.

101

God Works through Their Sin

Today's Scripture: Galatians 3:16, 18, 29

It never surprised the Lord that Jeroboam and Rehoboam would sin. In fact, God knew that free moral agents would, at some point, violate that freedom and therefore, they would be guilty and accountable before Him. So, Christ's sacrifice was planned before creation even occurred (1 Peter 1:20; Revelation 13:8). The church-kingdom was also in the "eternal purpose" of God (Ephesians 3:11). Thus, it was never thought that either Jeroboam or Rehoboam would be guilty before their Lord. The plight of humanity was clearly understood and clearly stated in Scripture (1 Kings 8:46; Ecclesiastes 7:20; 2 Chronicles 6:36; Romans 3:10, 23). The plan of salvation (sometimes called the "scheme of redemption") was planned from eternity by God. Men who were created as free (and, therefore, responsible for their actions) would eventually abuse this freedom and fall into sin. Such people would obviously need a Savior. Therefore, the sacrifice of Christ was planned as an answer to the need of the human family (Acts 2:22-24, 29-33).

Though in the mind of God from eternity, this plan took on specificity in the threefold promise the Lord made to Abraham (Genesis 12:1-7). He made a nation promise (fulfilled in Exodus 19:4-6), a land promise (fulfilled in Joshua 21:43-45), and a seed promise (fulfilled in the promised Messiah, Acts 3:17-26; Galatians 3:15-18). These promises were fulfilled historically, so history really and truly became "His story."

Jeroboam played an important role in this plan by putting the Israelites on a road that demonstrated the lengths to which God's people would go in rebelling against their Lord! They fell into the depths of sin, which eventually led to the Assyrian captivity in 722 B.C. Rehoboam, in spite of his horribly flawed character and his continual march away from God, helped to preserve the Davidic line that fulfilled God's plan in the coming of Christ and the establishment of His church-kingdom. The incredible plan of God took shape step by step until ultimately Scripture would say: "the promises were made to Abraham and to his offspring. It does not says, 'And to offsprings,' referring to many, but referring to one, 'And to your offspring,' who is Christ. ...For if the inheritance comes by the law, it no longer comes by promise; but God gave it to Abraham by a promise. ... And if you are Christ's, then you are Abraham's offspring, heirs according to promise" (Galatians 3:16, 18, 29).

Today, I will...celebrate the fact that without God's marvelous plan which is revealed in Scripture, I would never have come to know these amazing truths! I will pray that God will be glorified in all that I say, all that I am, and all that I do! And, I will praise Him in songs, like "The Precious Book Divine," by the esteemed brother, L. O. Sanderson.

WEEK #18

Elijah

ZACK MARTIN

Heeeeeeeeeeeeerere's Elijah

Today's Scripture: 1 Kings 17:1; I Kings 18:41-46; James 5:17-18

Unlike Johnny Carson, Elijah received no special introduction when he arrived on the scene in I Kings 17. In the Old Testament, the authors provide lengthy introductions of significant people, including biographies, genealogies, or even stories about extended family. Introductions give pertinent information about people and give the reader reasons why they should or should not be listened to.

However, Elijah just appeared, which would be part of his modus operandi (MO). Wherever he went, Elijah made a big impact. His sudden appearance probably came from his fast feet (1 Kings 18:46), but he also dressed like a wild man (2 Kings 1:8) and had no issue with dwelling in caves (1 Kings 17:3; 19:9).

So why study such an odd man? Because he, too, lived in a pagan culture but faithfully served God. This loyalty is reflected in the meaning of his name: "The Lord is my God." However, Elijah experienced some very low moments in his life. This sounds like my life. James wrote that he "was a man with a nature like ours" (5:17). Yet, he was able to do extraordinary things like pray for a drought, then pray for rain (James 5:17-18). James used Elijah as an example of a righteous man who did much through his fervent prayer life. James was saying that any righteous person can do the same thing! Let us dare to be like Elijah and pray with faith, knowing that God can do what we ask and much more because we are His!

Today, I will...pray with faith like Elijah. If I need more faith, I will pray for God to increase my faith.

Standing Up for God

Today's Scripture: 1 Kings 18

Elijah's first official act of ministry was to tell Ahab that God was withholding rain (I Kings 17:1-2). In 1 Kings 18:1, we are told that the rain stopped for three years. All the blame went to Elijah, of course. For this reason, Ahab called Elijah the "troubler of Israel" at their next meeting (1 Kings 18:17).

However, Elijah said that Ahab had brought this trouble to Israel because he had "abandoned the commandments of the LORD and followed the Baals" (1 Kings 18:18). This backsliding happened because of Ahab's wife, Queen Jezebel (1 Kings 16:31-33). Baal was the god of fertility and in charge of rain.

Stopping the rain was the first part of the challenge. Then, it was time to throw the gauntlet down and destroy Baal. Elijah told Ahab to gather all of Israel on Mount Carmel with 450 prophets of Baal and 400 prophets of Asherah. Two altars were built: one for Baal and one for God. However, Baal never showed up to the show that his prophets were putting on. So, Elijah repaired the altar of God. He prepared the sacrifice, then covered the altar and all its contents with the water of four jars three times. Then he called on God, who sent down fire to consume everything. This led Israel to turn their hearts back to God, resulting in God sending rain.

Although this challenge was between God and Baal, I bet Elijah felt the pressure that day and probably felt like he was all alone. Do you feel like that? Do you ever feel like you are the only Christian at your workplace, school, or in your family? Elijah stood courageous that day because he was on God's side. Martin Luther once said, "You plus God is a majority." Do not forget that! Keep standing for what is right! Keep being faithful in a faithless generation! Remember, with God, you can overcome everything!

Today, I will...remember that me plus God is a majority and continue to stand for the truth!

Mountain High and Valley Low

Today's Scripture: 1 Kings 19:1-18

Life is full of mountaintop experiences and valley lows. Yesterday, we showed a mountaintop experience with Elijah, literally and metaphorically. In 1 Kings 18, Elijah challenged the prophets of Baal on Mount Caramel. Elijah risked it all to stand up for God and he won! Then the rain came back after three long years! Elijah must have been on a spiritual high! Perhaps this is why he outran Ahab to Jezreel (I Kings 18:46).

But everything changed in Jezreel. Jezebel wanted Elijah's life because he took the lives of her prophets (1 Kings 19:1-2). Elijah very quickly found himself in a valley, metaphorically and literally. He traveled into the wilderness and asked God to take his life (v. 4). After a nap and some food, Elijah headed to another mountain—"Horeb, the mount of God (v, 8). But even there, he forgot the great victory, dwelt on his current situation, and asked God to take his life (vv. 9-10). God ignored this request and asked Elijah to go and "stand on the mount before" Him (v. 11). God passed by Elijah in several metaphysical ways but revealed Himself in "the sound of a low whisper" (v. 12) and spoke to him afterward. Elijah complained again, but God ignored him and gave him a job.

We learn valuable lessons on how to handle discouragement and situational depression. First, we should take care of ourselves physically. This may mean eating a favorite meal and taking a nap like Elijah. Furthermore, exercise is an excellent way to help us overcome discouragement by releasing endorphins. Second, we need to get to work. How many of us have visited a church member in the hospital and were helped more by the sick church member than we helped them? Finally, we must remind ourselves that God is always at work, even in small ways.

Today, I will...make sure that I am physically caring for myself to give my best to God. When I feel discouraged, I will remind myself that God is at work even when I do not sense Him.

THURSDAY
Who Will Fill Your Shoes?

Today's Scripture: 1 Kings 19:19-21

One day, unless Jesus comes first, you are going to die. The greatest preparation anyone can make is ensuring they have a good relationship with God. Another matter of preparation is ensuring we leave the right legacy for our children and grandchildren. However, have you considered who will fill your shoes at your local congregation when you are gone?

Yesterday, we looked at Elijah and his discouragement from I Kings 19. Part of the remedy to his discouragement was to eat and get some rest. But remember, God added something else to get Elijah out of his funk. God gives. Elijah was commanded to go and find "Elisha the son of Shaphat of Abel-meholah" and "anoint him to be prophet in your place" (1 Kings 19:16). Elijah went straight to Elisha. Perhaps it was a sign of importance.

How can you make sure that your shoes are filled? Discipleship or mentoring. This is the biblical way that we make sure our shoes are filled. Dr. Justin Rogers gives excellent advice on how to mentor. Firstly, Rogers suggests that mentoring is intentional. We see something in someone, and we intentionally invest in their lives. This intentional investment involves being personal, which is Rogers' second point. Finally, mentoring should be reciprocal. Everyone is made better because of the mentoring process. As Rogers discusses the process of leaders making leaders, he says it is important to understand that a leader does not want to form a copycat of himself. Still, our mentees should be better than the mentor. So as we think about filling our shoes, we want people to do better jobs than we ever could. No two people are alike. Elijah and Elishah were two different people with two different ministries. Still, Scripture clearly shows that Elisha was the successor.

Today, I will...think of someone at my local congregation that I can mentor or disciple. I will be an intentional person and form a reciprocal relationship.

Elijah and Christ

Today's Scripture: Luke 4:24-26

Judaism believed that Elijah would be the precursor to the Messiah based on Malachi's prophesy in Malachi 4:5-6. This role of a precursor to the Messiah happened through John the Baptist (Luke 1:17). However, Elijah himself gave full confirmation of Jesus being the Messiah on the Mount of Transfiguration (Matthew 17:4; Mark 9:5; Luke 9:33).

But it is in the role of prophet that Jesus identifies with Elijah the prophet. Remember that there were many who thought Elijah had come back as Jesus (Matthew 16:14; Mark 8:28; Luke 9:19).

Jesus made the connection between Himself and Elijah at the beginning of His ministry in Luke 4:24-26. Jesus illustrated His ministry in His hometown by using both Elijah and Elisha. Both of these prophets who were called to minister to God's people ended up ministering to Gentiles. The observation was that they had rejected Elijah and the God who sent him, even though they were in desperate need themselves. In applying it to His situation, Jesus was saying because of the skepticism or disbelief of His people, in Nazareth and later in Jerusalem, this rejection would lead to God's gracious gift of salvation to the Gentiles. The Jews thought they were good because they were God's people, but they actually needed healing and salvation—their loss but our gain as Gentiles.

So here is the final lesson I will leave with you this week: share the gospel with everyone. Do not let a person's background stop you from sharing the gospel with them. The Gentiles were not God's chosen people, but came to play a prominent role in the early church. As you read the New Testament epistles and early church history, there came a time in which the church changed from predominately Jewish to predominately Gentile. You never know who will obey the gospel. It is not our job to judge receptivity but to share the gospel with everyone.

Today, I will...intentionally share the gospel with someone who crosses my path.

WEEK #19

Elisha

GEORGE HULETT

How to Be a Social Influencer

Today's Scripture: 1 Kings 19:19-21

From early history most leaders were born to the position. Often, they were descended from the previous leaders. That's not how the history in the Bible goes at all. In fact, God seemed to have constantly been looking for leaders who had neither the qualifications nor the desire to lead. God chose these people, who were often nobodies, and raised them up as leaders. Then, He could demonstrate that it was through His power and will that the work actually got done.

Many of us are nobodies. We weren't born to luxury or power. But like those great leaders we read about in Scripture, God can work great influence through our lives. Perhaps that word of encouragement to a young man was just the motivation he needed to dedicate his life to preaching the gospel and resulted in hundreds of souls being saved. Perhaps that moment of caring and prayer was the deciding factor in a young lady's decision not to abort her baby. Perhaps that few extra dollars you tossed into the collection plate was used to dig a well and provide safe drinking water for a thousand people who praised God. You see, God can use us, no matter how insignificant we might think ourselves to be.

When God chose Elisha to succeed Elijah, he was a nobody. His father, Shaphat, had land and servants. But other than that we know almost nothing about him. When Elijah first encountered the young man, Elisha wasn't much to see. The workers were plowing, and he was just another plowman in the field. But when Elijah put the mantle on him, Elisha immediately dropped everything, sacrificed the oxen he was plowing with, and said goodbye to his family to follow Elijah. He spent the next sixty years influencing God's people.

Today, I will...do something intentional to influence a young person to dedicate their own life more fully to the Lord.

Open My Eyes

Today's Scripture: 2 Kings 6:15-17

"Ice cream! You have ice cream? Can I have some? Can I have two scoops?" It's amazing how excited children can get over simple things like ice cream. They will run and jump. It's very easy to keep their attention when they're excited about something like that. In fact, when they get all excited about something, it's often hard to get them to refocus their attention away from the excitement at hand.

But things change as we grow older. Maybe we've seen and done so much that we become jaded. Maybe the simple thrills of life don't hold as much appeal, because we already have so many things and are too busy to notice the wonder all around us.

Years ago, I took a friend from Siberia to the Walmart supercenter in Florence. We walked into the store and he was amazed. I remember him shouting my name and saying, "They have beans!" I tried to calm him down, but he was very excited. I told him of course they have beans. But he was not to be dismayed. He said, "They have green beans and black beans and white beans and red beans and cut beans and spicy beans!" Then his voice fell a little, he held up one finger and said, "In Russia, we have bean."

Sometimes it seems like we are so busy with our plenty that we forget to marvel at the awesomeness of God on display all around us. Remember the scene from the movie where they go to the Grand Canyon and stand there awkwardly for about ten seconds before moving on? But we must stop and remember that Jesus came so we could enjoy an abundance of life. Would that our coming together to worship could be as special to us as ice cream is to children.

Today, I will...pray that God will open my eyes like He did those of the prophet's servant so that I too can see the wonder and majesty of my Lord.

WEDNESDAY
Biscuits and Gravy
Today's Scripture: 2 Kings 4:8-37

"This is Tom Bodett for Motel 6, and we'll leave the light on for you." That's one of the most iconic advertising slogans of all time. Listeners knew immediately that when they arrived at their destination, no matter how weary they were from their journey, they would be welcomed and find a place to rest. Sam Walton founded an empire with a simple philosophy for all his employees: If a customer gets within ten feet of any employee, they are to smile and ask if they can help.

If you were to buy a new Corvette and ask to pick it up at the factory, you'd be amazed. Upon your arrival in Bowling Green, they'd take you on a tour of Corvette history through their museum, while an employee would be washing your new car to make it ready for you. After going through the museum, they'd take you on a tour through the factory, where you would meet some of the people who actually worked on your car. Finally, you'd be led outside to your shiny new Corvette, while all of the factory workers would take a break to come out and welcome you to the Corvette family.

The Shunammite Woman invited Elisha into her home for hospitality. Not only did she provide food and lodging for him, but she went a step further and actually made a room for him to stay in when he came to visit. She did these things out of the simple goodness in her heart. She could never have imagined that this itinerant Jew would be able to bless her so that she could conceive a son—let alone that this same wanderer would be able to raise her dead son to life again. She was just being hospitable. But her hospitality was rewarded.

Today, I will...open the doors of my heart to a stranger and share God's love with them.

THURSDAY
Trust and Obey

Today's Scripture: 2 Kings 5:1-14

"Rules were made to be broken." How many times have you heard that? An episode of the television series, Friday Night Lights really demonstrates the fallacy of this premise. The setting is a football game. One of the teams is notorious for playing dirty. As the game progressed there are numerous infractions and bad hits. But the referees never throw a penalty flag. The hits become more vicious and the retaliations become more blatant until finally the game ends in a huge brawl on the field.

We all know that was just a TV show. But the truth is, rules were made to be followed. Parents have a reason to set curfews and limit places or activities for their children. As infants, the rules are fewer (Don't touch — hot!). But as children grow and mature, the dangers are greater and more guidance is necessary to protect them. Bosses understand that there is a need for rules in the workplace. Coaches require following their rules if you want to play the game. Some rules are easy to understand, but sometimes you wonder what is the purpose of particular rule.

Some of God's commands throughout history have fallen into the latter category: Build a boat in the desert. Put the blood of a lamb on your doorposts and lintels. Walk around the city silently for six days. Go dip in the river Jordan seven times to be cleansed of leprosy. What? These rules make very little sense to us. But those who obeyed received their blessings.

What if we were to apply that same commitment today: Love one another by forgiving and forbearing. When you have a difference with your brother or sister, go to them and reconcile the issue. Worship God in Spirit, but also in truth. Be immersed for the remission of your sins. Study to show yourself approved. Remain faithful until death.

Today, I will...pray that God will allow me to appreciate the rules and commandments that will hep me to follow His will.

Who Do You Appreciate?

Today's Scripture: Luke 4:16-30

Everyone likes recognition. There are awards for everything. There are even awards for participation. In fact, there are actually awards that you can give to yourself by simply going online and ordering them. Folks like to be noticed and recognized.

When Jesus came back to Nazareth after beginning His ministry, you'd think He would have received all kinds of accolades. After all, here was the hometown Carpenter who had decided to dedicate His life to teaching people about God. But that didn't happen. Rather, they rejected Him.

After reading from the scroll of Isaiah, He told them that the Scripture He had just read was being fulfilled right then in their presence, and they were offended. Have you ever wondered why? Stop for a moment and read Isaiah 61:1. What could be offensive about that? Shouldn't every preacher everywhere be able to say those same words every week? But they were offended by Him.

Maybe it was their familiarity with Him that brought contempt. They knew Him as a carpenter, not a rabbi or teacher of the Law. Maybe it was the very idea of an untrained person claiming to speak or fulfill prophecy. At any rate, they hated Him for it.

And when they rejected Him, Jesus reminded them of all the times God had tried to send others, prophets included, to do this very same thing. They had been rejected as well. No prophet's miracles are so well documented as Elisha's. Yet almost all of them took place outside of Judah, because God's people rejected Him. No one in Scripture was involved in more miracles than Jesus was. Yet, rather than embracing the Son of God and sharing in His blessings, the hometown folks who knew Him best, rejected Him outright.

Today, I will...strive to help Jesus fulfill His mission of proclaiming the good news to people.

114

WEEK #20

Isaiah

JOHN McMATH

Isaiah, the Man

Today's Scripture: Isaiah 1

A couple of years ago, I immersed myself in an audiobook on the life of George Washington. I say "immersed," because it was forty-plus hours of listening. My family got tired of hearing about it.

But in those hours of listening, I learned a great deal about the "father of our country." I learned things I had not previously known. I had myths and misunderstandings corrected. Most of all, by learning more about the man, I learned more about why our country and our government is shaped the way that it is.

I am convinced that the more you know about a person, the more you will understand his mission, his motives, and his accomplishments.

Unfortunately, very little is told to us about the personal life of Isaiah the prophet. He was the son of Amoz (Isaiah 1:1). His wife was a prophetess (8:3), and he had two sons (7:3; 8:3).

Perhaps the deepest insight we have into the man Isaiah was in his encounter with God in chapter six of the book that bears his name. There, in the presence of the thrice holy God, Isaiah came to realize how deeply in need of God he was. "Woe is me! For I am lost; for I am a man of unclean lips, and I dwell in the midst of a people of unclean lips" (Isaiah 6:5).

It was this realization of his deep need for God, and his realization of his condition without God, that opened him up to his greatest usefulness. "And I heard the voice of the Lord saying, "Whom shall I send, and who will go for us?" Then I said, "Here I am! Send me." (Isaiah 6:8)

Today, I will...see myself as God sees me. I will acknowledge my deep need for Him. I will open myself to being a useful instrument for God.

Isaiah, the Prophet

Today's Scripture: Isaiah 6

The term prophet has been used widely in diverse contexts. The ancient Egyptians used it in reference to everything from priests to psychics and palm readers. A.G. Auld asserts that most of them saw themselves as poets. but the Hebrew terms to describe them suggest a loftier purpose. In the Old Testament, prophets are referred to as seer, man of God, man of the Spirit, watchman, and messenger.

The most common term for prophet is *nabi*, which literally means "to bubble forth." J.A. Brewer contended that the word connoted an individual pulled or carried away by the influence of another. "For no prophecy was ever produced by the will of man, but men spoke from God as they were carried along by the Holy Spirit." (2 Peter 1:21)

The late Homer Hailey wrote, "Never perhaps has there been another prophet like Isaiah, who stood with his head in the clouds and his feet on the solid earth, with his heart in the things of eternity and his mouth and hands in the things of time, with his spirit in the eternal counsel of God and his body in the very definite moment of history. Truly, Isaiah may be called the dean of all the prophets."

As a prophet, Isaiah was a man of the people but more so a man of God. He spoke to the matter of the day and current issues of the Jews, but he also spoke of the future and particularly the coming of the Messiah. He spoke to kings (Isaiah 1:1; 2 Chronicles 26:22; 32:32), to priests (Isaiah 28:7), and to the common man (Isaiah 6:9).

In his call, recorded in chapter 6, Isaiah's response was also his responsibility. "And I heard the voice of the Lord saying, ''Whom shall I send, and who will go for us?' Then I said, 'Here I am! Send me.'" (Isaiah 6:8) In verse 11, he asked, "How long?" God's response was until My will is accomplished. And that is the essence of a prophet. He did not look for results; he fulfilled his responsibility to God. Isaiah was one of the best.

Today, I will...seek the will of God. Learn from these men of God His character, nature, and will. I will mold my life to more closely reflect that of the Messiah of whom Isaiah prophesied.

Isaiah, a Family Affair

Today's Scripture: Isaiah 7

We are often not told much about the families of the prophets. It would seem that some did not have a family. Then there were prophets like Hosea and his constant travails with his unfaithful wife, Gomer. Our hearts break over his heartbreak.

In the book of Isaiah, we learn that Isaiah had a wife. In chapter 8, verse 3, she is referred to as "the prophetess." He also had two sons "Shear-jashub" (7:3) and my personal favorite, "Maher-shalal-hash-baz" (8:3). Honestly, it's just a fun name to say. Go ahead. Try it. Five times fast. Okay, you can just refer to him as "MSHB."

Seriously, however, each of these sons became a central part of Isaiah's message by their names and by their presence when certain prophecies were revealed. One for redemption and restoration, and the other for ruin. Let's focus for a moment on the first, as it is one of Isaiah's most prominent prophecies.

We do not have time or space here to discuss the meaning of *almah* in 7:14, whether it is "young woman" or "virgin." One thing that is abundantly clear is that the Holy Spirit, through the pen of Matthew, made it clear that the "young woman" of Isaiah 7:14 was to be a "virgin" (*parthenos*). Matthew's language is very specific. Thus the prophecy rings true with Jeremiah's words, "For the LORD has created a new thing on the earth: a woman encircles a man" (Jeremiah 31:22).

What a prophecy! The sign the Lord would show was the coming of the Messiah—Immanuel—God with us. And Shear-jashub was right there as a witness to this momentous prophecy.

Parents, this is a wonderful lesson for us. Do not just send your children to worship, or camp, or VBS, or Bible class. Take them. Let them see in you a model of what the Lord desires throughout their lives. You hear a great deal today about mentoring. Your greatest opportunity to mentor (disciple) someone is right within the walls of your own home. Do not let that opportunity slip away.

Incidentally, Shear-jashub was very young when this took place. It is never too early to start!

Today, I will...model Christianity before my children. I will mentor them in the ways of the Lord. And I will disciple them to be followers of Jesus.

Isaiah, the Diplomat
Today's Scripture: Isaiah 50

In his commentary on the book of Isaiah, Homer Hailey wrote that Isaiah was "not only a prophet but also a great statesman." A statesman is a wise, skillful, and respected leader who has developed the art of diplomacy. Hailey noted that English statesman, Edmund Burke, habitually read from Isaiah before attending parliament.

Isaiah was an advisor to kings. He dealt with the rising power of Assyria, and the problem of Egypt. He navigated relations with three political parties of the time: the pro-Egyptian party, the pro-Assyrian party, and a "Jehovah" nationalist party led by Isaiah himself that promoted loyalty to God.

One of my favorite verses in Isaiah highlights the characteristic that enabled Isaiah to negotiate such delicate situations. "The Lord GOD has given Me the tongue of the learned, that I should know how to speak a word in season to him who is weary" (Isaiah 50:4, NKJV). When, what, where, and how we speak to others has a lot to do with human relations. In the New Testament, Paul put it this way: "Let your speech always be gracious, seasoned with salt, so that you may know how you ought to answer each person" (Colossians 4:6).

We live in a world where people always seem to be at each others throats, constantly bickering with one another. We see this behavior in politics, families, and sadly even in our churches. We could use a few diplomats to help navigate the turbulent waters of disagreement. Jesus said, "Blessed are the peacemakers" (Matthew 5:9). Paul exhorts us, "If possible, so far as it depends on you, live peaceably with all." (Romans 12:18). The people of God should bring peace to the world by being peaceable in the world, and part of that is learning how to use our words for "great things" rather than "a world of unrighteousness" (James 3:5-6).

Today, I will...choose my words wisely and use my words for good (Ephesians 4:29). I will speak encouragement, love, and salvation. I will be a diplomat for the kingdom of God in a world that needs peace.

Isaiah and the Suffering Servant of Galilee

Today's Scripture: Isaiah 53

In his monumental sermon before the chief priests, Stephen made the following charge against the Jewish establishment: "'You stiff-necked people, uncircumcised in heart and ears, you always resist the Holy Spirit. As your fathers did, so do you. Which of the prophets did your fathers not persecute? And they killed those who announced beforehand the coming of the Righteous One, whom you have now betrayed and murdered," (Acts 7:51–52).

The great faith chapter of the Bible comes to a close with these stirring accolades for men of faith: "Others suffered mocking and flogging, and even chains and imprisonment. They were stoned, they were sawn in two, they were killed with the sword...destitute, afflicted, mistreated— of whom the world was not worthy" (Hebrews 11:36–38). Many scholars believe that the phrase "sawn in two" refers specifically to Isaiah, based on the tradition of Isaiah's gruesome death. King Ahaz certainly was not a fan of Isaiah prophecies (cf. 7:3-13).

When Isaiah describes the Messiah as "despised and rejected by men, a man of sorrows and acquainted with grief" (Isaiah 53:3). It was a concept to which Isaiah and many of God's prophets could relate.

In the epic chapter Isaiah 53, the one "acquainted with grief," was to be "stricken, smitten by God" (v. 4) due to sin (v. 4-6), shame (v. 7), separation (v. 8), and suffering (v. 9). It was really no accident that when Jesus asked his disciples, "Who do people say that the Son of Man is?" (Matthew 16:13) that part of the response was "one of the prophets" (Matthew 16:14). Isaiah was eager to speak to the people for God once he realized God's holiness and their sinfulness (Isaiah 6). He came to know their shame (Isaiah 30:5), their separation (Isaiah 59:1-2), and their suffering (Isaiah 24:6). Isaiah gave his life (41+ years) to point his people to the remedy for sin, shame, separation, and suffering.

Isaiah is the most quoted prophet by New Testament writers. He is widely regarded as the Messianic prophet. One writer referred to the book as the Romans of the Old Testament. The message of Isaiah is to wait for the Lord, with expectation, hope, and faith. Because the only answer for our sin, shame, separation, and suffering is the suffering servant of Galilee who would give his life for all.

Today, I will...put my full faith in Jesus, the suffering servant of Galilee. I will wait on the Lord. I will trust Him, and him alone for my salvation.

WEEK #21

Josiah

BARRY GRIDER

Josiah, Who Did That Which Was Right

Today's Scripture: 2 Kings 22:1-2

Many of us turn to the Bible with complete confidence that it not only contains helpful information, but it is in fact the Word of God. Jesus said, "Sanctify them in the truth; your word is truth" (John 17:17). God's commands are "true, and righteous altogether" (Psalm 19:9). Whatever God says about anything, you can be sure it is right.

Among the good kings of Judah was Josiah, the son of the wicked Amon. Josiah was eight years old when he began to reign. Unlike his father, Josiah was a good king. "And he did what was right in the eyes of the LORD, and walked in all the way of David his father, and he did not turn aside to the right or to the left" (2 Kings 22:2). This passage is such a beautiful summation of Josiah's life. Would it not be wonderful if it could be said of each of us that we did what was right in the sight of the Lord?

Can we really know what is right and wrong today? All one must do is listen to what God says. For example, Paul wrote, "Children obey your parents in the Lord, for this is right" (Ephesians 6:1). The number one reason to obey one's parents is that doing so is the right thing to do. Parents must once again instruct their children in that which is right. However, even when parents fail to do this, it does not lessen the responsibility of children to learn and apply God's standard of right and wrong. Josiah's father was a wicked man, but Josiah did not use the wickedness of his father as an excuse for him to engage in wrongdoing. He did not subscribe to the idea that sin was something inherited or that bad behavior was a "family tradition."

Today, I will...choose, as did Josiah, to do what is right.

Josiah: the Seeker

Today's Scripture: 2 Chronicles 34:3

People by their very nature are seekers. Foolish people are looking for something even though they are unsure what that is (Proverbs 18:2). It seems a vacuum exists in man that only God can fill, but most people are searching for anything and everything but God. As a result, man comes to the end of his days unfulfilled and depressed. God created us for Himself and placed a spiritual desire within us that will not allow temporal things to satisfy (Ecclesiastes 3:11). Augustine wrote, "You have made us for yourself, O Lord, and our heart is restless until it rests in you."

Josiah was a good king because he was a God-seeker. "For in the eighth year of his reign, while he was yet young, he began to seek after the God of David his father" (2 Chronicles 34:3 KJV). I recall as a teen, perhaps about the same age as Josiah, I responded one Sunday evening during the invitation hymn. The preacher kindly asked how he could help me, and I told him that I did not think I was growing as a Christian ought, and I wanted to be closer to God. Before he led the prayer, I remember he said to the congregation, "Barry is a wise young man." The statement struck me as odd. I did not feel very wise, especially while I was sitting on the front pew making a public confession. He then explained. He said, "Barry is seeking God at a young age, and that is the wisest thing a young person could ever do."

Josiah's success came as he began to seek after God. "The fear of the LORD is the beginning of knowledge" (Proverbs 1:7 KJV). The good news is that God is not hard to find (Acts 17:27). However, do not delay. "Seek the LORD while he may be found; call upon him while he is near" (Isaiah 55:6).

Today, I will...seek the Lord.

Josiah: the Purger

Today's Scripture: 2 Chronicles 34:3-7

When I preach, I prefer proclaiming the positive aspects of Christianity that, if applied, will make life better for every Christian. However, preaching the gospel or the good news of salvation implies that something exists that is not good. Sin is the transgression of God's law (1 John 3:4). Nothing sinful has ever been advantageous or beneficial in anyone's life. When man sinned in the garden, he willingly and deliberately gave the allegiance that belonged rightly to God to the devil. Now God has given man a plan whereby he can be reconciled, but to do so one must travel the pathway called repentance.

King Josiah, while seeking after God, realized that God must be God alone. There was no room in the land for idolatry. Therefore, Josiah knew that humble repentance in Judah demanded that all idols be destroyed. "And in the twelfth year he began to purge Judah and Jerusalem" (2 Chronicles 34:3). This demanded not only denouncing the idols but the tearing down, pulling up, burning, and cleansing of all that was evil (2 Chronicles 34:3-7).

When something is purged, it is purified. Dear reader, perhaps you need to be purged from sin. Idols in your heart will hinder your relationship with God. You probably have never bowed down to an idol made of wood or stone, yet you still may have idols in your heart (Ezekiel 14:3). In fact, idolatry really is a heart problem. Whatever we place above God has become our idol. Paul wrote, "Put to death therefore what is earthly in you: sexual immorality, impurity, passion, evil desire, and covetousness, which is idolatry" (Colossians 3:5).

Through the blood of Jesus, we can have our sins purged. "Let us draw near with a true heart in full assurance of faith, with our hearts sprinkled clean from an evil conscience and our bodies washed with pure water" (Hebrews 10:22). The one who does this will then let God reign supreme upon the throne of his heart.

Today, I will...purge my heart of every idol that stands between me and my God.

Josiah: the Repairer

Today's Scripture: 2 Kings 22:3-20

When one begins to seek after God and purges himself from sin, it leads to positive action. "Now in the eighteenth year of his reign, when he had cleansed the land and the house, he sent Shaphan the son of Azaliah, and Maaseiah the governor of the city, and Joah the son of Joahaz, the recorder, to repair the house of the Lord" (2 Chronicles 34:8). Because of the wickedness of Judah's previous rulers, which led to apathy among the people, the temple of God was in much need of repair. Josiah was not content just to rid the land of idols, but also desired to restore the temple worship which meant "repairing the house" (2 Kings 22:5).

During this time, the book of the law was found inside the temple, and Shaphan the scribe delivered it to the king and read to him from the book. "When the king heard the words of the Book of the Law, he tore his clothes" (2 Kings 22:11). One should not be surprised to note that if God's house is neglected, it is because His Word has been neglected. Josiah's reaction to the reading demonstrates the penitent attitude of the king on behalf of all of Judah.

Whether it be in the nation, the church, or the individual, revival, restoration, and renewal will not take place without repentance. Josiah, like the psalmist, could say, "my heart stands in awe of your words (Psalm 119:161). Josiah's decision to fully comply with the Word of the Lord would bring God's blessings upon him and the nation, just as it shall today. "But this is the one to whom I will look: he who is humble and contrite in spirit and trembles at my word" (Isaiah 66:2).

It is never just enough to get rid of sin and wickedness in our lives. We must replace the emptiness with something good. As we diligently seek God through His Word, through prayer, through worship, through the church, our lives will start to radically change as we begin to bear the image of the Christ who redeemed us and who set us free.

Today, I will...renew my commitment to Christ and give Him complete control of my life.

The Healer of Broken Hearts

Today's Scripture: 2 Kings 22:20

Names mean things, which was especially true during biblical times. The name of Josiah means "God supports and heals." In recent years, many parents have selected this name for their own sons. Considering that Josiah was the good and righteous king of Judah, it is an honorable name for a young man to wear.

Remember Josiah did that which was right in the sight of God. He was a seeker of God. He purged the land of idolatry. He repaired the breaches of the temple, restoring the ancient worship. He respected and obeyed the law of the Lord. As a result of his good and righteous reign, he brought healing to the land of Judah. While ultimately the nation would once again drift into apostasy, which included the practice of idol worship, Josiah would not have to witness this. "'Therefore, behold, I will gather you to your fathers, and you shall be gathered to your grave in peace, and your eyes shall not see all the disaster that I will bring upon this place.' And they brought back word to the king" (2 Kings 22:20).

Just as Josiah, through his submission to the divine will, brought spiritual healing to a broken people, so the King of kings, Jesus the Christ, brings spiritual healing to us today. He came to do the will of the Father (Hebrews 10:7). His mission is clear in the following passage. "The Spirit of the Lord is upon me, because he has anointed me to proclaim good news to the poor. He has sent me to proclaim liberty to the captives and recovering of sight to the blind, to set at liberty those who are oppressed, to proclaim the year of the Lord's favor" (Luke 4:18-19). A major part of Jesus' ministry was to heal the sick, afflicted, diseased, and demon possessed. This same One is compassionate toward us and invites us to come to Him that He may bear our burdens, especially our burden of sin, and heal our broken hearts.

Today, I will...bring all the broken pieces of my heart to Jesus and let Him put it all back together again.

WEEK #22

Jeremiah

CHUCK MONAN

MONDAY
Going Where You Don't Want to Go
Today's Scripture: Jeremiah 1:1-3; John 21:18

Years ago, a friend was preaching to the inmates in the prison in Jackson, Michigan Telling the men about the faith of God's servant Abraham, he emphasized the mettle of a man willing to leave his home to go "to a place I will show you." He asked the audience, "How many of you would have the faith to get up and go right now to an unknown place?"

Every single person raised his hand. You've got to know your audience.

Jeremiah was from Anathoth, a Levitical city three miles north of Jerusalem. Like most people of his era who rarely left their home or village, Jeremiah probably would have been content to live out his days in his ancestral homeland. The Lord had other plans.

The tumultuous career of Jeremiah as God's prophet saw Judah circling the drain for the last time. God's patience with the wickedness of the people had run out, and the bill would be served by Nebuchadnezzar. In contrast to the optimistic lies of his contemporaries, Jeremiah's words proved true as the city fell and the people were reduced to servitude. Jeremiah was broken in spirit but treated well by the Babylonians.

Just when things couldn't have gotten worse, the acting governor of Judea, Johanan, fled to Egypt, taking with him Jeremiah and his scribe, Baruch. The prophet spent the rest of his life seeking in vain to turn his people back to God.

Tradition holds that Jeremiah spent the remainder of his life in Egypt, a long way from home. A stalwart for God surrounded by idols.

Despite our best plans, life often takes unexpected turns. Sometimes we end up living in places we had not sought or anticipated. As Jesus told Peter, sometimes we end up being led to places and circumstances we do not want to go (John 21:18). Still, we can serve God anywhere and everywhere.

Today, I will...give God my very best, despite whatever circumstances I am facing.

Seeing What You Don't Want to See

Today's Scripture: Jeremiah 8; Lamentations 1

By the spring of 1945 as the Allies were advancing on Germany from the West, American soldiers discovered firsthand the horrors of Nazi atrocities. Upon seeing the Ohrdruf concentration camp, General Dwight Eisenhower testified, "I have never felt able to describe my reactions when I came face to face with indisputable evidence of Nazi brutality and ruthless disregard of every shred of decency...I visited every nook and cranny of the camp because I felt it my duty to be in a position from then on to testify at first hand about these things in case there ever grew up at home the belief or the assumption that the stories of Nazi brutality were just propaganda..." General George S. Patton refused to go inside as he claimed he would get sick.

Too often life forces us to see things we would just as soon not see. Jeremiah watched his countrymen reject God, then watched God's justice reduce Jerusalem to charred ruins. Even now, the words of the prophet drip with pain:

> The harvest is past, the summer is ended, and we are not saved.
> For the wound of the daughter of my people is my heart wounded;
> I mourn, and dismay has taken hold on me (Jeremiah 8:20-21).

> For these things I weep; my eyes flow with tears; for a comforter
> is far from me, one to revive my spirit; my children are desolate,
> for the enemy has prevailed (Lamentations 1:16).

Like Jeremiah, we cannot avert our eyes from painful images. Every day we are confronted with brutal examples of man's inhumanity to his fellow man, or sickness, plague, and disease, and of nature itself red in tooth and claw. We long for a day when God will put the world back to rights, when He will wipe away every tear from our eyes, and when the lion will lie down with the lamb.

Hang in there, friends. That Great Day is coming.

Today, I will...feel the pain of my fellow man, do my best to comfort the brokenhearted, and encourage people with the good news of Jesus.

WEDNESDAY
Doing What You Don't Want to Do
Today's Scripture: Jeremiah 1:4-19

How many times have you heard someone proclaim, "God just wants me to be happy"? Most of us have likely lost count. And no matter how many times you search the Scriptures for this pearl of wisdom, you won't find it.

The Dalai Lama says, "The purpose of our lives is to be happy." But Qoheleth counters, "The end of the matter; all has been heard. Fear God and keep his commandments, for this is the whole duty of man" (Ecclesiates 12:13).

God calls us to be faithful, not to go through life grinning like monkeys riding jet skis to Banana Island. Few would be more qualified to weigh in here more than Jeremiah.

God's call to the prophet from Anathoth was to preach to the nations, "for to all to whom I send you, you shall go, and whatever I command you, you shall speak" (Jeremiah 1:7).

It didn't take very long to discover that this commission would be a brutal undertaking. Jeremiah not only had his message rejected, but he was rebuffed with extreme prejudice by his hostile audience:

They threatened him (26:8).

They mocked him (18:18).

They beat him (20:2).

They restricted his movements (36:5).

They burned his message (36:1-32).

They put him in public stocks (20:2).

They imprisoned him for years (32:2-3).

They threw him into a cistern to die (38:1-6).

Keep in mind that Jeremiah didn't want to preach in the first place (20:14-18). He didn't want to continue. He complained repeatedly to the Lord (11, 12, 15, 17, 18, 20). And as far as his calling making him deliriously happy, he was known as the weeping prophet (9:1; 10; 14:17; Lamentations 1-5).

Yet through it all, Jeremiah persevered. He was faithful: "If I say, 'I will not mention him, or speak any more in his name,' there is in my heart as it were a burning fire shut up in my bones, and I am weary of holding it in, and I cannot" (Jeremiah 20:9). By God's measure of a life, Jeremiah was a success.

Today, I will...remember that the purpose of life is to fear God and obey His commandments.

THURSDAY
Preaching What They Don't Want to Hear
Today's Scripture: Jeremiah 3:10-14

Jesus said, "The truth will set you free" (John 8:32). Aldous Huxley noted, "You shall know the truth, and the truth shall make you mad." Both statements are correct, incidentally.

Long before the apostle Paul asked the brethren, "Have I then become your enemy by telling you the truth? (Galatians 4:16), Jeremiah was telling the nation the truth...which they did not want to hear. And telling them the truth made him their enemy.

Jeremiah pulled no punches in delivering God's Word to the people:
> He called on them to repent and turn back to the Lord (3:10, 12).
> He told them to walk on the ancient paths (6:16).
> He reminded them that a man's life is not his own (10:23).
> He warned them that the heart is deceitful above all things (17:9).
> He defied the false prophets preaching lies (28:15-16).
> He advised the exiles to build new lives in a new home (29:1-14).
> He condemned the idolatry of the land (23:9-15).
> He promised God's imminent punishment on the wicked (25:1-38).

Martin Luther King, Jr. said, "The ultimate measure of a man is not where he stands in moments of convenience and comfort, but where he stands at times of challenge and controversy." In such times as these, Jeremiah did not flinch. He faced down kings, their representatives, and the powerful religious establishment of the day and told them the truth, for which he paid a heavy price.

Commenting on Paul's admonition to "Preach the word, be ready in season and out of season..." (2 Timothy 4:2), Marshall Keeble explained that meant "when they want it, and when they don't." The latter was true for most of Jeremiah's life.

No matter. "The truth does not change according to our ability to stomach it emotionally" noted Flannery O'Connor. Today millions are under the delusion that we determine truth, when the reality is that the truth sits in judgment of us: "The one who rejects me and does not receive my words has a judge; the word that I have spoken will judge him on the last day" (John 12:48). Thank God for fearless proclaimers of the truth like Jeremiah.

Today, I will...speak and live for the truth.

I Have Come to Do Your Will, O God

Today's Scripture: Hebrews 10:5-7

There is no more succinct summation of the life of Jesus than that given by the Hebrews writer: "When Christ came into the world, he said, 'Sacrifices and offerings you have not desired, but a body have you prepared for me; in burnt offerings and sin offerings you have taken no pleasure.' Then I said, 'Behold, I have come to do your will, O God, as it is written of me in the scroll of the book'" (Hebrews 10:5-7). "I have come to do your will, O God..." No one who ever lived did this like Jesus.

But among those who have strived to do God's will, Jeremiah succeeded more than most. This relentless pursuit of the Lord's way resulted in Jeremiah having much in common with Jesus:

Both told the people things they didn't like. Jeremiah countered the lies of the false prophets, telling the people that the exile would be very brief (Jeremiah 29:4-9). Jesus reminded His audiences that they were wrong in making void the Word of God for the sake of their traditions (Matthew 15:1-9).

Both suffered through declining ratings. Jeremiah not only failed to convince the masses of his message, but he was considered a traitor and killjoy by, well, everyone save Baruch. Jesus initially had great crowds following Him until He told them some things they didn't like, and the crowds dwindled.

Both used innovative teaching methods. Jeremiah used a linen belt, a misshapen pot, a broken jar, a yoke and crossbars, and a rock to reach the people. Jesus mastered the parable, which opened God's message to the ordinary while annoying the arrogant.

Both cried over his people. Jeremiah, the Weeping Prophet, was crushed by the hard-heartedness of the nation (Jeremiah 13:17). Jesus, the Man of Sorrows, wept over Jerusalem and its future (Matthew 23:37-39).

Both failed to have a storybook ending. Jeremiah died an exile in pagan Egypt. Jesus died a pariah among His people at the hands of pagan Rome.

Both were ultimately vindicated by God. Jeremiah was proven right by God in the exiles' return (Ezra 1:1; 2 Chronicles 36:22). Jesus was proven right by God through the resurrection (Acts 2:22-41).

Today, I will...rededicate myself to doing God's will, as Jeremiah and Jesus did so faithfully.

WEEK #23

Daniel

JOHN MOORE

Daniel: He Was Different

Today's Scripture: Daniel 1:8-17

Daniel is perhaps one of the greatest heroes of the Bible, and some of my earliest memories of great Bible stories come straight from the book which bears his name. As a young man, Daniel was removed from his homeland and relocated to Babylon, thousands of miles away from the country and surroundings he loved and knew so well. While in captivity he was faced with the temptation to be like everyone else, and to partake of food that would somehow defile him (Daniel 1:8). Despite a life-threatening situation, Daniel stood firm and courageously spoke to the king's officials about an alternate plan for eating and drinking food that was kosher. Even at such a youthful age, he trusted in God and was determined to be faithful to the religious teachings he had received from his youth. He wasn't afraid to be different, and as a result, God rewarded him with the skills and knowledge he needed to complete his task as required within the king's court. Daniel was truly a person of conviction.

Like Daniel, we must also have the courage to be different. Christians are called to be a peculiar nation and show forth good works (1 Peter. 2:9). We must never conform to the world (Romans 12:1-2) or be in fellowship with unfruitful works of darkness (Ephesians 5:11). But being different is rarely easy, and we can often encounter ridicule because of it. Rest assured, though, that when we are faithful to God and aren't afraid to do the hard things, the right things, and what others consider to be the strange things, God will ultimately reward us. He is faithful and He has promised that when we become "doers of the word", we will be blessed in our deeds (James 1:22-25). This is exactly what happened to Daniel. He was blessed because he stood firm and wasn't afraid to be different. As a result, God gave Daniel what he needed.

Today, I will...not be afraid to be different. I will serve the Lord with courage (Psalm 27:14) and look forward to His rewards.

Daniel: A Man with Camel Knees

Today's Scripture: Daniel 9:1-23

In Book II, chapter 23 of Eusebius' *Ecclesiastical History*, the story is told about a man named James "the Just" (the same James, the brother of Jesus, who likely wrote the book of James), who was known for his habit of going into the temple to pray. Eusebius said that James "was frequently found upon his knees begging forgiveness for the people, so that his knees became hard like those of a camel, in consequence of his constantly bending them in his worship of God, and asking forgiveness for the people." We might say today that James had camel knees.

I wonder...do you think Daniel had camel knees? I think we could say with a fair degree of certainty that he did. He was a man known for his praying. No less than three times the book of Daniel reveals to us the value Daniel placed on prayer (Daniel 2:17-18; 6:10; 9:3-19). Because he was so regular and persistent in praying, it became the means by which his detractors could entrap him (Daniel 6:7). Even though a legal decree had been signed by the king that made it illegal to pray, Daniel "entered his house (now in his roof chamber he had windows opened toward Jerusalem); and he continued kneeling on his knees three times a day, praying and giving thanks before his God, as he had been doing previously" (Daniel 6:10, NASB 1995).

Praying on your knees three times every day would certainly make your knees a little more calloused and perhaps a bit knobby. But, as with so many things, when we are willing to sacrifice there are often great rewards. Repeatedly, Daniel was rewarded with God's favor and deliverance simply because he both obeyed and reverenced God. As a result, God used him in ways that brought hope for believers, both in his age and in ours. Prayer changes things (James 5:16; Mark 11:24), and it will change your outlook and bring blessings to you as well.

Today, I will...work on acquiring camel knees.

Daniel: A Faithful Messenger

Today's Scripture: Daniel 4:27

It's one thing to say what is on your mind to those who are afraid of you, but it is an entirely different matter to speak the truth to a superior—or even worse—to someone who has the power over life and death. It takes courage and conviction to say what has to be said, especially to kings and to people in positions of authority. Daniel was just such a man. He spoke what was true and was a faithful messenger in proclaiming the commands of God?

On two different occasions, Daniel had to deliver a message of doom and disaster to kings who had become filled with pride and irreverence. First, before King Nebuchadnezzar, Daniel faithfully interpreted the king's dream and revealed that God would punish him through a most humiliating means (Daniel 4:24-25). He also called the king a sinner and instructed him to repent of his misdeeds. Years later, Daniel was called upon years later to interpret the writing on a banquet wall that had been written by a mysterious finger during a feast organized by King Belshazzar (Daniel 5:13-28). Vessels from God's temple were being used in worship to the gods of Babylon, and Daniel was called upon to interpret what turned out to be a condemnation of the king. In both cases, Daniel did not waver nor shrink from saying what God had revealed. He delivered God's warning without one adjustment or change to the message. Daniel was a faithful messenger of God, even in a threatening situation.

As Christians, we too are called upon to faithfully proclaim the message of truth (2 Timothy 4:1-5). Despite what may or may not be popular, we must contend for the faith (Jude v. 3), and hold fast to the traditions of the apostles, whether in word or in deed (2 Thessalonians 2:15). We must have the courage of our convictions to be faithful servants of God, and to carefully guard and protect the truth of the gospel. We must preach the truth in love, but it must always be done in love (Ephesians 4:15).

Today, I will...remain faithful to God's Word and preach all that He commands.

Daniel: An Influencer

Today's Scripture: Daniel 5:13-14

In March of 2008, something incredible happened in the California town of South Pasadena. In an unprecedented act, the city council voted to proclaim the first week of March a "No Cussing Week." South Pasadena's mayor Michael Cacciotti said the ordinance "provides a reminder to be more civil, and to elevate the level of discourse." The ordinance was created because of the influence of a fourteen-year-old boy named McKay Hatch. His story has been told on nearly every major news network throughout the U.S. McKay was, in many ways, one of the first "influencers" in the social media world.

Some 2,600 years ago, the first city council influencer arose within the ancient nation of Babylon. Like McKay Hatch, Daniel had the ear of some very important people—people far more powerful than any city council member of a democratically elected society. In Daniel's case, he was able to influence one of the most powerful men on earth to give praise and glory to God (Daniel 4:34-37). Daniel's honesty, integrity, courage, and devotion to God influenced Daniel's friends, King Nebuchadnezzar, and the royal palace. His legacy of good works and the prophecies he made about the kingdom (Daniel 2) continue to influence us still. Any child growing up in the church today knows about Daniel, and each of us have been taught to be like him.

Whether we like it or not, everyone has influence. Let none of us be guilty of thinking that what we do and say goes unnoticed, for as Paul revealed, "none of us lives to himself, and no one dies to himself" (Romans 14:7 NKJV). He also said that Christians must be "lights in the world" (Philippians 2:15). Our walk of faith must be characterized by love and righteous works so that others will be caused to glorify our "Father which is in heaven" (Matthew 5:16 NKJV). Through our good behavior we can cause even our enemies to "glorify God in the day of visitation" (1 Peter 2:11-12 NKJV).

Today, I will...influence others to give glory to the God of heaven.

Daniel: He Reminds Us of Jesus

Today's Scripture: Daniel 7:13-14

After meeting someone for the first time, my wife and I will often say to one another, "who does she [or he] remind you of?" It might be an old friend, someone famous, or perhaps a family member. Of course, my opinions don't always coincide with hers, but occasionally we agree and a peculiar trait or mannerism might be observed that causes us to think of someone else. This occurs between us quite often, and sometimes we can even make those connections between God's people found in the Bible.

In many ways, Daniel should remind us of Jesus. Just as he carefully observed the law of God (Daniel 1:8), Jesus did as well (Matthew 5:17; Romans 8:3-4). Just as Daniel was regular in prayer, Jesus consistently prayed to the Father (Luke 18:1). And, when Daniel was entombed in the lion's den, we remember that in a similar way Jesus conquered death and emerged from the tomb victoriously (Romans 6:9). Above all, Daniel reminds us of Jesus because he spoke so readily about Him. The Son of Man who received an everlasting kingdom is a topic that stands at center stage in this marvelous book. Daniel pointed people to Jesus by the way he lived and by things that he taught. It's actually very hard not to think of Jesus when we look at Daniel. He lived like Him and talked about Him.

When others look at you, what or who is it that they see? Do you remind people of Jesus in the way that Daniel reminded others about Christ? As Daniel talked about the Son of Man, do you talk to others about the Son of God? As a Christian, you are called to be like Jesus. You must bear the image of Christ (Colossians 3:10), follow His example (1 Peter 1:22), and have within you the heart of a servant (Philippians 2:1-5) and the mind of obedience (Luke 22:42).

Today, I will...remind people of Jesus, and endeavor to be like Him in all that I do.

WEEK #24

Shadrach, Meshach, & Abednego

DAVID DUNCAN

What Do I Do When Bad Things Happen?

Today's Scripture: Daniel 1:1-7

Do you know of Hananiah, Misael, and Azariah? We usually call them Shadrach, Meshach, and Abednego. I can imagine them being tempted to ask why bad things happen to good people.

Everything seemed to be going their way early on. According to Daniel 1, they were healthy, good looking and extremely intelligent. They were even from royalty. All was good until Babylon invaded Israel and hauled the men off to a foreign country.

Imagine the frustration they could have felt. Before captivity, people listened when they talked, noticed when they walked in a room, and when a problem needed to be solved, they were up for the test. They were the best their nation had to offer. Then, because of no fault of their own, their world completely changed.

A world leader forever changed their lives. Nebuchadnezzar crumbled their country and tore the men from their homeland. Their geography changed. The culture was unusual. The food was weird. The religion was idolatrous. Shadrach, Meshach, and Abednego lived daily without knowing why their lives had been turned upside down.

What should we do when bad things happen to good people? Shadrach, Meshach and Abednego would tell us to stay faithful to God. The men refused to eat the king's food and refused to worship an idol. Even when threatened with a horrible death, they stayed faithful to God. Daniel 3:17-18 (NIV) states, "If we are thrown into the blazing furnace, the God we serve is able to deliver us from it, and he will deliver us from Your Majesty's hand. But even if he does not, we want you to know, Your Majesty, that we will not serve your gods or worship the image of gold you have set up."

Real-time living is more difficult than looking back at history. What do I do if one of my family members gets sick? How should I react if I lose my job? What is my response to disappointment? I may not know why things are occurring, but I know what to do.

Today, I will...vow to stay faithful to God. Keep praying. Keep worshiping. Keep studying. Keep depending on God.

TUESDAY
Choose God

Today's Scripture: Daniel 1:8-21

Shadrach, Meshach, and Abednego knew the ways of the Lord but found themselves living in Babylon. Not only did they live there, Daniel 1:5 states they were to be trained for three years in the ways of the king of Babylon.

Our children seem to be under the tutelage of Babylon today. There is a sense, however, that children are not the only ones being educated by anti-Christian teachings. Adults, even Christian parents and grandparents, are lifelong learners and practitioners of sin.

Babylon's voice is not just heard in public education, although it is sometimes. Nebuchadnezzar's ways are sometimes espoused through social media, political rhetoric and conversations with friends. So called "Christian" preaching has even been known to be a funnel of information that leads to worship of things rather than God.

How did Shadrach, Meshach, and Abednego survive Babylon's ungodly babbling? The young men did what old men need to do as well. They resolved to stay faithful. They were polite in their conviction but unmoving. The young men did not lose their tempers or storm Nebuchadnezzar's palace when they disagreed with the order to eat the king's food. They, along with Daniel, respectfully sought a resolution. Finally, even when they refused to bow to an idol set up by the king, they did so quietly. Their quietness should not be mistaken for a lack of boldness. Their resolve led them to a punishment in a fiery furnace where, saving a miracle, they would have lost their lives for their biblical convictions.

What do I do as the ways of Babylon are all around me? Like the young men, I must be resolute not to fall to temptation. I will not be moved by the devil's schemes. I will keep my eyes on Jesus, the author and perfecter of our faith (Hebrews 12:2). I may not be able to decide where I live, but I can determine how I live.

Today, I will...choose to look to the God of heaven rather than to the empty earthly promises that Babylon offers me.

I Know My Identity

Today's Scripture: Daniel 1

Have you known people that have lost their identity? It happens all the time. An eighteen-year- old leaves home for a giant university and feels like a number. A man gets transferred to a new office across the country that looks very different from home. A faithful Christian family leaves their small congregation for a larger one with a stronger youth group. Instead of connecting, they become disenfranchised from the Lord.

Hananiah, Mishael, and Azariah were taken from their earthly father but not from their Heavenly Father. They lost their names, but they did not lose their identity. They could have melted into the new culture, but they chose to stand out.

How can I stay faithful through the chaos and change, like the men we usually call Shadrach, Meshach, and Abednego?

First, I need to prepare before there is a crisis. Prayer, Bible study, worship, fellowship, and ministry involvement will help me know the Lord. It is usually too late to dig the foundation and build the house when the storm has already blown in.

Second, I need to decide my non-negotiables before someone expects me to negotiate. The devil will probably not initially ask me to give up everything. I would resist such a suggestion. He will instead try to get me to move my "line in the sand" just a little bit. Such a move is harder to resist.

Third, I need to cast all my anxiety on the Lord. Peter reminded his persecuted audience that God is still alive and active even amid my confusion.

Fourth, as Peter also wrote, I need to remember other believers have been threatened with identity loss and stood strong. Shadrach, Meshach, and Abednego maintained their convictions, Elijah was reminded of other faithful prophets, and Jesus, Himself, was true to His mission.

Today, I will...declare my identity is in Jesus.

The Importance of Doing the Right Thing

Today's Scripture: Daniel 3

In 1952, Harry Volkman and Frank McGee, unlawfully repeated information of a possible tornado outbreak on WKY-TV in Oklahoma City that they heard at Tinker Air Force Base. Weather information was considered classified information. Why would Volkman and McGee knowingly break the law? They seemingly had a commitment to humanity. They believed the information could save lives.

Shadrach, Meshach, and Abednego disobeyed an order from the king. They could have given in to political and social pressure. Or, they could have secretly followed God and said, "We will bow but think about Yahweh while we do it." The three enslaved Israelites chose to refuse the king's idol, or even appear to worship it.

Why would Shadrach, Meshach, and Abednego intentionally break the law? They broke man's law because they had a commitment to the law of the Lord. While God was honored with their bravery and conviction, humanity also continues to benefit from the young men's decision. Millions of people of numerous languages, races, and locations for thousands of years have gained insight into God and courage to face persecution, because Shadrach, Meshach, and Abednego decided it was better to go into a fiery furnace than to get their knees dirty bowing to a statue.

My morality and spiritual conviction are challenged every day. The things I put in my body and brain can tempt me to go the way of Babylon. There is sometimes an urge to go with the culture rather than the Creator.

Decisions I make today will have an impact on others, one way or another. My anger may mean the elders spending needed time away from children to pray with me. The money I flippantly spend now may cost me later. My sin may bring division in the church.

On the positive side, through the help of God, I can help change generations for good. My Bible study can lead me to praise, prayer can lead me to resolve, and service can lead me to the salvation of others.

Today, I will...stand up for God because it is the best decision I can make.

More Like Jesus

Today's Scripture: Luke 22:41-42

I have felt persecuted before. I was not invited to some parties in high school. I have been called a "goody two shoes" more than once' which hurt my feelings. I have even felt like a suffering servant when church members have not agreed with my sermons. Yes, I know, that is not persecution. It may be annoying and slightly hurtful, but my life has never been threatened. I have experienced nothing like Shadrach, Meshach, and Abednego.

No human would normally desire to die. We gasp for breath when we come up out of the water, and we move when a ball is flying toward our head. God has put it in us to live.

People who are willing to die do so only when deeply convicted or they love profoundly. Shadrach, Meshach, and Abednego were convicted of God's sovereignty and loved Him with all their heart, soul, mind, and strength. They willingly went into the furnace because their loyalty to Yahweh was unmatched.

There is another individual that is deeply convicted and loves wholeheartedly. His name is Jesus. His fiery furnace came in the form of a cross.

The words of Jesus in the garden of Gethsemane should give strength to all, "Not my will, but Your will be done" (Luke 22:41-42). Jesus was convicted of the mission with such an almost incomprehensible love for His Father and the world that He suffered persecution.

Shadrach, Meshach, and Abednego went through emotional trauma as they went into the fire but God did not let them burn or even smell like smoke. Another being even went through the escapade with them.

Jesus, on the other hand, felt the Roman whip, heard the jeering crowds, experienced the abandonment of His disciples and knew when His Father turned away. On the cross, He must have felt something like shooting fire go through His nerves from His hands and feet, racing up and down His body.

The three young men, like Jesus, took on persecution because it was nothing compared to the love and conviction they had for the Father.

Today, I will...ask the Lord to help me be more like them.

WEEK #25

Ezra

JUSTIN GUIN

Ezra: A Faithful Servant of God

Today's Scripture: Ezra 7

We are introduced to the faithful servant Ezra in the book that bears his name. However, he does not appear in the story until Ezra 7. In Ezra 1-6, the faithful scribe recounted the return of Israel to Jerusalem and the rebuilding of the Temple. As Ezra wrote about himself, we learn several important facts about him. First, his lineage was impressive. He could trace his roots back to Aaron, the brother of Moses. This lineage uniquely qualified him to be the spiritual leader Israel needed as they resettled their land. Second, the text described him as "skilled in the Law of Moses." He lived and taught God's Word. Third, the Persian king commissioned Ezra to carry out whatever he needed him to do as Israel returned from captivity (7:25-26). Ezra 7:6 ends "for the hand of the LORD his God was on him." Who else in the Old Testament enjoyed this divine privilege? Joseph, Moses, Samson, and David, just to name a few. Artaxerxes, Israel, and the Lord could rely on him, because Ezra was a faithful servant who sought to serve God with every fiber of his being.

Faithfulness is the goal of every Christian. We are instructed to be "steadfast, immovable, always abounding in the work of the Lord" (1 Corinthians 15:58). At the end of our earthly sojourn, we desire to hear "well done, good and faithful servant." The challenge with faithfulness is the consistency it demands. Christianity is not something you do in a season of life, then move on to something else. It is a lifetime commitment (James 1:12). Ezra's example of unwavering faith reminds us that it can be done with God's strengthening power. Paul wrote, "be strong in the Lord and in the strength of his might" (Ephesians 6:10). God can use servants who are faithful and strengthened by Him to accomplish His purposes.

Today, I will...resolve to become more faithful in my service to the Lord, relying on His strengthening power.

The Heart of the Matter

Today's Scripture: Psalm 119

Psalm 119:2 says, "Blessed are those who keep his testimonies, who seek him with their whole heart." From Genesis to Revelation, you can see examples and study principles relating to giving your "whole heart" to God. For the Hebrew people, the heart was the center of emotions. It is the source of thought and devotion. Giving your whole heart to God symbolizes giving your entire being to the Lord.

Ezra was a man whose heart was given wholly to God. Note the most well-known passage about this godly man, "For Ezra had set his heart to study the Law of the LORD, and to do it and to teach his statutes and rules in Israel" (Ezra 7:10). "Set his heart" refers to being firm, ready, or certain. It describes the devotion that Ezra made to studying and interpreting the law. His task consumed him.

What have you set your heart to do? Different seasons of life bring different roles and opportunities. Five years ago, what was important to you is no longer at the forefront of your mind today. Regardless of life's changes, a Christian must set their heart to serve the Lord. This focus will require a shift in attitude. You must strive to view things from an eternal standpoint. Paul stated, "So we do not focus on what is seen, but on what is unseen. For what is seen is temporary, but what is unseen is eternal" (2 Corinthians 4:18, CSB). Setting your heart to serve the Lord puts temporary things in their proper perspective. Also, you align your desires with God's. Note Psalm 37:4, "Delight yourself in the LORD, and he will give you the desires of your heart." When you delight in the things the Lord does, you will know joy, and your heart will seek His divine will for your life.

Today, I will...begin taking delight in the things God delights in, aligning my desires with His.

A Living Bible

Today's Scripture: Nehemiah 8

John Maxwell said, "A leader is one who knows the way, goes the way, and shows the way." Ezra resembled this leadership principle in every way. Returning to Ezra 7:10, note how the text describes him, "For Ezra had set his heart to study the Law of the LORD, and to do it and to teach his statutes and rules in Israel." Ezra was faithful to three simple tasks—study, live, and teach God's Word.

Study means to inquire or seek. Perhaps the idea of "studying" get a bad rap because we view it almost as a punishment. We all dreaded studying for tests when in school. We must not allow this attitude to affect our love for learning God's Word. Ezra had such an attitude. He devoted himself to searching out God's Word and became "skilled in the Law of the Moses" (Ezra 7:6). May we seek to be like the Psalmist, "With my whole heart I seek you; let me not wander from your commandments" (Psalm 119:10).

Next, the text says Ezra sought to "do it." Learning God's Word is excellent but not enough. We can have a head full of Scripture and a heart full of sin. It must become our life's duty to apply it to life. The Bible equips us for faithful service in "rightly handling the word of truth" (2 Timothy 2:15). Our lives become a living Bible.

Finally, considering Ezra's example, note that he taught it to Israel. In Nehemiah 8:2-3, Erza's teaching ministry was in full effect. He taught the Word of God to the people for several hours. His teaching led to a revival among the children of Israel (Nehemiah 8:13). If we want to effect real change in our world, we must be about teaching God's Word.

Our lives are to proclaim the excellencies of the Lord (1 Peter 2:9). When we seek to become a living Bible like Ezra, we will do just that.

Today, I will...seek to become a living Bible following Ezra's example of studying, living, and teaching God's Word.

THURSDAY
If You Mess Up, You Must "Fess" Up
Today's Scripture: Ezra 9:5-15

When he began his ministry among the Israelites, Ezra found several spiritual deficiencies. They were largely ignorant of the law of Moses and hadn't kept its feasts (Nehemiah 8:13). They had intermarried with pagans who brought in idolatrous practices (Ezra 9-10). The people were willing to learn and apply (cf. Ezra 9:4) but more needed to be done. Ezra 9:5-15 records one of the most beautiful prayers in Scripture as God's faithful priest confessed the people's sin.

What happens when you try to hide sin? Note David's experience, "For day and night your hand was heavy upon me; my strength was dried up as by the heat of summer" (Psalm 32:4). It is a harrowing experience. There are constant reminders of the mistake you made. You become paranoid because you think people are "on to you." Add to these things the guilt you feel because you know you have hurt your God, who loves you. What is the solution to relieve such a terrible state? Note Psalm 32:5-6, "I acknowledged my sin to you, and I did not cover my iniquity; I said, 'I will confess my transgressions to the LORD,' and you forgave the iniquity of my sin. Therefore let everyone who is godly offer prayer to you at a time when you may be found; surely in the rush of great waters, they shall not reach him."

Confession brings about ownership and responsibility. It also leads to forgiveness from our gracious God. He is faithful and just to forgive when we confess our sins to Him. He cleanses us from all unrighteousness (1 John 1:9). Let us resolve to confess our sins to God, who desires to forgive us.

Today, I will...resolve to quit holding on to sin. I will confess it to God and seek His forgiveness.

Christ, Our Intercessor

Today's Scripture: Ezra 10

In the Old Testament, the priest interceded between God and the people. Ezra fulfilled this task well. After confessing their sins, he had the people make a covenant with the Lord. Ezra 10:3 says, "Therefore let us make a covenant with our God to put away all these wives and their children, according to the counsel of my lord and of those who tremble at the commandment of our God, and let it be done according to the Law." Solving the spiritual problem of intermarriage required revival, renewal, and resolve. The people had to make a solemn promise in the presence of God to faithfully keep the law where their ancestors failed. The covenant sought to bring the people closer to God and stronger in faith.

The work of Ezra, and other priests before him, foreshadowed the priesthood of Christ. In the New Testament, the role of priest and intercessor is fulfilled in Jesus Christ. First John 2:2 describes Him as our advocate who offered Himself as our atoning sacrifice. His priesthood is unlike Ezra and others in the old covenant (Hebrews 7:23-25). His is eternal. Note the blessing of His eternal priesthood, "Consequently, he is able to save to the uttermost those who draw near to God through him, since he always lives to make intercession for them" (Hebrews 7:25). Therefore, we can confidently come before God as He intercedes on our behalf.

Christ has also made a covenant with God's people. It is a better and abiding covenant, in which He secured eternal redemption (Hebrews 9:13-14). The old covenant required the continuous offering of bulls and goats that brought about a reminder of sin. Christ's covenant is based on the once-and-for-all sacrifice of Himself for sin (Hebrews 10:3-4, 12-13).

Today, I will...have a greater appreciation of Christ's work as our High Priest and Intercessor.

WEEK #26

Nehemiah

JAMES HAYES

MONDAY
A Bad Report
Today's Scripture: Nehemiah 1

Even though the Bible is filled with good news—like the gospel itself—there are also many accounts of bad news. Ten spies gave a bad report about the Promised Land (Numbers 13:27-29); three messengers told Job that his children, servants, and livestock had been destroyed (Job 1:13-19); and John the Baptist's disciples told Jesus that John had been decapitated (Matthew 14:10-12).

In Nehemiah 1, we see that Nehemiah received a bad report: the walls were broken and the gates to the city of Jerusalem were burned down. Then Nehemiah did a human thing—he cried. He was living hundreds of miles away in Susa of Babylon, with the exiles from Jerusalem, and his heart was torn to pieces. But after weeping, he did a Christian thing —he prayed.

Nehemiah's prayer had three basic elements. First, he acknowledged who God is. He called the Lord a "great and awesome God" who maintains His covenants and His love for His people (1:5). Second, acknowledged his sins and the sins of his people (1:6). Lastly, he acknowledged God's promises (1:8-9).

You would not understand a world that contained only good news. In the last 24 hours, you have likely heard of divorces, disabilities, and deaths. As Anne Murray sang about many years ago, we all could use some good news today.

When you receive a bad report, remember Nehemiah. That faithful man of God wept when he heard about Jerusalem. God made us emotional beings. It is always okay to cry. If our perfect Savior did not suppress His emotions when He was in pain, neither should we.

Take your pain to the Lord. Remember who He is. Remember, He watched His Son be tortured, so He knows your pain as well. But on top of all that, remember His abiding promises—when you confess your sins, He is faithful to forgive (I John 1:9). He will supply the grace if you run to Him in your time of need (Hebrews 4:16).

Today, I will...weep with those who weep and take my pain to my Lord.

TUESDAY

A Blessed Request

Today's Scripture: Nehemiah 2:1-8

Richard Griffin spent thirty years in Buckingham Palace in London as a royal protection officer for Queen Elizabeth II. He told the story of a weekend in which he and the queen were in Scotland at one of the queen's private residences. After having a picnic together, Griffin and the queen went for a walk through the Highlands. They came upon two American hikers, neither of whom recognized the Queen. They began telling her about their homes in America and how long they had been in the United Kingdom on vacation. At the end of the conversation, one of the Americans made an unusual request—he wanted the queen to take a picture of him and Richard Griffin. Then they took a picture of her and went on their way. Imagine their shock when they finally (hopefully) found out that they had asked the Queen of England to take a picture for them!

In the fourth century B.C., Nehemiah could not be that casual with King Artaxerxes. Even though Nehemiah worked as the king's cupbearer—a job of some importance—making requests directly to a king was neither advisable nor common. But in Nehemiah's sorrow, after he prayed, he said to the king: "If it pleases the king, and if your servant has found favor in your sight, that you send me to Judah, to the city of my fathers' graves, that I may rebuild it" (Nehemiah 2:5).

Nehemiah could have taken many different approaches that day. He could have run away to Jerusalem. He could have blamed the Babylonian kings for his predicament. But instead, he chose to ask, and he was blessed: "And the king granted me what I asked, for the good hand of God was upon me" (2:8).

No matter how upset you might be, it is always better to ask instead of demand, respect authority instead of rebelling against it, and wait for the answer instead of acting selfishly and impulsively.

Today, I will...respect those around me and thereby fulfill the Golden Rule.

A Bold Resolution

Today's Scripture: Nehemiah 2:11-18

It has been said that during the frontier days in America, a "buck" was used in card games to signify whose turn it was to deal the cards. The buck could be a knife stuck in the table or any other device to remind the players who the next dealer would be. If the designated player did not want to deal, he or she would "pass the buck" to another player. "Passing the buck" later became an expression that meant someone was trying to pass blame or responsibility to someone else. President Harry Truman had a sign in the Oval Office that read "The Buck Stops Here," indicating that the president makes the tough, final decisions.

Nehemiah was not a buck-passer. He spent three days secretly evaluating and investigating the destruction of Jerusalem's wall and gates. He did not like what he saw. In Nehemiah's day, if a city had no wall, it had no protection. Today, you might drive from one town to another without knowing where one town ends and another begins. Not so in ancient Israel. There were no sprawling suburbs. There was the city and the desert. Without a wall, Jerusalem could not be Jerusalem.

So, Nehemiah took on the responsibility of rebuilding the wall. He said: "You see the trouble we are in, how Jerusalem lies in ruins with its gates burned. Come, let us build the wall of Jerusalem, that we may no longer suffer derision" (2:17).

Nehemiah took on a tremendously difficult task when he made that bold resolution. He could have passed the buck after determining the work would be too hard. But he didn't. He trusted that the same God who had been favorable to him in the past would be favorable to him in the future (2:18), so he went to work.

Too many Christians sidestep their God-given responsibilities. Paul wrote: "Whatever you do, work heartily, as for the Lord and not for men" (Colossians 3:23). Nehemiah worked heartily for the Lord. So should we.

Today, I will...rededicate myself to fulfilling my responsibilities to the Lord.

A Belittling Resistance

Today's Scripture: Nehemiah 4:1-8

The greatest feeling in the world is acceptance, and the worst feeling in the world is rejection. We want the group, the person, the organization, or the boss to endorse and celebrate us. We want to be in the "in crowd," because the sting of rejection never fully fades. Remember the girl or guy who wouldn't date you? Remember the job you didn't get? Remember the offer on the house that wasn't accepted? Of course you do. You remember the pain even if you don't feel the pain anymore.

Nehemiah was harassed while he rebuilt the wall. Sanballat the Horonite and Tobiah the Ammonite mocked and despised Nehemiah (4:1-3). Their anger burned against Nehemiah and his workers so badly that they conspired to stir up all of Jerusalem against them (4:8). But Nehemiah was not deterred. He stationed half of his men around the walls as a security team while the other half worked. "Those who carried burdens were loaded in such a way that each labored on the work with one hand and held his weapon with the other" (4:17).

As we can see, Nehemiah took the threats seriously, but he also took his God seriously. Before arranging his men to defend the rebuilding project, he prayed. He then encouraged the Jews by saying, "Do not be afraid of them. Remember the Lord, who is great and awesome, and fight for your brothers, your sons, your daughters, your wives, and your homes" (4:14).

Paul teaches us to take everything to the Lord in prayer (Philippians 4:6). When times are good, pray. When times are bad, pray. When you are belittled even though you are doing a good thing, pray. And as you are praying, use God's blessings to continue to serve Him, just like Nehemiah did. "Be steadfast, immovable, always abounding in the work of the Lord, knowing that in the Lord your labor is not in vain" (I Corinthians 15:58).

Today, I will...ignore the criticisms, pray about it, and serve God no matter what.

A Beautiful Reconstruction and Reconciliation

Today's Scripture: Nehemiah 6:15-19; Ephesians 2:14-16

The Bible states that the wall was completed in fifty-two days. Nehemiah wrote: "When all our enemies heard of it, all the nations around us were afraid and fell greatly in their own esteem, for they perceived that this work had been accomplished with the help of our God" (6:16).

Throughout Nehemiah's work, he prayed and gave glory to God. Even his enemies conceded that God had blessed him. It reminds us of Jesus' teaching about the result of our work for Him: "Let your light shine before others, so that they may see your good works and give glory to your Father who is in heaven" (Matthew 5:16).

Nehemiah's work resulted in a wall that would give the Jews protection. Spiritually, we need to continue to build walls for our protection. We need to build a wall against the schemes of the devil by putting on the whole armor of God (Ephesians 6:11). We need to build a wall against fleshly desires and behaviors (Galatians 5:19-21). We need to build a wall of peace around our hearts through prayer (Philippians 4:7).

Jesus, however, tore down the strongest wall—the one between us and God—and created reconciliation. As Paul stated, "He Himself is our peace, who has made us both one and has broken down in his flesh the dividing wall of hostility" (Ephesians 2:14). Sin builds walls. Only Jesus can tear them down. Not our good works. Not our self-righteousness. Not our rationalizations or excuses. Only through Christ can we have peace with God (Romans 5:1). Only in His righteousness can we stand justified before God (2 Corinthians 5:21).

Build walls that protect your faith. Tear down walls that divide souls. And praise Jesus that He tore down the one wall we couldn't destroy—the wall of sin! Therefore, as the Hebrews writer said, let us shake off the tangles of sin and run with endurance all the way to our heavenly reward.

Today, I will...be a minister of reconciliation for my fellow man.

WEEK #27

Esther

DALE HUBBERT

Bloom Where You Are Planted

Today's Scripture: Esther 2:19-23

The accounts found in the book bearing her name give us reason to be impressed and encouraged. Esther and Ruth are the only two books of our Bible that bear the name of women. Abraham, Moses, and David are among a list of remarkable spiritual stalwarts that do not have a book named after them. The chronicles of Ruth and Esther relate circumstances that provided significant challenges.

When we first met Esther she was among a group of Jews captive to the Persians. Her mother and father were dead (Esther 2:7). The major influence and role model in her life was Mordecai, a relative who took her as his own daughter (Esther 2:7). How seemingly obscure and insignificant!

God, however, had an amazing role for one who was willing to listen and respond with courage and faith. There is no record of Esther whining, complaining, or hosting a pity party for her station in life. She was patient and willing to be utilized by God to overturn a plot to destroy her and all of the Jews. It is unlikely she had any foreknowledge of how the situation would unfold or what the next steps would be. She simply took one day and one opportunity at a time.

Who could have known that the removal of Vashti as queen would lead to Esther being chosen as her replacement (Esther 1:19-22)? Who could have known that Mordecai through Esther, would have an opportunity to save the king (Esther 2:19-23)? Who could have known that Esther would have such a powerful influence upon the king (Esther 7:2)? Esther truly bloomed where she was planted!

What about me? What about you? What circumstances in our lives do we wish were different that God is waiting to use for the good of others and to His glory? May God help us to live not in the "what if" world but in the "what is" world. Like Esther—bloom where you are planted.

Today, I will...focus on my current station in life and bloom where I have been planted!

Use What You Have

Today's Scripture: Esther 3

The book bearing her name finds Esther herself captive in a foreign land. It is not very likely that her financial net worth statement was very impressive. She did not begin occupying a place of prominence in society. She did not have her parents to lean on for guidance and support. So, what did she have?

Esther was beautiful and lovely (Esther 2:7). She had the ability to gain grace and favor (Esther 2:17). She had an advisor, Mordecai, who gave her wise counsel and discernment (Esther 4:13-14).

Beauty can be both external and internal. Esther was both beautiful on the outside and the inside. Being lovely is often a combination of attitude and action. Esther used was able to obtain grace. She was also able to find favor.

It was not what Esther did not have, but rather what she did have which God utilized in an amazing way to save the Jews from destruction at this time (Esther 3:5-6).

Esther was content and willing to use the talents and resources she had rather than focus on what she did not have. What a novel lifestyle! Satan knows it is easier (and counterproductive) to spend valuable time in thought of what we don't possess and what others do possess.

Have your ever taken inventory of the areas God has blessed you? Where are your strengths? What do you do well? What ways do you connect best with others? How willing are you to partner with God in this?

A parable Jesus teaches points out that all received something (Matthew 25:15). In the same setting Jesus also identified six areas of service that afford opportunities for us to use our gifts (Matthew 25:35-36). If we will use our gifts, we are certain God will do His part (1 Corinthians 3:6).

Today, I will...like Esther use the gifts God has given me to His glory.

Such a Time as This
Today's Scripture: Esther 4:14

The amazing events chronicled in the book of Esther are a reminder of the unlimited ability of our God to use His people to accomplish things we cannot sometimes conceive. As a captive Jew, Esther seemed an unlikely person to preserve and protect a group of people from which Jesus would later be born.

One of the blessings to Esther was the aid and guidance of her relative Mordecai. It was Mordecai that challenged her when there was a plot to kill and destroy all of the Jews. Esther had a decision and an opportunity. She could stay silent and die or speak up and potentially live.

Mordecai asked her: "who know whether you have not come to the kingdom for such a time as this?" (Esther 4:14). We never know when we will have an opportunity or what impact that opportunity will have.

Esther took advantage of that "time." Through a series of events, she was able to expose a man's wicked plan to destroy the Jews. How often do we spend time in prayer that God will provide opportunity and open doors in our lives? How open are our eyes to see when God provides in this way? Is it a conversation? Is it a benevolence situation we come upon? Is it a tragedy? Is it chaos in the life of someone? Is it a family difficulty?

Providence is real and somewhat challenging to identify. God can take us, like Joseph and Esther, wherever we are to accomplish His will and bless others. We do not have the insight to know how large or small the effects will be when we submit to God's calling.

It took the words of a friend for Esther to see challenge and opportunity. Have others shared with us? Have we shared with others? God does not want anyone to be lost eternally, but He needs our partnership (2 Peter 3:9).

Today, I will...look for the opportunities God places in my path.

"If I Perish, I Perish"

Today's Scripture: Esther 4

In the 10 chapters and 167 verses in the book of Esther, there are a number of twists and turns. The book begins with Esther, a Jew, in obscurity, but she rises to be the queen following Vashti's dismissal. Esther was beautiful and lovely, finding grace and favor with King Ahasuerus. Haman was a man who despised Mordecai and the Jews. He connived a plan to destroy all Jews and was able to convince Ahasuerus to allow him to carry out the plan (Esther 3:8-11).

Esther had initially not made known her Jewish nationality (Esther 2:10). Even as the queen, she was not exempt from the consequences of the decree of the king. Mordecai explained to her that deliverance could come to the Jews from another place, but she and her family would die (Esther 4:14).

Esther faced a difficult quandary. If she approached the king without being invited, she would stand to die if he did not extend to her his golden scepter (Esther 4:11). If Esther did not convince the king to revoke his decree, she would die because of the order of the decree Haman tricked Ahasuerus into signing.

Esther responded with courage. She made the decision to approach the king with the mindset, "if I perish, I perish" (Esther 4:16).

God's people have always been called upon to act with courage. Sometimes the results may seem small, and sometimes the results affect an amazing number of people. Esther chose to do the right thing in the face of potentially fatal consequences.

She was encouraged by Mordecai, her mentor. Courage is always enhanced when we receive strength and confidence from others. God makes promises for those who will be courageous (Deuteronomy 31:6). Because Esther's courage propelled her to take a risk, the lives of many people were saved.

Today, I will...act with courage, truly trusting God to stand with me.

One for Many

Today's Scripture: Galatians 4:4; Hebrews 7:27

The book of Esther does not mention God by name, but His presence, providence, purity, and promises immersed the events, which took place in Susa. A most unlikely Jewish woman wisely and courageously set things in order to preserve the Jews from death plotted by the wicked Haman. God can still use ordinary people to do extraordinary things today.

Esther lived almost five hundred years before Jesus lived on the earth. There are some parallels that link Esther and Jesus to our goals and aspirations. Our knowledge of Esther begins with her living in relative obscurity. Jesus was born in Bethlehem. He was laid in a manger because there was no room in an inn for Mary and the family. His childhood was seemingly without great notice.

When the timing of God was right, there was a plan and purpose for Esther and for Jesus. In what seemed a hopeless situation, Esther acted courageously in seeking the presence of the king to overturn a deadly decree. She put her own life at risk to save the lives of many. She petitioned for the lives of all the Jews.

Jesus arrived on God's terms and His timing (Galatians 4:4). Jesus lived a sinless life and not only put His life at risk, but gave His life (John 3:16). Jesus died "once for all when he offered up himself" (Hebrews 7:27). We can have hope because of Jesus' courage and love. One died for many.

We are thankful for the example of Esther. She used her gifts and acted courageously when the opportunity presented itself, which resulted in the salvation of the Jews. Even greater is Jesus love and grace. He humbled Himself and became one of us, so that One could die for and save many. Hallelujah what a Savior!

Today, I will...live in such a way that reflects my gratitude for Jesus who died for all.

WEEK #28

Job

WAYNE JONES

Job in Chaos

Today's Scripture: Job 1:1-5, 13-22

James assumes his readers have "heard of the steadfastness of Job" (James 5:11). Have you? In order to appreciate his steadfast patience, you must be aware of the intenseness of his tragedy.

Job's story may be the most popular in the Old Testament. It is one of heartbreak, loss, conflict, and resolve. It is likely, even if you have not read all of the speeches that comprise most of the book, you know about his swift and tragic fall.

Job was the greatest man in the east. You could measure his wealth in vast numbers of livestock and servants. You could measure his success by his family's loyalty and unity as they regularly shared meals together. You could measure his spiritual awareness by the daily sacrifices that he offered just in case sin had been committed. You could measure his personal righteousness by God's own assessment of him – "blameless and upright, one who feared God and turned away from evil" (Job 1:1).

Then, in what appears to be just a matter of minutes, Job lost it all. Fire from heaven, Chaldean raiders, and a great wind from the wilderness took Job's livestock, servants, and children. Chaos invaded and devastated Job's life.

The human response to such chaos was alive and well in the heart of Job. In devastation and sorrow, he tore his clothes and shaved his head. However, Job did not allow the physical response to his suffering to overwhelm and override his spiritual reaction. In addition to grieving, Job also worshiped amid chaos. It is not that he praised God for his loss but despite it.

What is our first reaction to chaos and tragedy? Do we ever allow our emotional pain to cloud our spiritual perspective? If so, let us remember the steadfastness of Job.

Today, I will...look for the positive in every negative. I will praise when tempted to complain. I will sing even if my joy is diminished.

TUESDAY

Job in the Dark

Today's Scripture: Job 1:6-12

There may not be a more awkward social situation than being in the middle of a conversation without knowing the subject being discussed. Have you ever walked into a room while others were in discussion and assumed you knew the theme and direction of the conversation? However, when you offered a comment or asked a question, it became obvious that what you thought they were talking about was not it at all.

Sometimes being in the dark can lead to more than embarrassment or increased awkwardness. Being in the dark could have meant emotional and spiritual surrender for Job.

Job's loss was even greater than one might first consider. Yes, he "lost it all." But he was also in the dark as to the "why" of that loss. As readers of Scripture, we have information that helps us understand why God would allow these devastating losses in Job's life. We are privy to the conversations between God and Satan. We are allowed behind the veil to witness the accusations of Satan against Job and to witness the confidence that God placed in Job to withstand such tragedy.

Interestingly enough, God never told Job (at least in the book itself) about this cosmic war. Despite remaining in the dark, Job was patient and faithful to God.

What about us? How badly do we want to know why things happen and how they are going to turn out? How many times does a lack of information hinder our ability to endure the struggle that we are unsure about?

What Job teaches us is simple, but powerful. God can and should be trusted even when we are in the dark about the things that we are suffering or the uncertainty of their end. Has God ever let us down? Has there been a promise that God didn't keep? David affirmed, "I have been young, and now am old, yet I have not seen the righteous forsaken or his children begging for bread" (Psalm 37:25).

Today, I will...turn uncertainty over to God. I will list the things that I struggle to understand and share those things with God. I will commit my trust to Him, even while I am still in the dark.

Job in the Whirlwind

Today's Scripture: Job 42:1-6

How many conversations do you have on an average day? How many questions do you answer (that number will increase exponentially if you are a parent)? How many explanations do you have to give, or corrections do you have to make? How many words do you speak in any one day?

Answers to these questions are staggering and exhausting. But we all agree that the words of some are more important than the words of others. For example, when a police offer speaks, when a judge gives a ruling, when a witness provides testimony, when a child speaks for the first time, and when a marriage ceremony ends with "I do," those words carry much more weight than the idle talk of mundane, everyday conversation.

This distinction is certainly true in the book of Job. His story is one that is almost exclusively told through dialogue. Job talked. His wife talked. His friends talked. Their assertions, conclusions, and applications were often misguided and sometimes outright wrong. Even Job spoke in the book without full knowledge and with incomplete understanding. But eventually, God spoke from the midst of a whirlwind and His words are recorded in chapters 38 through 41.

God's words are, without question, the deepest, truest, most powerful, and most accurate words in the entire book. God began by telling Job, "Dress for action like a man; I will question you and you make it known to me" (Job 38:2). He put Job in his place while defending His own sovereignty and autonomy. From the whirlwind, God reminded those listening, and now those reading, that He truly is God and that He is worthy of praise not complaining.

Job's response was full of humility and wonder. He was in awe of God's presence, purposes, and power.

Today, I will...seek a deeper knowledge of God's presence, purpose, and power.

Job in the Right

Today's Scripture: Job 42:7-17

Living righteously in a world of unrighteous people can wear you down and test your mental strength. Jesus said that because of Him we would be hated by the world (John 15:18). Christians are often misunderstood and, as a result, the worst is believed and assumed about our motives, beliefs, and intentions.

Did you know that much of the dialogue in the book of Job reflects this tension? Maybe not for the same reasons, but Job's friends started with the assumption that Job was a terrible sinner and they never really looked at him any differently. No matter how much he argued with them and no matter how much evidence he provided to the contrary, in their eyes, Job was wrong. His fight for vindication wore him down even more.

Then it happened. One day (which probably seemed like a lifetime), God stepped in and vindicated Job. God not only restored Job's lost material possessions by giving him double what he had lost, but God spoke in vindication of His servant Job. God said to Eliphaz, "My anger burns against you and against your two friends, for you have not spoken of me what is right, as my servant Job has" (Job 42:7).

Can you imagine the relief and satisfaction that Job must have felt? He just wanted the world to know that he was not suffering because of sin nor was his terrible plight due to God's rejection of him. Now they knew. Now he was proven right, and they had been wrong about him all along.

Every faithful child of God will have a moment like this. There will be a point in time when God will make everything right and our faithfulness will be vindicated. It may not be as soon as we would like or even in this life at all, but it will happen. Until then, remember the words of Paul: "If possible, so far as it depends on you, live peaceably with all. Beloved, never avenge yourselves, but leave it to the wrath of God, for it is written, 'Vengeance is mine, I will repay, says the Lord.'" (Romans 12:18-19).

Today, I will...pray for those who assume things about Christians that are not true. I will live in peace if possible and allow God to handle what I cannot change.

Job in the Savior

Today's Scripture: Psalm 73

The battle between God and evil began long before any of us were ever born. The struggle for the allegiances and hearts of mankind was first fought in the paradise of God shortly after the creation of the world.

In the story of Job that battle continues, but this time Job IS the battlefield. God allows Satan to take from and touch Job so that we might be able to see through the many lies that Satan will throw at us. It is only because of people like Job that we can truly say, "we are not ignorant of his designs" (2 Corinthians 2:11).

One of the most powerful lies that Satan tells the world is that material blessing and physical health are directly tied to a person's level of spirituality. In other words, only the unrighteous will suffer and only the righteous will prosper. When a man believes this lie, the world around him will make no sense. In today's Scripture, David lamented, "For I was envious of the arrogant when I saw the prosperity of the wicked" (Psalm 73:3).

God also knew that this lie would have an impact on how the world viewed the cross of Christ. If only the ungodly suffered, what would that say about the sinless Son of God on the cross? If God did not provide ample proof that this theory was merely a ploy of the devil to confuse the hearts of men, what would they say about the cross? What would they believe about Jesus?

So, God, in His infinite wisdom and foresight, soundly defeated Satan's lie all the way back in the book and life of Job. If Job suffered all he suffered and it was not because of his sinfulness, then the same could and would be true for Jesus and His cross. Job's suffering serves as a vindication of Jesus that we might trust in His righteousness.

Thanks be to God for that vindication.

Today, I will...thank God for revealing the schemes of Satan so that I might not be ignorant of his schemes. I will thank God that I can put my trust in the righteousness of Jesus.

WEEK #29

Micah

NEAL POLLARD

Corrupt Leaders and the Persecuted Poor

Today's Scripture: Micah 1-3

Micah was from Judah, the southern kingdom. Moresheth was southeast of Jerusalem and close to Goliath's hometown of Gath (1:10). But he spoke to both parts of the divided kingdom, addressing their capital cities (1:1). Yet, he dated his writing based on the reigns of the southern kings (1:1). Two of them were wicked and one was righteous. Yet, his was a general proclamation to all (1:2). The news wasn't good! He declared judgment against both kingdoms, though the end was very near for Israel (the north). Micah wrote in the last half of the eighth century BC, and in 722 Israel fell to Assyria. Toward the end of Micah's time of prophesying (Jeremiah 26:18-19), Hezekiah barely dodged the bullet with Sennacherib (Isaiah 36-38), though through the pagan king's siege of Lachish Micah's hometown was ravaged. What was Micah's concern?

The theme of the entire book is found in Micah 3:8 (NASB 1995), as the prophet said he was filled with God's power "to make known to Jacob his rebellious act, even to Israel his sin." Why such weeping and lamentation from Micah, whom P.C. Craigie calls "the conscience of Israel"? Because those who knew better and had the most power and influence abused their position! The heads, rulers, seers, priests, and prophets (3:1, 5, 7, 11) were blowing it! How? By stealing houses and inheritances (2:1-2), hurting their heroes and evicting their women and children (2:8-9), and ravaging the powerless (2:1; 3:1-7). Why? They hated good and loved evil (3:2). They practiced evil deeds (3:4). God warned all of these leaders, "On account of you Zion will be plowed as a field, Jerusalem will become a heap of ruins..." (3:12). Jack P. Lewis tells us that Micah's "burden is the lot of the small farmer in the area of Moresheth-Gath, the oppressions he suffered, and the impact of the Assyrian invasion upon him" (33).

God is concerned with the nation's most powerful governing its people with fairness and compassion. In Psalm 33:10, 13, the writer reminds us that "The Lord nullifies the counsel of the nations" and as "He looks from heaven, He sees all the sons of men." Just because somebody has the ability to do something does not mean that they should (2:1). When the powerful become cutthroat, enriching themselves on the backs of those they lead, God will not ignore it! The leaders did not want to hear the truth (2:6), although it was their only hope of remedy (2:7).

The hope of a nation is not its military, its constitution and government, its wealth, its education, or its territory. Its hope rests in abiding by God's governing principles, from the top down. When greed and power become the chief motivators of its leaders, it is destined for destruction. So, we should not take lightly the New Testament's urging "that entreaties and prayers, petitions and thanksgivings, be made on behalf of all men, for kings and all who are in authority, so that we may lead a tranquil and quiet life in all godliness and dignity" (1 Timothy 2:1-2).

Today, I will...pray for the leaders of my nation and those of every nation, that they will exercise their power with righteousness so that the gospel can spread to all men.

In the Last Days

Today's Scripture: Micah 4-5

It may be helpful to read Micah with a book marker in Isaiah. They prophesied at the same time. Micah 4:1-3 and Isaiah 2:2-4 are virtually identical. After Micah's decidedly negative message of judgment in the first three chapters, his focus shifted to the hopeful future of all who are faithful to God's message. Micah loved his people and wanted them spared from harm, but he loved God even more. He's thrilled that God's message included more than judgment, but also deliverance. What he and Isaiah foresaw would "come about in the last days" (4:1) and benefit "many nations" who could enter "the house of the God of Jacob" to learn "about His ways...that we may walk in His paths" (4:2). This would come via God's Word (4:2). It would be a time of peace, faithfulness, and restoration (4:5-8).

Inseparably tied to the hope which would come through the church is the coming of the One who would be Head of the church. The Ruler of that holy nation would be the One who would come via Bethlehem of Judah (5:1-2). While there is a strong hint of who this is even in the context, Matthew clears up any doubt by quoting this passage and applying it to Jesus Christ (2:6).

What a contrast the hopelessness incurred by ruthless, materialistic rulers with God's reign and rule. Though He had been rejected by Micah's generation, the steadfast love of God would fling open wide the door of hope and salvation. He would be the good shepherd (5:4; John 10:11). In this prophecy about the Prince of Peace, Micah gave us His place (5:2—Bethlehem), person (5:2—One; everlasting), position (5:2—Ruler), provision (5:4—He shall stand and feed), power (5:4—strength and majesty), and peace (5:5).

There is no present so hopeless and discouraging that we cannot be undaunted when we look at the future. For us, the future is not about the first coming of the Messiah! Praise God, that has already occurred. Micah's foretelling proved correct. We await the better day (2 Peter 3:13) when we live in the presence of God forever (Psalm 23:6; Revelation 21:1-8). Can you hang on through the present difficulties? Jesus is coming again (Matthew 25:31-34)!

Today, I will...focus intently on the promises God's Word contains for my eternal future!

What Does God Want?

Today's Scripture: Micah 6

With the purpose statement in Micah 3:8, God has set out His case against the transgressions of His people. There is great hope for the future, but the current situation and the consequences of their sin is grim. So, you will find Micah detailing the rebellion and wickedness of Israel and Judah, and the doom they would soon face. But in the end, he said, "Who is a God like you, pardoning iniquity and passing over transgression for the remnant of his inheritance? He does not retain his anger forever, because he delights in steadfast love. He will again have compassion on us; he will tread our iniquities underfoot. You will cast all our sins into the depths of the sea. You will show faithfulness to Jacob and steadfast love to Abraham, as you have sworn to our fathers from the days of old" (7:18-20).

In the immediate context, Micah told the people how they would enter into a covenant relationship with Him. He told how it wouldn't happen (6:6-7). He's not saying that He doesn't want sacrifice, but He doesn't want empty ritual. He also doesn't want anyone to think that they can bribe Him or earn His salvation through their works. Then, in Micah 6:8, he showed how one enters into that relationship with Him—three great qualities—justice, kindness, and humility. The problem was that the people weren't practicing those three qualities. They divorced their vertical relationship from their horizontal relationships.

They weren't practicing kindness (2:8-9; 3:10-11; 6:12). They weren't practicing humility (2:3). Above all, they weren't practicing justice with their fellow man (2:1-2; 3:1-3; 6:11). They lost sight of their own law; it should have been embedded in their hearts and their collective consciousness. There was a guide for their relationship with God (Deuteronomy 6:5). But, directly related to it was a guide for their relationship with one another (Leviticus 19:18). Because they departed from these two beacons, they had gotten lost in both relationships. They didn't fear and honor God. No wonder they lost sight of how to treat their neighbor.

Today, I will...concentrate on building a better relationship with God and those made in His image.

Who Is a God Like You?

Today's Scripture: Micah 7

What a contrast between God and me. As I read through Micah, I see myself more often than is comfortable. Even in chapter 7, as the condemnation of the people, is summarized, I am there. I can struggle with my ethics and morality (v. 3). I can hurt others (v. 4) and be less than trustworthy (v. 5). I can be a problem for my family (v. 6). What is my hope of improvement and salvation?

Micah said, "But as for me, I will look to the LORD; I will wait for the God of my salvation; my God will hear me" (v. 7). In context, he held onto this hope when he was on the receiving end of people like I just described in the first paragraph. Sometimes I need God to save me from others; at other times, I need Him to save me from me. Whether I'm facing those who mock my God (v. 10) or facing a God who has seen my mocking, He is my hope. Why?

The last three verses say it best. "Who is a God like you?" (v. 18). What does He do? What is He like? He is ready and eager to take away my sin and pass it by (v. 18). He is ready and eager to let go of His righteous anger. He delights in lovingkindness (v. 19). He is ready and eager to step on and throw our sins so that they are crushed and drowned (v. 20). This is not cheap grace. Micah made it clear that repentance is at the core of his message, but what should motivate repentance? Isn't it what God is ready and eager to do with our sins? He wants to forgive them and erase them from His mind. I may struggle to forget them, but He stands ready to do so (Acts 2:38)!

Today, I will...be defined by His grace and not by my guilt.

Where It Would All Begin
Today's Scripture: Micah 5:2

Bible scholars have long touted that over 300 Messianic prophesies fill the pages of the Old Testament. All of them are significant, though they point to different powerful aspects of the coming Christ. Only Micah 5:2 refers to the place where the Messiah would be born. That the Jews anticipated this is made clear in John 7:42 (NASB 1995), where some who were doubting Jesus asked, "Has not the Scripture said that the Christ comes from the descendants of David, and from Bethlehem, the village where David was?" Of course, this was their own ignorance about His birth and background (John 7:41).

Yet, Matthew 2:6 faithfully recorded the birth of "Immanuel" (Matthew 1:23), quoting Micah 5:2. Matthew told Jesus was born in Bethlehem of Judea in the days of Herod the King (Matthew 2:1). The gospel writer highlighted the kingship of Jesus, in keeping with his purpose in convincing his Jewish audience that Jesus was the promised Messiah. He cited the fact that out of Bethlehem "shall come forth a Ruler who will shepherd My people Israel" (NASB 1995). Micah's prophesy also points out His deity, saying, "His goings forth are from long ago, from the days of eternity" (NASB 1995).

God coming to earth as King sounds regal, but Luke showed us the humble humanity of "God with us" (Luke 2:4-7). Mary had to give birth to Him outdoors. Lowly as she and Joseph were, they had to make the burnt offering and the sin offering of the poor in the temple when the days of their purification were completed (Luke 2:21-24; Leviticus 12:8). This was the life of the Royal Redeemer (2 Corinthians 8:9).

He defied the materialistic and militaristic fantasies of the earthly-minded. Those looking for such a Messiah missed the Savior. Such still miss Him today. Yet, we must imitate His example (John 13:12-17). We must lower ourselves to be exalted (1 Peter 5:6). We must humble ourselves in obedience to receive what only He can give. What kind of Savior and what kind of deliverance do we seek? The place to begin our search is a passage like Micah 5:2. God is teaching us so much about discipleship and greatness by how He chose to bring our Deliverer into this world.

Today, I will...measure greatness by using God's perfect "ruler."

WEEK #30

Habakkuk

JEFF JENKINS

A Praying Preacher

Today's Scripture: Habakkuk 1

Have you ever prayed about something repeatedly, all the while wondering if God is listening? Why haven't I received the answer I want? Is God paying attention? Is He concerned? Does He care?

Some would tell you that those kinds of questions show a lack of faith. Others would say that this is an understanding of our humanness. However one wishes to describe it, what we know is that there are people of great faith throughout Scripture who have pondered the same questions.

One of these is a man of God by the name of Habakkuk. This prophet lived somewhere around 600-650 years before Christ was born. Listen carefully to the words he spoke to God from his heart.

"How long, O LORD, will I call for help, and You will not hear? I cry out to You, "Violence!" Yet You do not save. Why do You make me see iniquity, and cause me to look on wickedness? Yes, destruction and violence are before me; strife exists, and contention arises. Therefore, the law is ignored, and justice is never upheld. For the wicked surround the righteous; therefore, justice comes out perverted" (Habakkuk 1:2-4 NASB 1995).

Does any of this sound familiar? Many of God's people in our day have prayed similar thoughts about their own nation. And many leaders in the church of our Lord have felt these same concerns about the Kingdom and have carried similar thoughts before our Father's throne.

In the next few verses, we read God's response to His man. "Look among the nations! Observe! Be astonished! Wonder! Because I am doing something in your days—You would not believe it if you were told" (Habakkuk 1:5 NASB 1995). God basically was telling Habakkuk that He was doing His work, and that He was still in charge. The message is as clear today as it was more than 2,500 years ago. God is often working behind the scenes in ways we cannot imagine or even understand.

Today, I will...pray about something significant in my life, and I will trust God to answer my prayer according to His will and His timing.

TUESDAY

A Proclaiming Preacher

Today's Scripture: Habakkuk 2:1-3

After God informed His prophet concerning the work He was doing to bring repentance to the nation, Habakkuk said, "I will stand on my guard post and station myself on the rampart; and I will keep watch to see what He will speak to me, and how I may reply when I am reproved" (Habakkuk 2:1 NASB 1995).

God's response to this preacher's waiting posture was that God was doing His part and would continue to do so. Then He told Habakkuk what he should do. "Record the vision and inscribe it on tablets, that the one who reads it may run. For the vision is yet for the appointed time; it hastens toward the goal and it will not fail....For it will certainly come, it will not delay." (Habakkuk 2:2-3 NASB 1995)

God reminded His preacher that He was doing exactly what He said He would do, and that Habakkuk had work to do himself. The mission of men of God, indeed the entire nation of God's people is the same for all ages. We are to clearly proclaim the Word of God. First and foremost, our work is to "preach the Word" (2 Timothy 4:2 NASB 1995). We are to preach the Word all the time.

In our day, the proclamation of the Word has fallen on tough times. Many are afraid that biblical teaching isn't popular, that people in our day will not listen, so all too often we have diminished the teaching and preaching of Scripture. May we never forget that Jesus came to seek and save the lost. May we never forget that His mission was focused on the Words He read to the people. "The Spirit of the Lord is upon Me, because He anointed Me to preach the gospel to the poor. He has sent Me to proclaim release to the captives, and recovery of sight to the blind, to set free those who are oppressed, to proclaim the favorable year of the Lord." (Luke 4:18-19 NASB 1995) And so, all His followers have been sent to proclaim this good news to the world.

Today, I will...tell the good news to someone who has not become a child of God. I will pray for people who have not yet obeyed the gospel, and I will do my part to clearly proclaim God's Word.

A Preserving Preacher

Today's Scripture: Habakkuk 2:4-20

In addition to telling Habakkuk that He should clearly proclaim the Word, God also reminded him that if we want to be righteous, there is a certain way we must live. Notice the contradistinction between those who follow God and those who do not. "Behold, as for the proud one, his soul is not right within him; but the righteous will live by his faith" (Habakkuk 2:4 NASB 1995).

In a world where many give up too easily and quickly, those who follow God have numerous opportunities to show what it means to be faithful. We can teach our children, our grandchildren, our fellow Christians, and the world what it means to be faithful in our marriage, in our relationships, as well as in our commitment to the Lord. Jesus taught us that if we would be faithful even if it means dying, we can receive a crown of life (Revelation 2:10). Of course, He is our greatest example of overcoming. "He who overcomes, I will grant to him to sit down with Me on My throne, as I also overcame and sat down with My Father on His throne" (Revelation 3:21 NASB 1995).

When life is tough, when we feel as if we are all alone, when we are weary, when satan turns up the heat, and when we wonder if we are doing anything worthwhile, the Lord comforts us. Our Savior teaches us that whatever we do in His Name, will be properly rewarded in eternity (Matthew 10:40-42).

We are blessed to be able to choose whether we will live by faith or by fear. Hebrews 11 gives us some wonderful examples of people who, "Died in faith, without receiving the promises, but having seen them and having welcomed them from a distance, and having confessed that they were strangers and exiles on the earth" (Hebrews 11:13 NASB 1995).

Today, I will...choose to live by faith rather than fear and be counted among those who are just.

A Praising Preacher

Today's Scripture: Habakkuk 3

What began as a complaining prayer, ended as a chorus of praise. After Habakkuk complained in prayer to God, he heard the Words of God and saw the work of God, then he praised God. "Even if the fig tree does not blossom, and there is no fruit on the vines, if the yield of the olive fails, and the fields produce no food, even if the flock disappears from the fold, and there are no cattle in the stalls, yet I will triumph in the LORD, I will rejoice in the God of my salvation. The Lord God is my strength, and He has made my feet like deer's feet, and has me walk on my high places" (Habakkuk 3:17-19 NASB 2020).

This man of God got to a point in his life where he recognized that God should be praised, even if everything didn't go the way he wanted it to go. Can we praise God no matter what happens? When our prayers seem to go unanswered, or we don't get the answer we want, can we praise God anyway?

It requires a great amount of faith to trust God during difficult and trying times. We are reminded of the words of three teenage boys when their faith was tested. Shadrach, Meshach, and Abednego knew that God could and trusted that He would deliver them from Nebuchadnezzar's fiery furnace. But they were not sure He would. Listen to the faith in their response. "If it be so, our God whom we serve is able to rescue us from the furnace of blazing fire; and He will rescue us from your hand, O king. But even if He does not, let it be known to you, O king, that we are not going to serve your gods nor worship the golden statue that you have set up." (Daniel 3:17-18 NASB 2020) This is the type of faith that can and will lead us to praise God, no matter what comes our way.

Today, I will...trust God no matter what and I will praise Him even during the most trying seasons of life.

It Is Still Good News

Today's Scripture: Romans 1:16-18

Long before Habakkuk lived, another man of faith became a Preacher of Righteousness. Noah lived during a time when our Maker recognized that the people He created had turned their hearts away from Him. "Then the LORD saw that the wickedness of mankind was great on the earth, and that every intent of the thoughts of their hearts was only evil continually" (Genesis 6:5 NASB 2020). Noah not only preached the righteousness of God, but he also lived according to God's righteousness. "So Noah did these things; according to everything that God had commanded him, so he did" (Genesis 6:22 NASB 2020).

Somewhere around 650-700 years after Habakkuk, another man of God decried the ways of the people of the world in which he was living. Among other comparisons to the people living during the days of Habakkuk, note Paul's description of his world. "For even though they knew God, they did not honor Him as God or give thanks, but they became futile in their reasonings, and their senseless hearts were darkened. Claiming to be wise, they became fools, and they exchanged the glory of the incorruptible God for an image in the form of corruptible mankind, of birds, four-footed animals, and crawling creatures" (Romans 1:21-23 NASB 2020).

No wonder Paul highlighted the importance of preaching the good news, quoted the words of Habakkuk concerning faith, and reminded us that in that faith the righteousness of God is revealed (Romans 1:16-18).

The description of the world given by God in the days of Noah, mentioned in the prayer of Habakkuk, and detailed in Paul's letter to the Romans, reads like the headlines of any major newspaper or website in our world today. Brothers and sisters, the answer is the same today as it has always been. It is not our duty to try to fix everyone and everything. Neither should we hide our heads in the proverbial sand. Today and always, people of God should clearly proclaim the message of God and live our lives by faith!

Today, I will...do my best to let others know the gospel of God and I will live my life by faith.

WEEK #31

Haggai

SONNY OWENS

Heroes

Today's Scripture: Haggai 1:3

"My Heroes Have Always Been Cowboys" Do you remember that song? It was "recorded by Waylon Jennings on the 1976 album Wanted! The Outlaws, and further popularized in 1980 by Willie Nelson as a single on the soundtrack to The Electric Horseman" (Wikipedia).

"My heroes have always been cowboys and they still are." I like cowboys, too. That's telling my age and generation. I still like and almost daily watch: Gunsmoke, Rawhide, and any older cowboy show that I can find on TV.

In 2010, I had a staph infection to infect a knee replacement that I had in 2006. Every day I watched Bonanza. In fact, I watched several episodes of Bonanza every day. When I was able to get back to the pulpit and back to working, I met with the elders and told them that I had an "addiction." I didn't know if I could stop watching Bonanza every day. Of course, they didn't seem to see the humor as I did.

I like cowboys, but they are not my heroes. For many years, I have said publicly that my heroes are young preachers and the prophets.

Oh, just think about the prophets! God called on people to help, teach, and lead His people through difficult times. He called them "prophets," and Haggai was one of them. In a real way, these prophets said, "I will climb the hills, swim the rivers and help Your people out of sin and degradation." And they did. They stood in the gap.

The prophets taught pointed lessons, told truths, and held no punches. They loved God's people. In the beginning of their writings, many of the minor prophets would scorch the people, but in the last days would soothe their wounds.

Today, I will...listen to God's Word by listening to God's prophets.

[I give credit to Ray Reynolds, Mike Jones, and Gary Davenport (and possibly others) for the material written in these lessons. These good brothers helped provide me with good material to build these five lessons. To God be the glory!]

Haggai, The Writer

Today's Scripture: Haggai 1:7

The short book of Haggai: Chapter 1 has only fifteen verses. Chapter 2 has twenty-three verses, which makes this whole book only thirty-eight verses.

Headings for chapter 1: 1. The Command to Rebuild the Temple; 2. The People Obey the Lord.

Headings for chapter 2: 1. The coming glory of the temple; 2. Blessings for defiled people; 3. Zerubbabel chosen as a signet ring

The Jews had been in captivity in Babylon for seventy years (Jeremiah 25:11). They were first deported in 606 BC. The final destruction of the temple was in 586 BC. When the Persians defeated the Babylonians in 539 BC, Darius took over and changed the foreign policy concerning captive peoples. In 538 BC, he decreed that the Jews could return to their homeland and rebuild the temple (Ezra 1-3).

Haggai dates each of his sermons to the day. His precision is similar to maintaining a journal. Since Darius began his rule in 522 B.C., Haggai's proclamations are from 520 B.C., two years following.

In the book of Haggai, we see that God is precise. He demands and expects our lives to work in concert to His plans. Haggai rebuked them for having misplaced priorities and pointed out the results which were dissatisfaction with the things of this world and discipline from God.

Remember the words of Paul, "for whatever was written in former days was written for our instruction, that through endurance and through encouragement of the Scriptures we might have hope" (Romans 15:4).

Today, I will...look at God's plan for my life and recognize His preciseness in how to live my life according to His plan.

[I give credit to Ray Reynolds, Mike Jones, and Gary Davenport (and possibly others) for the material written in these lessons. These good brothers helped provide me with good material to build these five lessons. To God be the glory!]

Nice Home, New Cars, and Empty Church Buildings

Today's Scripture: Haggai 1:4-7

I read the title of this lesson on another lesson about the Minor Prophet book of Haggai. Is this an accurate picture of America today? Worse, is this an accurate picture of "Christian" America today? Let's get worse than that. Is this an accurate picture of the churches of Christ today?

Honestly, I don't think so, but just look at her members' houses and cars. We have struggled with empty church buildings. COVID did a number on us. Well, satan did a number on us (Ephesians 6:12). But as of late (June 2023), I personally am seeing our meeting houses filling up. I am seeing (FB) and hearing of conversions and restorations on a weekly basis.

It is encouraging to see people coming to the Lord, coming back to the Lord, and filling His house for assemblies and Bible classes. satan wrangled us in; but through Christ we are breaking free of his devices.

Haggai rebuked the Jews for having misplaced priorities and pointed out the results which were dissatisfaction with the things of this world and discipline from God. Their response was to obey God's message and resume the work on the temple. Their obedience (repentance and confession) cleared their conscience so that they could worship God, and brought the Spirit's enablement on them so they could do the work of God. Their courage and motivation were to come from the promise of God's presence and His peace. This is the peace of mind that comes from knowing that God is in control.

Haggai also dealt with the issues of living clean and godly lives so God's people would not defile their work and sacrifices. He also urged them to depend on God for life. Finally, Haggai gave them hope for the future by revealing that God was going to destroy their enemies and establish His kingdom with them, His chosen people.

Today, I will... listen to God and move forward in faith.

[I give credit to Ray Reynolds, Mike Jones, and Gary Davenport (and possibly others) for the material written in these lessons. These good brothers helped provide me with good material to build these five lessons. To God be the glory!]

THURSDAY

THURSDAY

What a Man of God!

Today's Scripture: Haggai 2:7-9

1. Don't procrastinate in the work of the Lord (1:3). [So true, never]

2. Don't seek the unimportant—it holds back the work of God (1:4, 9). [They truly do.]

3. Remember God's work always aims to glorify himself (1:8). [Ephesians 1:5, 9; Philippians 2:13; 2 Thessalonians 1:11]

4. Let calamities serve as spiritual wake-up calls (1:6, 10, 11).[Yes, He does.]

5. Trust and obey God, then see his spiritual blessings appear (1:12-14). [Living holy lives]

6. Don't put off obeying God's commands (1:12-15). [Until it's too late. It is true that as long as there is breath it is not to late.]

7. Be certain of God's presence and find your boldness in Him (2:1-4). ["I will never leave you nor forsake you." (Hebrews 13:5)]

8. See things from God's perspective to alleviate your discouragement (2:6-7). [Open our eyes and hearts to Him.]

9. Submit to God's control, because everything belongs to Him (2:7-8). [He owns it all, even a thousand cows on a thousand hills.]

10. Do not assume that righteousness is passed down automatically (2:11-12). [Your holy living for God is yours. My holy living is mine.]

11. Don't allow sin to ruin everything (2:13-14). [Everything]

12. God rebukes disobedience and rewards submission (2:15-19). [If we allow our disobedience to discipline us. Yes, blessings come from obeying God.]

13. Take courage in God's authority over the world's kingdoms (2:20-22). [Man must recognize God's sovereignty.]

14. Secure your faith to God's certain covenant promises (2:23). [God's pledge to man and His promises are guaranteed.]

What a man of God! Aren't you glad Haggai said "yes" when God called (Haggai 1:3)?

Today, I will... search His Word, listen to His prophet, and thank Him for these Holy Spirit moved people.

[I give credit to Ray Reynolds, Mike Jones, and Gary Davenport (and possibly others) for the material written in these lessons. These good brothers helped provide me with good material to build these five lessons. To God be the glory!]

185

FRIDAY
Haggai and Jesus

Today's Scripture: Matthew 1:23; 4:17; 16:18; Luke 1:19; 2:10-13; Matthew 16:18.19

Haggai the prophet prophesied 500 years before Jesus left heaven and came to earth. When Scripture announced Jesus' birth, we are told He would bring great joy. Jesus would be given the name Immanuel, which means "God with us", and we would all have opportunity to know that great joy. In Hebrew Haggai's name means "my feast" or "festival." Some suggest it can also mean "joyous one." This almost unknown man that God chose to preach brought great joy to His people in His day.

Jesus came preaching "repent, for the kingdom of heaven is at hand" (Matthew 4:17). Haggai, also called on God's people to "consider your ways" (Haggai 1:3-5).

As Jesus came into the region of Caesarea Philippi, He told Peter that He (Jesus) would build His church and that He (Jesus) would give Peter the keys to the kingdom of heaven (Matthew 16:13-19).

Haggai was given the call to rebuild God's house the temple. Haggai's preaching motivated the people to work and finish God's house. Aren't you glad God put people in our lives to motivate us to work and serve under the reign of God? In His kingdom, we have men called through the gospel to exalt Jesus and preach the kingdom of God.

Let us pray daily for God's preachers and teachers to help people consider their ways, repent, and come to Jesus through an obedient faith being born again that they also may be added to God's church. Like the people of Haggai's time, we must go to work. Please read Haggai 1:12-15. Consider your ways!

Today, I will... look again at my life that I may also consider my ways.

[I give credit to Ray Reynolds, Mike Jones, and Gary Davenport (and possibly others) for the material written in these lessons. These good brothers helped provide me with good material to build these five lessons. To God be the glory!]

WEEK #32

Malachi

PAUL SHERO

"Where Is My Honor?"

Today's Scripture: Malachi 1:6, 10, 14

Malachi is the last of the Minor Prophets. He preached a short, powerful sermon on worship. He started by showing worship in his day was without love. Worship, by its very definition, is praise and adoration. Their worship was without love and honor. So, God asked, "where is my honor?" (Malachi 1:6).

Even priests despised God's name. They were not careful to sacrifice properly. They brought blind, sick animals to the altar, showing no respect to God and making the entire event a joke. But God was not smiling. A sacrifice like this was worse than no sacrifice at all. In fact, God said He would prefer the temple be closed. "Oh that there were one among you who would shut the doors, that you might not kindle fire on my altar in vain! I have no pleasure in you, says the LORD of hosts, and I will not accept an offering from your hand" (Malachi 1:10).

God is not interested in any old worship. He demands worship in spirit and truth. When we offer vain worship, bringing trash rather than sacrifice, we waste God's time, and He will not receive it. Instead of worship, it becomes an insult. God looks for proper honor in worship, or else shut it all down. Put out the fires, close the doors, and stop pretending.

Malachi described a process where a lack of love grew into boredom. Becoming bored with worship and tired of the encounter with God. Snorting and scoffing in the presence of God is a one-way trip to death. Surprisingly enough, things got worse. These people believed they could cheat God. Fool Him. God knows everything. This attitude is no sign of spiritual maturity but rather complete ignorance. " For I am a great King, says the LORD of hosts, and my name will be feared among the nations" (Malachi 1:14).

The first thing we bring to God is our heart. God does not need our stuff. He wants us. If our heart is filled with conceit and lies, nothing we bring will be accepted. Our heart must be full of love and honor. Then our gift will be accepted and our worship will be successful.

Today, I will...count my blessings and show the love I should to the one who made me and saved me.

TUESDAY

You Know Better Than This

Today's Scripture: Malachi 2:1-12

I am the oldest of four brothers. You can imagine the trouble we were able to get into. Sometimes when Dad began to dish out judgment on us, I got more punishment. I would ask how is this fair when we all did it, but I got more punishment. Dad would say, "Johnny, you know better." It made no sense at the time, but now I know he was exactly right. Jesus explained it this way. "And that servant who knew his master's will but did not get ready or act according to his will, will receive a severe beating. But the one who did not know, and did what deserved a beating, will receive a light beating. Everyone to whom much was given, of him much will be required, and from him to whom they entrusted much, they will demand the more" (Luke 12:47-48).

"And now, O priests, this command is for you" (Malachi 2:1). Malachi went on to say they must listen to the word of God. They must take it to heart. They MUST give honor to His name. He even said if the don't there will be a severe curse. This punishment was really serious.

God intends all men to honor Him and love Him. Those who are in a covenant relationship with Him are held to a higher standard. This is not bad. It is not only fair since "we know," but an honor because we wear His name.

God said to the priest, "But you have turned aside from the way. You have caused many to stumble by your instruction. You have corrupted the covenant of Levi, says the LORD of hosts," (Malachi 2:8). You turned away. You caused many to stumble. You have corrupted the covenant. This was serious.

When the people of God live like pagans, it is worse than when pagans live like pagans. "Judah has been faithless, and abomination has been committed in Israel and in Jerusalem. For Judah has profaned the sanctuary of the LORD, which he loves, and has married the daughter of a foreign god" (Malachi 2:11).

When we break the covenant of worship, God calls it an abomination. But it does not stop there. Bad worship produces bad living. This evil behavior in worship and in daily life produces serious punishment. "May the LORD cut off from the tents of Jacob any descendant of the man who does this, who brings an offering to the LORD of hosts" (Malachi 2:12)! In such a situation our worship becomes vain. God does not show up. We are left on our own.

Today, I will...be careful to obey God's commands. I know better, so I am determined to take worship seriously and not profane my time with God.

Bringing It Home

Today's Scripture: Malachi 2:13-17

Since God takes covenant making and keeping seriously, we should too. God was there when you made your marriage vows. "But you say, 'Why does he not?' Because the LORD was witness between you and the wife of your youth, to whom you have been faithless, though she is your companion and your wife by covenant. Did he not make them one, with a portion of the Spirit in their union? And what was the one God seeking? Godly offspring. So guard yourselves in your spirit, and let none of you be faithless to the wife of your youth" (Malachi 2:14-15).

God was not only there, He was a part of the ceremony. He was part of the covenant. A covenant between the man, his wife, and God's Spirit. When this covenant is violated, more happens than a new address. Malachi called divorce a violent act. God hates divorce. We should too. Everything in our lives affects everything else. Our moral actions affect our worship, our prayers, and our future. "For the man who does not love his wife but divorces her, says the LORD, God of Israel, covers his garment with violence, says the LORD of hosts. So, guard yourselves in your spirit, and do not be faithless" (Malachi 2:16).

Love is not what we feel; it is what we do. When we break our faith in one area (home) the cracks spread to all areas (worship, children, even the future). The attitude of indifference to God's will in our personal lives spreads to every area of our lives. We even begin to believe lies about the covenant we made with God. "You have wearied the LORD with your words. But you say, 'How have we wearied him?' By saying, "Everyone who does evil is good in the sight of the LORD, and he delights in them.' Or by asking, 'Where is the God of justice?" (Malachi 2:17).

God expects and demands our obedience to the covenant we made. The first offering we bring to God is our self. "I appeal to you therefore, brothers, by the mercies of God, to present your bodies as a living sacrifice, holy and acceptable to God, which is your spiritual worship" (Romans 12:1).

If God will not accept the sacrifice of a blind or damaged beast, how can we expect Him to not notice our life? Holiness does not just happen. We have to be diligent in our efforts to be obedient. We must make an effort to know God's will and submit to it. We must never resist His will or make our life a lie. We must never become master of "double talk" (Matthew 7:21-23). Words are not enough. We must obey the will of the Father.

Today, I will...make my life more than words. I will obey the commands of God.

THURSDAY
Judgment Is Coming

Today's Scripture: Malachi 3

Malachi breaks forth in a direct statement from God. "Behold, I send my messenger, and he will prepare the way before me. And the Lord whom you seek will suddenly come to his temple; and the messenger of the covenant in whom you delight, behold, he is coming, says the LORD of hosts. But who can endure the day of his coming, and who can stand when he appears? For he is like a refiner's fire and life fullers' soap" (Malachi 3:1-2).

Wake up! The time is near. Remember the parables of Jesus? How many of them show the Lord returning? Many were not ready. The time for preparation is now. Malachi told us John the Baptist was their last warning. Would you want the Lord to come into His temple now? Are we ready? Is our life ready? Family ready? Is our worship ready? If not, now is the time to get ready.

When Jesus came most were not ready. John pointed this out, and many got ready. But many more were not ready. Peter thought he was ready. But when he saw Jesus, he said, "Depart from me, for I am a sinful man" (Luke 5:8).

This getting ready can be painful. This deep cleaning can hurt. Like refining ore, it involves melting and removal of impurities. But if you are willing, the one doing the refining is able to remove the sin and save the sinner.

This is not new carpet; this is a restoration. Every rotten board removed. Nothing from satan left. No lies, no theft, no meanness, no covetousness. Nothing! You may think you can't live through such a process, and you would be right. You have to die! That old man you were dies. He is buried and raised as a new person.

This process involves all parties. On our side we must repent—change our thinking, our directions, our actions. From God's side, there is pruning, cleansing, restoration. Though difficult, the end result is life with God— peace. Our "walk" and our talk are in agreement.

Today, I will...open my life to God. I will stop resisting, quenching, and grieving the Spirit. I will become a "living sacrifice."

191

The Gospel Is Still the Gospel

Today's Scripture: Malachi 4

Have you noticed that even when God is declaring judgement, He reminds us of His good news? Even when He speaks of hell, we are reminded that God does not want us to go.

You see, God hates sin but loves sinners. God hates murder but loves murderers. God hates lies but loves liars. God hates homosexuality but loves homosexuals. God hates divorce but loves the divorced.

When judgment comes who can survive? Who can survive judgment? Those who fear Him will survive (Malachi 3:5). Those who return to the Lord will survive (Malachi 3:7). Those who return to obedience will survive (Malachi 3:8). Those who belong to the Lord will survive. (Malachi 3:17). Not everything burns up!

Even though this process is painful and difficult, it is good news. "For I the LORD do not change; therefore you, O children of Jacob, are not consumed. From the days of your fathers you have turned aside from my statues and have not kept them. Return to me, and I will return to you, says the LORD of hosts. But you say, 'How shall we return?'" (Malachi 3:6-7).

It is actually possible to come back to God. To obey His commands. To live by faith—Trust God. To Repent—Stop Sinning. To pray again. To live righteous lives. How is this possible?
- God is in charge (Malachi 3:6).
- God hears our prayers (Malachi 3:16).
- God promises (Malachi 3:17).
- God is the judge (Malachi 3:18).
- Those who serve the Lord will survive (Malachi 3:18).

Today, I will...give God honor by loving Him and obeying Him. I will trust His promises and obey His commandments.

WEEK #33

Zechariah

BILLY SMITH

Zechariah's Character

Today's Scripture: Luke 1:1-17

It is one thing for a man and his wife to be described as righteous and blameless, but it is a completely different matter when Zechariah and Elizabeth are introduced to us as "both righteous before God, walking blamelessly in all the commandments and statutes of the Lord," by the Holy Spirit (1:6)! This lesser-known couple, the aged parents of John the Baptizer, defines what it means to be people of Christlike character, what you really are, not what people think you are. Do not mistake people of genuine character with those who are "characters"! We delight in the one but despise the other. One may appear to be one way but in reality are another—deceivers. Life eventually reveals the difference, and even if someone is not exposed in life, he will be in the judgment.

"Righteous" means Zechariah lived that which was right in the eyes of God continually, daily obedient to each of His commandments and statutes. "Blameless" refers to the absence of evil in one's life, against whom even God Himself finds no fault. No finer human example can be given than that of Job, "a man in the land of Uz [who] was blameless and upright, one who feared God and turned away from evil" (1:1), an Old Testament model of a New Testament Christian. When the time came for God to choose the parents of the one who would be the forerunner of the Christ, He did not choose haphazardly. Rather, He chose the ideal couple in Zechariah and Elizabeth, who had not been blessed with children before. They were righteous and blameless in the eyes of the Lord, providing a godly home for John while keeping their eyes on what he might become.

In addition to outstanding Bible examples, God has placed in our lives those whose life is worthy of imitation. We have followed them as they followed Jesus, our Savior and Lord. The daily task before us is to become such a "God's person," who knows the way we must go, who shows the way, and who teaches the way in our journey to Heaven.

Today, I will... rededicate myself, by the wonderful grace of God, to being righteous and blameless in the eyes of God and others, that in saving my soul, I might also save others.

Zechariah's Doubt

Today's Scripture: Luke 1:18-25

My students were given the assignment of sharing with me the title and text of the lesson they each planned to present in class. One young man responded, "I'm not really sure, but I am thinking about 'Doubt.'" He had doubt about speaking on doubt! Doubt is a form of unbelief, for true faith has no room for doubt (2 Timothy 1:12). It is a sign of uncertainty, where truth or the facts of a matter or of a person lack evidence. When we are sure, we are prone to say, "I have no doubt!" When we are not sure, we say, "I have my doubts."

When the angel Gabriel appeared to the elderly priest Zechariah in the temple, he was the bearer of good news: "Do not be afraid, Zechariah, for your prayer has been heard, and your wife Elizabeth will bear you a son, and you shall call his name John" (1:13). You can imagine Zechariah's shock, as revealed in his question: "How shall I know this? For I am an old man, and my wife is advanced in years" (1:18). Gabriel assured him the birth of John was going to happen, but "because you did not believe my words" (1:20), he would be silent and unable to speak until the child was born. Zechariah was putting himself in good company in questioning God, for so did Abraham and Sarah, Moses, Gideon, Job, David, Jeremiah, and Habakkuk before him, along with Mary (Luke 1:34) and eventually his son John (Matthew 11:3).

We, too, are in good company when we occasionally experience doubt in this life of faith. We do not sin when we have questions, as long as we take those questions to the right source, God the Father, with whom every question is answered, every problem is solved, and every doubt is destroyed. This is especially true when we practice the following steps:

- Admit your doubts and ask for help. Share your questions and concerns with seasoned saints who have studied the Word and have lived the faith longer.
- Act on your faith, not on your doubts. You must know what you believe, and why you believe it. When the test comes, rely on the evidence of what you know to be true rather than what may appear to be true.
- Always doubt your doubts, not your faith. Instead of questioning the evidence that led you to faith, challenge your doubts and put them to the test. Is there any evidence to support them?
- Anchor your faith in the certainty of what you know, of the One you know! We know God as our Father, Jesus as our Savior, the Bible as our guide, and Heaven as our home.

Today, I will... pray this prayer, "Lord, increase my faith; I believe, but help my unbelief."

Zechariah's Surrender

Today's Scripture: Luke 1:57-66

The birth of a child is one of the most wondrous moments to be experienced in life. As we raise them in the Lord and grow older, we no longer anticipate the birth of children but of grandchildren, who teach us just how great and good God is! We sometimes refer to childbirth as "a miracle," because the whole process is so amazing. However, in our story of Zechariah and Elizabeth, the birth of John really was miraculous because, even though they had prayed for a child, they were now advanced in age and Elizabeth had always been barren. This is not to be confused with the virgin birth of Jesus, the ultimate miraculous birth, because no human father was involved. Mary's conception was from the Holy Spirit.

Though a righteous and blameless man serving as a priest, Zechariah's lack of faith in Gabriel's message caused him to be stricken mute for the length of the pregnancy (Luke 1:20). Imagine losing the joy of vocally sharing this excitement with Elizabeth, their family, and the people they served! Of course, he communicated through writing, but that can't compare with expressing yourself from the heart through the voice. However, the point here is that Zechariah learned his lesson; he completed his service in the temple and returned to his home in the hill country of Judea, surrendering his will to the gracious will of the Father in anticipation of the child's birth and raising him to fulfill God's purpose.

When Gabriel first informed Zechariah that Elizabeth would bear a son, he also specifically stated, "you shall call his name John" (meaning "God is gracious"), with the promise the child would "be great before the Lord" (1:13, 15). On the day John was circumcised, the eighth day after birth, Elizabeth stunned her family and friends by announcing his name would be "John," not "Zechariah" after his father. In submission to Gabriel's command, Zechariah had earlier made it clear to Elizabeth that the boy would be named John, which she both accepted and stood firm in announcing it. When the relatives appeared to Zechariah asking what he wanted the child to be named, he took a tablet and wrote, "His name is John" (1:63), at which time God returned the gift of speech to him. He used his voice first to bless God, again revealing his surrender to all the wishes of God for the child, as others asked, "What then will this child be?" (1:66a), for it became clear to them "the hand of the Lord was with him" (1:66b).

May we always remember the following lessons: while the surrender of our will to God's is often hard, it is all the more necessary for our good; that the reward of surrender to God are His blessings beyond our imagination; that with the gift of a child comes the responsibility of raising him in the instruction and discipline of the Lord; and, though the way forward may seem dim to us, it is crystal clear to the Father who loves us, now and forever.

Today, I will... resolve to surrender my will to the will of my Father, to make the goal of pleasing Him my number one priority, and to raise the children He has given me to love, obey, and serve Him.

Zechariah's Praise and Prophecy
Today's Scripture: Luke 1:67-69

When the Lord returned to Zechariah the power of speech, he was "filled with the Holy Spirit and prophesied" (1:67). By inspiration Luke has recorded for us twelve of the most beautiful verses in all of literature, known as the Benedictus, words from the heart and mouth of this good and faithful man that begin, appropriately, with praise for God followed by a prophecy for John.

In this sterling and stirring presentation, little-known Zechariah became the first prophet of the New Testament, the first prophetic voice of God since the close of the Old Testament with Malachi, a span of four hundred years. We will note how his message, his psalm, develops through four stages:

First, he praises God for keeping His promise to David, whose kingdom would last forever through his divine descendant, Jesus, "the horn of salvation" (1:68-71).

Second, he praises God for keeping His promise to Abraham, that from his seed all the nations of the earth will be blessed through the coming of Jesus (1:72-75).

Third, he praises God for blessing himself and Elizabeth with John, their beloved son who would serve as the forerunner of the Christ, calling people to repent (1:76-77).

Fourth, he praises God for the promise of Jesus, "the sunrise who visit us from on high" (1:78-79). Notice the beautiful tribute he ascribes to the Lord in this final verse:"He will "give light to those who sit in darkness and in the shadow of death, to guide our feet into the way of peace."

The significance of this story for us is that God is behind it all, even from eternity (Ephesians 3:11). After a perfect creation of the world and humanity, He carefully planned the formation of a special race, beginning with Abraham, through whom the Savior of the world would eventually come to save the world from itself. He chose and prepared ordinary people to carry out His extraordinary plan of redemption. Zechariah and Elizabeth perhaps thought their life together would soon end, but God had plans for them they could not have imagined, to give birth and raise the son who would blaze the trail of the long-awaited Messiah!

Have you given thought as to how God can use you, whether young or older, for outstanding contributions to His cause? There is much work for each of us to do before the Lord appears to take us home to glory. Are you ready to answer His call? Will you be ready for that great day that is coming?

Today, I will... seek out opportunities to serve God by serving others, bringing them the light of Jesus so they may know the way of peace.

Zechariah, John, Jesus, and You

Today's Scripture: Luke 1:80; 2:41-52

If it were not for Luke's inspired account of the gospel story, we would not have known of this humble couple who loved and faithfully served their God, Zechariah and Elizabeth. In doing so, they have done their part in changing the world forever. Praise God for these shining lights whose story will continue to bless the world until the Lord comes. It is so often the case that the greatest truths and principles in Scripture are best seen in both the faith and the failings of its characters.

It is no secret why the lives of John the Baptizer, the son of Zechariah, and Jesus the Christ, the Son of God, are intertwined. It was the divine plan of God for one to prepare the way for the other, and the greater of the two to build on the foundation laid by the labors of the lesser. Not only is there a parallel between their miraculous births, but so is the mission distinctly given to them. The same messenger, Gabriel, portrayed what each would accomplish, speaking first of John: "He will be filled with the Holy Spirit, even from his mother's womb. And he will turn many of the children of Israel to the Lord their God, and he will go before him in the spirit and power of Elijah, . . . to make ready for the Lord a people prepared" (Luke 1:15-17). And of Jesus Gabriel promised: "The Holy Spirit will come upon you, and the power of the Most High will overshadow you; therefore the child to be born will be called holy—the Son of God" (Luke 1:35).

Once their respective ministries began, the greatest words to proceed from the mouth of John were, "Behold, the Lamb of God, who takes away the sin of the world" (John 1:29)! And, while John was imprisoned, the greatest compliment Jesus ever gave to anyone was, "Truly, I say to you, among those born of women there has arisen no one greater than John the Baptist" (Matthew 11:11). And most importantly, John gave his life for Jesus, and Jesus gave His life for John and the entire world.

What about you? Are there some life lessons you can apply to your life? I think so:
- First, we must always remember that God is in complete control of the universe and life.
- Second, God is working providentially in our lives, even when we do not know.
- Third, when it is the most difficult to believe God's promises, we must trust Him, always.
- Fourth, God will use what appears to be the most obscure life in the world to His glory.
- Fifth, even when we momentarily doubt and fail Him, His grace is sufficient to forgive us.

Today, I will... say a special prayer of gratitude for those God has used throughout the Bible story to accomplish His purposes, including the life He has graciously given me to live.

WEEK #34

Joseph & Mary

CHRIS PRESSNELL

If Not Mary, Then Who? (Part 1)

Today's Scripture: Luke 1:26-38

If you are a business owner, administrator, or in management of some kind, then more than likely, at some point, you have poured over the resumes of multiple job applicants, searching for that one individual who you believe bests meets the criteria needed to fill the position for which you are hiring. Once that person is identified, then it is time to contact them about the job.

When God looked through the ages of time searching for the perfect mother for his Son's earthly sojourn, He chose a young woman named Mary from the insignificant city of Nazareth in Galilee. She met the criteria for the job description physically speaking; she was a virgin (Isaiah 7:14, Luke 1:27), a child of Abraham (Genesis 12:3), of the tribe of Judah (Genesis 49;10, Isaiah 11:7) and a descendant of King David (Jeremiah 23:5), if you accept that one of the genealogies in the gospels of Luke or Matthew reference the lineage of Christ from His mother's side. She also lived during the time of Roman imperialism. This is significant because the prophet Daniel envisioned that the coming universal and everlasting kingdom (which obviously would need a king) would be set up while the Romans were in power (Daniel 2:44). But more importantly, she met the criteria of what our Heavenly Father was looking for in a mother, spiritually speaking. It was time to make contact.

Paul says in Galatians 4:4-6, "But when the fullness of time had come, God sent forth his Son, born of woman, born under the law, to redeem those who were under the law, so that we might receive adoption as sons. And because you are sons, God has sent the Spirit of his Son into our hearts, crying, 'Abba! Father!'" This means that Jesus was sent at the proper time. Luke 1:26 tells us that the angel Gabriel was sent by God to Mary to inform her that she would be the mother of the Messiah. What an amazing honor and awesome responsibility!

Do we meet the criteria that God has for people He wants to employ in His service? If we had been a woman living during the time when God planned to send His son, would we have been a candidate for the job?

Today, I will...pray to God to help me be ready to answer His call.

If Not Mary, Then Who? (Part 2)

Today's Scripture: Luke 1:26-38; 46-55

Not only did Mary meet the physical criteria to be the mother of the Messiah, but she also was a woman who spiritually met the criteria desired by God for the mother of His Son. So, what honorable characteristics did Mary exhibit that made her God's selection and a woman to be emulated?

First, Mary was a woman of purity. Prophecy dictated that the Messiah would be born of a virgin. From her response to Gabriel, it appears that this was something she valued and was concerned about protecting. Unfortunately, in our society, the idea of sexual purity before marriage has become something people ridicule and ignore rather than admire and pursue. In 2020, the United States Census Bureau collected data that revealed 4 out of every 10 children are born to unwed mothers. This new trend was unheard of decades ago but has become the new reality. In I Timothy 5:1-2, Paul told his co-laborer to encourage older women of the church to teach the younger women about purity. Make no mistake about it, Mary was a woman of purity and this was pleasing to God.

Second, Mary was a woman of humility. After Gabriel's revelation regarding her pregnancy, her response was, "Behold, I am the servant of the Lord" (Luke 1:38). This word for servant in the text would be better translated as bond-servant. She continued to acknowledge her lowly estate in Luke 1:48 and recognized that the great things done for her were from the Almighty. Paul told us in Philippians 2:5, to have a mind that is humble just like Christ. Mary was a woman of humility.

Third, Mary was a woman of faith. As a bond-servant of God's, she was ready to do whatever He needed her to do. She knew that God would honor and show mercy to those who fear Him. Something else that she knew was God's Word. That makes sense seeing that "Faith comes by hearing, and hearing by the word of God" (Romans 10:17 NKJV). Luke 1:55 lets us know that she was familiar with the Hebrew Scriptures, making reference to the fact that God had spoken to Abraham and his offspring.

Fourth, Mary was a woman who loved her God and praised His holy name. The beautiful words found in the song she sang forever echo the heartfelt sentiments of God's people and remind us of the true blessing it is to be a Christian.

Today, I will...work to be a person of purity, humility, faith, and love.

Mary: Devotion to Her Son and Savior

Today's Scripture: John 19:25; Acts 1:14

To watch your child die must be the most awful experience a parent could have. The thought of such a prospect is hard to imagine and gut-wrenching. Recently, a precious lady and dear sister in our congregation lost both of her children over the span of one week due to unrelated circumstances. Her daughter was killed in a car accident, and about five days later her son was found dead in his room. I have no words to describe the grief she experienced and continues to experience. Furthermore, I have no basis for comparison to even know what she is going through.

In the same vein, I can not imagine what Mary was feeling and thinking as she stood by the cross and watched her perfect little boy die in such a horrific way. I wonder if she and Jesus ever previously talked about this day. I wonder if she were ever present when He preached about the eventuality of His being put to death. Well, either way, there she stood. Not ashamed that He was being punished like someone guilty of committing a heinous crime. Just a loving mother doing the best she could to be there for her Son at this most terrifying and painful time.

I also wonder about the internal struggle that she might have been experiencing. To think that spiritually speaking, she was also responsible for what was taking place. It was her sins too that He was bearing. The roles were now reversed. The mother who had protected and preserved her Son all of His life would now be protected and preserved for all of hers because of His death.

Well, His death for her would not be in vain. She would do everything in her power to see His kingdom established and grow. After his resurrection and appearances, you will find her in Acts 1:14, devoting herself to prayer alongside the apostles and her other children.

Today, I will...dedicate myself to making sure that Jesus' death for me was not in vain.

Joseph the Just

Today's Scripture: Matthew 1:18-25

Not much is said in the Scriptures about the earthly father of our Lord, Jesus Christ. However, the small section of Scripture that does introduce him speaks volumes about the quality of his character.

The very first thing that is said about Joseph is that he was a just man. The Greek term for this word, according to Strong's Exhaustive Concordance, means a person who is "equitable in character, holy, right, innocent." An examination of his thoughts and behaviors upon hearing that his espoused wife was pregnant and the subsequent visit by the angel of the Lord lead us to the following conclusions:

First, Joseph was a man of compassion and kindness. Even before the revelatory dream, Joseph had decided to act with mercy regarding Mary. He did not want to shame her or retaliate with spite even when this seeming betrayal would have most certainly caused him sadness and possibly embarrassment. He was going to divorce her quietly and privately.

Second, Joseph was a man of courage. The angel told him not to be afraid to take Mary as his wife. There might have been ridicule that came as a result of traveling with a wife who became pregnant before he married her. Or the uncomfortable feeling he might have gotten around people who looked at him with judgmental eyes. There might also have been the disconcerting feeling of knowing that he would be raising a child that physically wasn't his own. How was that dynamic going to play out? It would take courage to marry a pregnant woman carrying a child that was not his own and to be the physical guardian of the Son of God.

Third, Joseph was a man of compliance. When he woke up from his dream, Matthew 1:24 said that "he did as the angel of the Lord commanded him" and took Mary to be his wife. He always followed God's directives. In Matthew 2:13, the angel appeared to Joseph again in a second dream with a new command. He was told to take Jesus to Egypt. He obeyed and went. In Matthew 2:19, there is a third dream and visit from the angel instructing Joseph to take Jesus back to Israel. Matthew 2:21, says "And he rose and took the child and his mother and went to the land of Israel." At every turn, Joseph obeyed the voice of the Lord.

Fourth, Joseph was a man of control. Certainly, one of the greatest joys of life is the physical relationship enjoyed by husbands and wives. This is especially true when you consider the anticipation of your wedding night. However, Joseph did not engage in sexual relations WITH HIS WIFE until after the birth of Jesus. He would deny himself in order to make sure that God's word was fulfilled.

Fifth, Joseph was a man of conviction. Joseph made sure that he observed the law of Moses with regards to this son. Luke 2 also verifies that Joseph was intent on worshiping God as he went every year with his family to the Passover feast in Jerusalem.

Today, I will...ask the Father to help me to be a man of God like Joseph.

Joseph: Like Father, Like Son

Today's Scripture: Matthew 2:13-15

The invasion of Russia into the Ukraine in 2022 sent thousands of people scrambling to seek shelter in other countries. Among those who left their homes, jobs, and educational institutions were four ladies from Kamyshin, Russia. These four Christian women and dear loved ones of ours were so frustrated and heartbroken about their country's tyrannical decision to attack their neighbor, that they refused to live in their homeland any more. Such a move was difficult and took lots of courage. The anxiety associated with going to an unknown place not knowing where you will live or how you will support yourself must be scary beyond explanation.

More than two thousand years ago, a man named Joseph was instructed by God to leave his homeland and go to Egypt with his family in order to avoid the tyrannical leadership of Herod, the king. This move came following a visit from some wise men bearing gifts for his young son, who Herod saw as a threat to his throne and decided to search for and kill. Joseph left the comforts of home and faced the difficulties of living in a foreign land and the uncertainties of what that would involve in order to save his family.

Shortly, before this move to Egypt, God, in the form of a little baby, left the splendor of heaven (His home) to sojourn in a foreign land to save His family. Such a move was difficult and took lots of courage and love. This foreign land cost Him the perfect peace and comfort that He had previously enjoyed with His Father and the Holy Spirit and subjected Him to sin and suffering associated with living on earth. Yet, He obeyed the will of His Heavenly Father just like His earthly father did in order to provide salvation for us from our mortal enemy, satan, the ruler of this world (John 14:30). Praise God for such a sacrifice as this.

Today, I will...pray that God will give me the strength and courage to go where He needs me to go and do what He needs me to do, wherever it is, to help bring salvation to those who so desperately need it and who are so tremendously loved by Him.

WEEK #35

John the Baptist

SCOTT HARP

Great Purpose!

Today's Scripture: Luke 1:5-25, 57-80

William Shakespeare wrote in *Twelfth Night*, "Be not afraid of greatness. Some are born great, some achieve greatness, and some have greatness thrust upon them." These words certainly could be said of John, the forerunner of Jesus. Much intrigue and mystery surrounded the birth of this great man of God. His parents were old and beyond child-bearing years when an angel revealed they were to have a son. And, when his father heard the heavenly promise, he questioned and was struck speechless until the child was born. But, perhaps the most intriguing of all was the purpose the child would be set to fulfill. Preparing God's people for the Lord's coming was no small task.

Did you know that God had a purpose in your birth? You share this purpose with every child that has been or will be born. He created the world as a place for soul-making. Hebrews 2:10 says, "For it was fitting that he, for whom and by whom all things exist, in bringing many sons to glory, should make the founder of their salvation perfect through suffering." God, who made everything by and for Himself did it all for one reason and one reason alone— "sons in glory." So much was His commitment to it that He allowed His Son, "the founder of their salvation" to die on the cross. Every child that enters the world, God sees as having the potential of being a son in glory with Him. From birth until death, you are being called by the gospel of Jesus Christ, (2 Thessalonians 2:14).

There is so much uncertainty with expectant parents. Beyond the hopes of ten fingers and ten toes is the potential for greatness. Dreams of grandeur and success invade the mind because every child is special. John was special! You are special! And, God's hope for you is success in life, even more, the life to come.

Today, I will...take time to think about the purpose God has for my life, and pray thanks for the joy of living for Jesus.

TUESDAY

Great Testimony!

Today's Scripture: John 1

The years 1947-1957 were considered transitional days between radio and television. The voice of CBS News was Walter Cronkite. During this period, he conducted a series on historical events called *You Are There.* At the end of each episode, the anchor would say, "What sort of day was it? A day like all days, filled with those events that alter and illuminate our times...and you were there."

John, the writer of the book of John, gave us many scenes of the life of Jesus. One was when John the Baptist, in the presence of many people, saw Jesus coming to him. Visualize it! We don't know what he looked like, but see yourself, maybe standing on the banks of the Jordan River, and Jesus is walking toward you. The Bible says that when John saw him, he said, "Behold, the Lamb of God, who takes away the sin of the world" (John 1:29). He saw him again and repeated the testimony in verse 36.

The Lamb of God! What did he mean? In Old Testament times, an unspotted lamb was chosen for sacrifices. Yet, no matter how many lambs were sacrificed on alters, they could never take sins away (Hebrews 10:4). The testimony of John said to the world that Jesus was going to be the final Lamb—the perfect, sinless Lamb—that, when sacrificed, would make it possible for all sins of all people to be forgiven.

In another place, the apostle Paul wrote, "For we walk by faith, not by sight" (2 Corinthians 5:7). In other words, what John saw, you too can see, not with your eyes, but with your thoughts. In your mind's eye, look down through history and see what John saw! What sort of day was it? It was a day like all days, filled with those events that alter and illuminate our times, and you were there.

Today, I will...see Jesus through the eyes of faith and point Him out to others.

WEDNESDAY
Great Honor!

Today's Scripture: Matthew 3:13-17

Several years ago, it was probably my life's greatest thrill and honor to baptize my children into Christ. All three, individually, as they realized their sins were why Jesus had to die, determined the need to be born again by the saving blood of Jesus. As a preacher, I have always encouraged dads to administer the baptism of their children when they are ready, for just that reason.

Imagine what it would have been like for John to have Jesus come up and say, "Hey, I need you to baptize me!" John had been baptizing many in Israel for the forgiveness of their sins. It was his mission to do so. Yet when Jesus came to him and requested it, he was like, "Whoa! Whoa! Whoa! Let's slow this thing down a minute! Are you saying you want me to baptize you?" Of course, he did not say it just that way, but you get the picture. John thought he was not worthy to baptize Jesus. Jesus was sinless! He always chose to do the right thing. That is one of the reasons He is so special. Yet, He asked John to baptize Him to "fulfill all righteousness" (Matthew 3:15). In other words, it was the right thing to do. And so, John baptized Him right then and there. Talk about your memorable moment!

John was special, and God used him to do great things for Him. He was put in the right place at the right time to do great things in preparing His people for the coming Messiah, Jesus. You, too, are precious in the eyes of God. As valuable as you are to Him, there is no telling what blessing He might lay upon you on any given day. If you serve Him, He will bless you in ways you never thought possible. If you have been born again through baptism, the Father's special Providence will give you good things in life.

Today, I will...allow the Lord to use me for His cause in service to others.

Great Tests!

Today's Scripture: Luke 7:18-35

How great was John in Jesus' estimation? He said, "For I say unto you, Among those that are born of women there is not a greater prophet than John the Baptist: but he that is least in the kingdom of God is greater than he" (Luke 7:28 KJV). How do you measure greatness? John was the great forerunner of the Messiah. Yet, as our passage tells us, John was in prison. History reveals that he never left his confinement and met with a horrible death, (Matthew 14:10).

Greatness comes at a cost. John paid the highest price—his life. Though serving God's purposes was his life commitment, it is easy to see how he could experience doubt. That might explain why he sent disciples to Jesus, asking if he really was the Messiah. Yes, this was the man who earlier said when he saw Jesus, "Behold, the Lamb of God, who takes away the sins of the world" (John 1:29). So, why the doubt?

Struggles have a way of making us question some of the most basic of our beliefs. In some ways, it is easy to think that the protective capacity of God's love for us will keep us from experiencing sorrow. But Jesus told His disciples, "I have said these things to you, that in me you may have peace. In the world you will have tribulation. But take heart; I have overcome the world" (John 16:33).

If you follow Jesus, you have chosen the way less traveled, (Matthew 7:13-14). It is the road with the greatest blessings. Hence, the comment of Jesus about the one who is least in the kingdom of God is greater than John. But this is the road satan loves to stand beside and shoot his flaming darts, (Ephesians 6:16). If he can cause you to doubt like he did John, then he can see the potential for victory. But remember, Jesus is stronger than satan! Never doubt, no matter what.

Today, I will...hold to my faith no matter what temptation satan hurls my way.

Great Beginnings!

Today's Scripture: Mark 1:1-8

Gospel is a word often used in the religion of Jesus Christ. Gospel message! Gospel preachers! Gospel meetings! The term *gospel* simply means good news. But what it involves is so much more. Mark began his book most insightfully. "The beginning of the gospel of Jesus Christ, the Son of God" (Mark 1:1). Here is where it gets interesting! For the next seven verses he spoke of John, the Baptist. Get the picture! To tell the story of Jesus, Mark had to start with John. You cannot tell the gospel of Jesus without John. God had foretold about John back in the days of the prophets of Israel (Luke 1:17). In other words, God talked about John hundreds of years before Jesus was born.

Without a doubt, Jesus is the object of our greatest affection, for He alone is the Author of our salvation, (Hebrews 5:8-9). But even Jesus could not have accomplished His work had John not been put in place to prepare the way. Visualize this crudely dressed wilderness preacher, who ate locusts and wild honey, crying out to the masses that they needed to be baptized for the forgiveness of their sins. Some might have thought of him as a crazy man. But he was popular. Jerusalem and all Judea and all the region about the Jordan were going out to him, and they were baptized by him in the Jordan River, confessing their sins. John was and always will be an integral part of the gospel.

Consider for a minute your part in this beautiful gospel. John lived and died before Jesus went to the cross. Millions have died since Jesus was resurrected and went back to heaven, many of whom continued to voice the good news of Jesus. Paul wrote that the gospel is that in which all people of faith stand (1 Corinthians 15:4). Jesus connected John with you and with all those who tell the good news of Jesus.

Today, I will...share the gospel of Jesus Christ and make straight His path to others.

WEEK #36

Peter

JAY LOCKHART

MONDAY

The Three Calls

Today's Scripture: John 1:35-42; Matthew 4:18-22; Luke 6:12-16

I like to think of him as the Big Fisherman—a robust man with muscles in his arms and calluses on his hands. He was a fisherman who was in business with his brother and three friends. He often was brash, always opinionated, and sometimes spoke and acted before he thought things through. But he was a passionate man and when he met Jesus, he was forever changed. His name was Peter and this man received three calls from Christ.

The call to be a Disciple (John 1:35-42). While he was still called Simon, his brother Andrew introduced him to Jesus as the Messiah. The first thing Jesus did when He met Simon was to change his name to Peter, which means "a stone." Simon, as a disciple, would spend the rest of his life trying to live up to this new name.

The call to be a Companion (Matthew 4:18-22). Peter's second call from Christ was to leave his fishing business and become "a fisher of men." Along with others, Peter became a constant companion of Jesus. He observed the perfect life of Jesus, heard Him speak with all the authority of God, saw the miracles He performed, and was convinced that Jesus is the Christ.

The call to be an Apostle (Luke 6:12-16). From the growing number of disciples Jesus chose twelve to be apostles, and Peter was one of these. Christ would one day place the gospel in their hands and trust them to take the message to the world (Mark 16:15-16).

We, too, have three calls from Christ. Through the gospel message Christ calls us to be disciples (learners, followers, and imitators), and gives us the name of "Christians" (Matthew 28:19-20; Acts 11:26). Second, Christ calls us to spiritual growth (2 Peter 3:18; Acts 20:32). Third, Christ calls us to faithful service (Matthew 25:21).

Peter accepted his calls from Christ. How are we doing in accepting Christ's calls to us?

Today, I will...pray for the determination and the strength to accept the invitations of Christ.

212

TUESDAY

The Three Friends

Today's Scripture: Luke 14:1, 12-14

From His disciples Jesus chose twelve and called them apostles "ones sent" (Luke 6:13). These apostles would be almost constant companions of Jesus over the next three years as He prepared them for the task of taking the gospel to the world. Obviously, Jesus was close to these men and called them "friends" (John 15:14). However, Jesus was closer to three of the apostles than He was to the others, and they became His inner circle of special friends. There are three events in the ministry of Jesus that especially emphasize His special relationship with Peter, James, and John: (1) the healing of Jairus' daughter (Mark 5:21-24, 35-43); (2) the mountain of transfiguration (Mark 9:2-3); and (3) the garden of Gethsemane (Mark 14:32-42).

Jesus had special friends. In addition to Peter, James, and John, there were others, such as Mary, Martha, and Lazarus, who were His special friends (Luke 10:38-42; John 11:1; 12:1-3). However, it should be remembered that Jesus loved and wanted to be the friend of all people. Even now, you and I are His friends if we obey Him (John 15:14). But the fact remains that Jesus did have special friends.

You may have special friends. In living the Christian life, you and I will have special friends and feel closer to some people in our church families than we do to others. We will be with these people more than we are with others; we have more in common with some than we do others; and we enjoy their company in a special way. And this is okay!

Do not forget to enlarge your circle of friends. When you are planning a get-together with your friends, seek out someone in your congregation who may be lonely, forgotten, or not feeling that they belong, and include them. Everybody will be blessed because this is the right thing to do.

Today, I will...pray that the Lord will give us eyes to see those who need us and the will to include them in our circle.

The Three Proofs

Today's Scripture: Matthew 16:13-17

Jesus asked His disciples two important questions. First, "Who do men say that I, the Son of Man, am?" (NKJV). It seemed everyone had an opinion about Jesus. The apostles answered, "Some say John the Baptist, some Elijah, and others Jeremiah or one of the prophets" (NKJV). These men were all held in high esteem by the people, and to say Jesus was the martyred John, who had come back to life, was a great compliment. To say Jesus was Elijah, the ninth century BC prophet, whom many in Israel believed would appear just before the Messiah came (Malachi 4:5) was to hold Jesus in high esteem. (See Matthew 11:12-14 for the true identity of this Elijah.) To say that Jesus was Jeremiah was to say He was someone great. However, Jesus was none of these. It is never enough to compliment Jesus unless we see Him as He really is. The second question was, "Who do you say that I am?" Peter answered for all of them when he said, "You are the Christ, the Son of the living God" (NKJV).

Jesus pronounced a blessing upon Peter for seeing Him for who He is. Jesus further stated that Peter did not learn His identity from men but from "my Father." How did the Father reveal to Peter the identity of Jesus? There are three answers to this question. First, Peter, in contrast to his own life, observed the perfect life of Jesus (Luke 5:8). Second, Peter witnessed the miracles of Jesus (John 20:30-31). Third, Peter heard the authority with which Jesus taught (Matthew 7:28-29).

In these three ways God revealed to Peter who Jesus is, and he believed. At this point he had not yet heard God acknowledge Jesus in the mountain (Matthew 17:1-5) or observed the greatest proof of all—the resurrection of Christ (Romans 1:4). In all of these ways the Father has revealed to us through the gospel the identity of Jesus. Will we believe?

Today, I will...pray for greater faith in Christ in order to obey Him better.

The Three Denials

Today's Scripture: Matthew 16:21-23; 26:69-75

Peter and the other apostles had difficulty in grasping many of the things Jesus taught them. Three times Jesus told them plainly that he would go to Jerusalem, would die, and on the third day would rise from the dead (Matthew 16:21-23; 17:22-23; 20:17-19). However, they did not understand what He was telling them. In the first of these instances, Peter responded by saying, "Far be it from you, Lord; this shall not happen to You!" Jesus said to Peter, "Get behind Me, Satan!" (NKJV) This may seem harsh, but Jesus wanted Peter to know that unless He died and was raised, the purposes of satan, not God, would be served.

Throughout the ministry of Jesus, Peter had difficulty understanding why Jesus had come into the world. His Christ-given name was Peter, meaning "rock," but often Peter was more like the shifting, drifting sand than a rock. Near the end of His ministry, Jesus warned Peter that satan would sift him as wheat, but Peter blurted out, "Lord, I am ready to go with You, both to prison and to death." It was then that Jesus said, "I tell you, Peter, the rooster shall not crow this day before you will deny three times that you know Me" (Luke 22:31-34 NKJV).

After Jesus was arrested, Peter stood in the courtyard of the high priest who conducted the first phase of Jesus' trial. A servant girl said to Peter, "You were with Jesus." And, Peter denied it. Soon, another girl saw Peter and said, "This fellow was also with Jesus." And, Peter denied it. Others came to Peter and said, "You are one of them, for your speech betrays you" (he must have spoken with the accent of Galilee). And Peter denied it, swearing by heaven and calling down curses upon himself if what he said was not true. It was then that the rooster crowed, and Peter went out and wept bitterly (Matthew 26:69-75).

Today, I will...pray that we may be bold in confessing our belief in Christ.

The Three Questions

Today's Scripture: John 21:1-19

Here are the facts: Jesus died, He was buried, and on the third day His tomb was empty. It is not an overstatement to say that when Jesus died the hopes of the disciples died with Him. Even though Jesus had told the apostles on at least three occasions that he would die and be raised, they did not comprehend what He said (John 20:9). Jesus appeared to the apostles twice within eight days following the resurrection, yet they were reluctant to believe. Possibly in despair, Peter and six other disciples went back to their nets. They fished all night and caught nothing. In the morning they saw someone standing on the shore who asked, "Have you any fish?" They said, "No." The stranger said, "Cast your nets on the other side of the boat." They did and pulled up 153 fish! They then knew the stranger was Jesus and hurried to shore.

After they ate together, Jesus asked Peter three questions, perhaps corresponding to the three denials of Jesus by Peter. Question 1: "Simon (the old name, not Peter the rock – JPL). . .do you love (*agapao* – the highest word in the Greek language for love – JPL) me?" Peter answered, "Yes, . . .I love (*phileo* – the affection of a friend) you." Question 2: "Simon. . .do you love (*agapao*) me?" Peter answered, "Yes, . . .you know that I love (*phileo*) you." Question 3: "Simon, . . .do you love (*phileo* – note the change in Jesus' word for "love" which could mean, 'Do you even love me as a friend?') me?" Peter, being grieved at the third time Jesus asked him about his love, said, "You know that I love (*phileo* – have affection for you." Peter was not quite as sure of himself as before he denied Jesus. But, Peter really did love Jesus supremely and would prove it by dying for Christ.

Today, I will...pray for greater love for the One who loved us and gave Himself for us.

WEEK #37

Andrew

KEITH HARRIS

Andrew: the Protoclete

Today's Scripture: John 1:35-40

Andrew holds a prominent place in Christian history as one of the twelve apostles chosen by Jesus Christ. While he stands among the twelve, he doesn't appear to be one of the more well-known figures of the New Testament. As a matter of fact, Andrew is only mentioned twelve times in Scripture. Four of those times simply lists him among the other apostles. As it is, very little is known about his life, though his impact is no doubt tremendous.

Andrew has been identified by some as "the protoclete," the first called. While Matthew and Mark both describe Jesus calling His first disciples, John 1 explains that Andrew was the first among those named to acknowledge and follow Jesus as the Rabbi and Messiah. "The next day again John was standing with two of his disciples, and he looked at Jesus as he walked by and said, 'Behold, the Lamb of God!' The two disciples heard him say this, and they followed Jesus. Jesus turned and saw them following and said to them, 'What are you seeking?' And they said to him, 'Rabbi' (which means Teacher), 'where are you staying?' He said to them, 'Come and you will see.' So they came and saw where he was staying, and they stayed with him that day, for it was about the tenth hour. One of the two who heard John speak and followed Jesus was Andrew, Simon Peter's brother" (John 1:35-40).

Though it appears that Andrew was first among those named and known followers of Jesus, his life and attitude seem to continually point to Jesus rather than himself. It is so easy for us to get consumed with self and status that we miss those opportunities to point to Jesus. But this is the very thing we ought to do each day. As we encounter others, as we experience those moments when opportunities to exalt ourselves appear, we must remember the example of people like Andrew. We must exalt Jesus.

Today, I will...take advantage of the opportunities to exalt Jesus.

TUESDAY

Andrew: the Brother of Simon

Today's Scripture: John 1:40

Have you ever thought of what it must have been like to be the brother of someone with such renown? Perhaps you have an older sibling that seems to excel in everything they undertake. Or maybe you have a friend that seems to always receive the praise and adoration from others. Whatever the case, we experience moments in life that open us up to the pitfalls of jealousy.

I wonder what it must have been like for Andrew. As we read about him in the Bible (and there are only a few times he is mentioned), we see him most often introduced as the brother of Simon Peter. For example, "One of the two who heard John speak and followed Jesus was Andrew, Simon Peter's brother" (John 1:40). Andrew is either identified as Simon Peter's brother or named after Peter, with the only exception being that of John 12:20-26. In this passage, Philip and Andrew are present, but Simon Peter appears conspicuously absent. While we do not know for certain, many believe that this indicates that Andrew was the younger brother of Peter. Some suggest that maybe this simply points to the fact that Andrew was somehow less important that Peter. However, that doesn't seem to be the case considering that John points to Andrew being the one who first followed. Most likely, Andrew was the younger brother of Simon Peter.

But again, what must that have been like for Andrew. Can you image the conversations? "Oh! Andrew, the brother of Simon Peter, right?"

It is possible that he never lived down his identification as Simon Peter's brother.

But one thing we never see is Andrew acting out in jealousy. From everything we know about him, Andrew was an important figure in the early church. He was chosen by Jesus as one of the twelve. And though he appears mostly in the shadow of his brother, we never see him complaining or falling into the pit of jealousy.

Today, I will...not let jealousy take hold of my life.

219

Andrew: the Fisher of Men

Today's Scripture: Matthew 4:18-20

Bethsaida was a town believed to be located on the northern shore of the Sea of Galilee, some five miles east of Capernaum. This town's name is Aramaic, meaning "house of fishing" or "house of the fisherman." It was essentially a fishing town. In the apostle John's account of the gospel, he wrote, "Now Philip was from Bethsaida, the city of Andrew and Peter" (John 1:44). From this, we come to know the hometown of Andrew. This certainly makes sense considering his vocation. Andrew was a fisherman. He was in partnership with his brother, Peter, and likely raised with an understanding that this was his calling.

However, Jesus had other plans for Andrew. "While walking by the Sea of Galilee, he saw two brothers, Simon (who is called Peter) and Andrew his brother, casting a net into the sea, for they were fishermen. And he said to them, 'Follow me, and I will make you fishers of men.' Immediately they left their nets and followed him" (Matthew 4:18-20). This event is also recorded in Mark's account of the gospel. He wrote, "Passing alongside the Sea of Galilee, he saw Simon and Andrew the brother of Simon casting a net into the sea, for they were fishermen. And Jesus said to them, 'Follow me, and I will make you become fishers of men.' And immediately they left their nets and followed him" (Mark 1:16-18).

Andrew immediately answered this play on words, this call from Jesus. While he likely did not understand everything this call would entail, he knew there was something special about Jesus. He was the one who first came to his brother stating with confidence, "We have found the Messiah" (John 1:41). He did understand that he would no longer be a fisherman, but as a follower of Jesus, he would be a fisher of men. This calling is one that extends to all followers of Jesus. The question is, will you answer this call?

Today, I will...answer the call to be a fisher of men.

THURSDAY
Andrew: the Missionary
Today's Scripture: John 1:41-42

Not unlike many Christians in the early church, Andrew had a heart for telling others about Jesus. We see this early on in his experience with Jesus. John wrote concerning Andrew, "He first found his own brother Simon and said to him, 'We have found the Messiah' (which means Christ). He brought him to Jesus" (John 1:41-42). Andrew was the one responsible for bringing his brother to Jesus. Some have referred to Andrew as the first domestic missionary. Scripture shows that he was the first to identify Jesus as the Messiah and the first to bring someone to Christ.

But Andrew's mission efforts were not confined to his own family or close associates. We also see him, along with Philip and Peter, presenting some Greeks to Jesus. In recording the events of Passover week, John wrote, "Now among those who went up to worship at the feast were some Greeks. So these came to Philip, who was from Bethsaida in Galilee, and asked him, 'Sir, we wish to see Jesus.' Philip went and told Andrew; Andrew and Philip went and told Jesus" (John 12:20-22). Because of this, Andrew has been named among the first foreign missionaries. Certainly, there is a mission mindset among the followers of Jesus, including Andrew.

While not much is recorded in the New Testament concerning the ministry and missionary work of Andrew, we know that he answered the call from Jesus to be a fisher of men. Even though there is not much evidence in the Bible, other writers such as Eusebius and Origen have written about the life and ministry of Andrew. These writings point to Andrew proclaiming the gospel to various ancient regions such as Scythia, regions around the Black Sea, and Achaea.

As evidenced by his running to Peter to explain that he had found the Messiah, Andrew possessed a heart for sharing Jesus with others. God desires His people to have this mission mindset. Andrew took every advantage to tell others of Jesus. Do you?

Today, I will...have a mission mindset.

FRIDAY
Andrew: the Follower of Jesus

Today's Scripture: Matthew 4:20

Andrew knew there was something special about Jesus. Because of this, his faith in Christ led him to release his fishing net, leaving all behind to follow Jesus. Think about these words from Scripture:

Immediately they left their nets and followed him. (Matthew 4:20)

And immediately they left their nets and followed him (Mark 1:18)

The next day again John was standing with two of his disciples, and he looked at Jesus as he walked by and said, "Behold, the Lamb of God!" The two disciples heard him say this, and they followed Jesus. Jesus turned and saw them following and said to them, "What are you seeking?" And they said to him, "Rabbi" (which means Teacher), "where are you staying?" He said to them, "Come and you will see." So they came and saw where he was staying, and they stayed with him that day, for it was about the tenth hour. One of the two who heard John speak and followed Jesus was Andrew, Simon Peter's brother (John 1:35-40).

There is no mistaking the fact that Andrew was intent on following Jesus, the Messiah. Certainly, he was not perfect, but Andrew displayed a striking resemblance to Jesus as he left everything for the sake of fulfilling the will of another. Jesus, "did not count equality with God a thing to be grasped, but emptied himself, by taking the form of a servant, being born in the likeness of men. And being found in human form, he humbled himself by becoming obedient to the point of death, even death on a cross" (Philippians 2:6-8). In a similar way, we see Andrew emptying himself of his old life of fishing (leaving behind his nets, etc.) and taking on the new life of following and submitting to the will of another.

This challenge lies before us even today. We ought to have the kind of spirit demonstrated in the life of Andrew, who left everything to be a follower of Jesus.

Today, I will...yield my will to the will of Christ.

WEEK #38

James

STEVE LOYD

James, the Author

Today's Scripture: James 1:1

James, the author of the New Testament book that bears his name, identifies himself as "a servant of God and of the Lord Jesus Christ," (James 1:1). Many sources identify him as having been the brother of Jesus.

The edition of the ESV I am referencing includes a paragraph introducing the book. It identifies the author in this manner: "One of the earliest of the New Testament writings (A.D. 40-50), it is believed to have been written by Jesus' brother James." This being the case, I find it intriguing that he did not makes reference to this fact when he identified himself. That seems to be the sort of thing I might highlight if I were a brother of Jesus, like James. But he did not. He simply identified himself as "a servant."

Again, drawing from the same edition of the ESV, there is a footnote for the word servant. The footnote reads, "or slave, Greek bondservant." It is the same word Paul used with reference to himself in the introductory line of his letter to the saints in Rome (Romans 1:1). So, both men, James and Paul, viewed themselves as "slaves" of Jesus Christ.

It is striking to think that Mary had another son, or other children (Matthew 13:55), when Jesus fills center stage. James could have capitalized on his familial relationship to his "brother"—but did not. He emphasized his commitment to Jesus by writing that he was a "servant (slave) of God and of the Lord Jesus Christ."

James could have emphasized other types of relationships he sustained with Jesus (e.g. brother or disciple), but he chooses to emphasize the fact that he is His slave.

Think about the various relationships you sustain with Jesus. While each one you could name may be legitimate, which relationship would you emphasize? Think about the implications of James declaring that he is a "slave."

Today, I will...consider the implications of being a slave of Jesus Christ (Romans 6:12-14).

A Cause for Offense

Today's Scripture: Matthew 13:55-57

There are two episodes recorded in the book of Matthew that involve James, the brother of Jesus. The first is in Matthew 12. Jesus was interacting with the Pharisees (Matthew 12:22-45), and his mother and brothers asked to speak to him (12:46). Jesus said,

"'Who is my mother, and who are my brothers?' And stretching out his hand toward his disciples, he said, 'Here are my mother and my brothers! For whoever does the will of my Father in heaven is my brother and sister and mother.'" (Matthew 12:48-50).

No doubt, some of what He said was motivated by the fact that He was not only their son and brother. He was also their God and Savior.

The second episode is in Matthew 13. The audience was "astonished and said, 'Where did this man get this wisdom and these mighty works?'" (Matthew 13:54). They thought among themselves,

"'Is not this the carpenter's son? Is not his mother called Mary? And are not his brothers James and Joseph and Simon and Judas? And are not all his sisters with us? Where then did this man get all these things?' And they took offense at him" (Matthew 13:55-57).

James became an inadvertent cause for others to take offense in the Lord. Due to the perception others had of Jesus' connection with Mary and her sons and daughters, Jesus' audience was puzzled. How could someone with such mundane connections to the world, astonish them with His teachings and mighty works?

Jesus' identity is a primary concern in all four gospel accounts. Each writer built the case for believing that Jesus is the Christ. They also record episodes in which Jesus' identity was denied or questioned. And, in the case of Matthew 13, James, unwittingly, became one of the reasons people took offense at Him.

Wittingly or unwittingly, deliberately or inadvertently, we can all become stumbling blocks. This makes the case of James all the more intriguing.

Today, I will...consider ways in which we might be the cause for someone to find offense in Him.

WEDNESDAY
A Collage of References
Today's Scripture: Galatians 2

There are eight references to James, the brother of Jesus in the New Testament—if indeed all eight passages refer to the same man.

When the angel delivered Peter from prison (Acts 12), Peter headed straight to the house of Mary, the mother of John, whose other name was Mark. Saints were gathered there to pray. They were utterly astounded by seeing Peter. He told them how the Lord delivered him from prison, and then said, "Tell these things to James and to the brothers" (Acts 12:17).

Paul referred to James in his letter to the Galatians. James is "the Lord's brother" (Galatians 1:19). James, Cephas and John "seemed" to be influential and "pillars" of the church (Galatians 2:9). When Paul retold the story of Peter's hypocrisy, we learn that "certain men came from James" (Galatians 2:12).

The epistle of Jude was written by an author who referred to himself as "a servant of Jesus Christ and brother of James" (Jude v. 1). Jude is mentioned under the name of "Judas" in Matthew 13:55.

If being mentioned first was any indication of prominence, he was mentioned first in three places—and in good company. He is named first among his brothers (Matthew 13:55), before the apostles (1 Corinthians 15:7), and before Peter and John (Galatians 2:9) .

I would not call James an obscure character in the New Testament. Some characters never get named. As a case in point, does anyone know the name of the Ethiopian eunuch in Acts 8? Some get named, like Melchizedek, yet are obscure in other ways.

I am persuaded that all of the people mentioned in the New Testament gain their significance by their connection to Jesus. You can work up an entire character sketch on Peter for example, but every instance his significance is seen in his connection with Jesus.

Today, I will...take time to consider what my significance in life is as it relates to Jesus.

THURSDAY

A Pillar

Today's Scripture: Galatians 2

The New Testament is replete with discussions concerning the place of the Law of Moses, circumcision, and early issues between Jews and Gentiles in Christ.

Luke opens Acts 15 informing the reader that men from Judea were pontificating, "Unless you are circumcised according to the custom of Moses, you cannot be saved" (Acts 15:1, 5). Paul and Barnabas had "no small dissension and debate with them..." (15:2). In response, several were appointed to go to Jerusalem to meet with the apostles and elders concerning this issue. Paul and Barnabas were among them.

This counsel had some significant participants: Paul, Barnabas, Peter and James to name a few, but it was James who put the capstone on the discussion. You can read what he said on that occasion in Acts 15:12-21. Instead of focusing on the debate itself, focus your attention on James. He was apparently one of the elders in Jerusalem (15:4, 6, 22, 23).

Paul reflects on the Jerusalem council in his letter to the Galatians. It was important for him to establish the fact that he was not in the least behind the other apostles in authority. So, he refers to those in Jerusalem as "those who seemed influential" (Galatians 2:2, 6) and adds that they contributed nothing to him. He also refers to James as one of those "who seemed to be pillars" (2:9).

To many, James was a pillar—along with Peter and John (Galatians 2:9—I find it interesting that James is mentioned first). But notice that Paul uses the word "seemed"—"seemed influential" (Galatians 2:2, 6), and "seemed to be pillars" (2:9). I do not believe this was intended to detract from any legitimate role James or the others played, but to place their roles in perspective so Paul could be seen to have equal voice with them. Paul even writes parenthetically "(what they were makes no difference to me)" (2:6).

Today, I will... make sure my understanding of other people's roles in the church is kept in perspective.

FRIDAY
James and Jesus
Today's Scripture: 1 Corinthians 15:1-11

How did James go from "brother" (Matthew 13:55) to "servant" (James 1:1)?

What was James' attitude toward his brother, Jesus, when he and his family asked to speak to Him (Matthew 12:46-49)? Was James supportive, or did he question Jesus' identity? Did he conclude, like Nicodemus, "Rabbi, we know that you are a teacher come from God, for no one can do these signs that you do unless God is with him" (John 3:3)? Was he jealous of the attention Jesus received? Was there any sibling rivalry on his part?

A reasonable question to ask might be: why did James become a "servant" (slave) of God and of the Lord Jesus Christ?

I would like to propose that the turning point for James was the resurrection of Jesus from the dead. If he entertained any questions concerning his Brother's identity, they would have been answered in His resurrection.

When Paul listed those to whom the resurrected Christ appeared, he wrote, "Then he appeared to James, then to all the apostles" (1 Corinthians 15:7). Notice that the Christ appeared to James, then he appeared to the apostles. Also remember that James' name appeared first in Galatians 2:9 —"James and Cephas and John." All three men were identified as those who "seemed influential" and who "seemed to be pillars" (2:2, 6, 9).

I am not sure anyone understood the implications of Jesus' resurrection when He was initially raised from the dead, but as the Spirit of God guided various ones into all truth, those implications were made clear. Those who believed were transformed. In the case of James, the transformation was from "brother" to "servant." Where we are concerned, we were transformed from sinner to saint.

Today, I will...reflect on the significance of Jesus' resurrection from the dead and how it transformed and continues to transform me.

WEEK #39

John

DENNY PETRILLO

Humble Beginning

Today's Scripture: Mark 1:19-20

I suspect most of us have gone fishing. It can be a unique combination of relaxing (beautiful day, clear water, peaceful) and frustrating (am I even going to get a nibble???). Fortunately, when I've been fishing my livelihood didn't depend on how productive I was. There were a few times that the family was back at the campground waiting for a fresh fish dinner, but that's a different story.

John was a professional fisherman. It was a noble profession, but certainly not one that had great admiration and fame attached. Professional fisherman had myriads of challenges. They had to deal with miserably hot days or horrific storms. They had smelly fish and broken nets. Their boats were not indestructible, either. Then, there was always the dreaded, "I have fished all night long and caught nothing" problem (Luke 5:5).

Yet on one amazing day, Jesus appeared and called John to follow Him. It is probable that Jesus repeated the words that He had said moments earlier to Peter and Andrew: "Follow me, and I will make you become fishers of men" (Mark 1:17). Like those two, John (and his brother James), left their father and followed Jesus.

While it is clear that all of the apostles had a mistaken understanding of what the Messiah would do (Acts 1:6), John certainly knew that his life was about to make a huge change. Why would the Messiah pick someone like John? The short answer is that John had the mentality and disposition to become what Jesus needed. He possessed a humility that enabled him to follow, listen, and learn (Matthew 16:24).

Would Jesus have chosen you to be one of His disciples? Do you have the humility and teachability that is required of all Jesus' disciples? May John's example encourage us all to be humble, to be learners, and to be teachable.

Today, I will...pray that I can practice humility by putting God's will above my own and truly demonstrating that He is the Lord of my life.

Son of Thunder

Today's Scripture: Luke 9:51-56

God's people have always been bothered, upset, and maybe even angry when they see open defiance of the God they love. David dealt with this when he wrote his famous Imprecatory Psalms. The souls who had been brutally slain for their faith asked God "how long before you will judge and avenge our blood on those who dwell on the earth?" (Revelation 6:10). Perhaps you also have had similar feelings when you witnessed Christianity being spit at, the Bible being shredded, and Jesus being openly mocked.

In Luke 9:51-56, we are told about a Samaritan village that was not welcoming to Jesus. They didn't want this Jew coming to their town. This rejection of Jesus angered James and John, so that they asked Jesus: "Lord, do you want us to tell fire to come down from heaven and consume them?" (Luke 9:54). Jesus even gave the two brothers an Aramaic name: Boanerges, which means "sons of thunder" (Mark 3:17). Jesus rebuked the two brothers (Luke 9:55).

Perhaps you are somewhat taken back by James and John's shocking willingness to annihilate an entire village. It is true that the hatred and animosity between the two peoples were great. It seems apparent that the two brothers shared the feelings of hatred toward the Samaritans, especially since they were rude and unwelcoming to Jesus. Yet Jesus showed no hatred to this Samaritan village whatsoever. He simply moved on to another village. Meanwhile, He had choice words of rebuke for James and John.

God's love for all of mankind is seen in His sending Jesus to be the Savior for everyone (John 3:16). He wants all to be saved (1 Timothy 2:4), including those who openly reject Him. Paul reminds us all of how we too were once God's enemies (Romans 5:10), but are reconciled by Jesus' blood, and are saved by His life. We can be grateful that God didn't zap us when we rejected Him.

Today, I will...appreciate God's love for me—as unworthy as I am.

John's Face Plant

Today's Scripture: Matthew 17:1-13

Occasionally there will be something which happens to us that ranks high on our "this was soooo cool!" list. I immediately think of turning the pages on one of the "Big Four" Bible manuscripts (created in the fourth century) or being able to move around some ancient Hebrew fragments (that predated Christ by over 150 years) like a jigsaw puzzle. What would be yours? Going to a magical place or seeing a famous person? Maybe being able to witness a once-in-a-lifetime event?

The Bible tells us that John was a part of an "inner circle" of Jesus' disciples. As a result, he was able to witness things that others, even some of the other apostles, were not able to witness. Jesus took his "inner circle" of disciples—Peter, James, and John—up on a high mountain. What John witnessed was one of those events that almost defy description. First, the text tells us that Jesus was "transfigured before them" (Matthew 17:2). John saw Jesus' face shine "like the sun" and saw his clothes become "white as light." Second, the Scriptures tell us that Moses and Elijah appeared and were talking with Jesus! Seriously? Moses and Elijah? Third, John heard the voice of God, saying "This is my beloved Son, with whom I am well pleased; listen to him." Imagine hearing, with your own ears, the very voice of God Himself!

Time for the face-plant. The text says that when John (and the others) heard this, "they fell on their faces and were terrified" (Matthew 17:7). This reaction shows a side of John that I really love. His humble, submissive reaction is noteworthy.

As we study a text like this we need to do a spiritual face-plant. We need to humble ourselves "under the mighty hand of God" (1 Peter 5:6). Great events in our lives are wonderful. Hopefully our experiences, like his, will lead us to humble ourselves before our great God!

Today, I will...make a concerted effort to practice humility, serving God as His faithful child.

The Disciple Jesus Loved

Today's Scripture: John 19:23-27

Some people! You know the type. They're the ones who will do and say things to make your life miserable. They almost seem to enjoy introducing troubles into our lives. It is hard to have good feelings about people like this!

The Bible teaches us to love everyone. Jesus even said, "love your enemies" (Matthew 5:44). This kind of love is that which God Himself demonstrated, having loved the world (John 3:16).

However, there are some for which we have a special love. It seems to be a closer, deeper more personal type of love. It might be the love a husband has for his wife, or the love a mother has for a child with special needs. That love is just on a different level. It is like you love everyone, but you REALLY love this person.

It is clear that Jesus loved all of His chosen disciples. He even made reference to His love for them (John 13:34; 15:12). The Bible affirms that He loved them "to the end" (John 13:1).

However, the Bible notes the special love Jesus had for John. On five different occasions John is identified as that disciple "whom Jesus loved" (John 13:23; 19:26; 20:2; 21:7, 20). This closer, deeper love was shared by Jesus and John. This love was also manifested in what happened at the cross. When Jesus was about to die, He entrusted His mother into the care of John (John 19:27).

Have you ever thought about what especially endeared John to Jesus? Was it his genuineness? His dedicated heart? Perhaps he had an attitude that Jesus found particularly appealing? We will never know the answer to that this side of eternity. However, what we do know is this. God loves those who are committed to keeping His commands (John 14:15). Our life purpose is to "fear God and keep His commandments" (Ecclesiastes 12:13). God will love us when we fulfill that purpose!

Today, I will...demonstrate my love for God by obeying His Word.

The Last Word

Today's Scripture: Revelation 1:9-10

A little fun fact: The word valedictorian (the person that is honored at graduation for being top of the class) actually comes from the Latin vale dicere which means "to say farewell" or "to say the final goodbye." This person would frequently be the last person to speak before the graduates received their diplomas.

Not everyone gets to say that last word. In some cases, that privilege is reserved for someone special. This is the case with God's Word. The final book in all of Scripture was written by John. Imagine: 66 books written over 1,500 years by approximately 40 men. However, it was John who got to record the last word.

John was, by this time, an old man (3 John 1). He had endured much in his years as an apostle of Jesus. In Revelation 1:9 he noted that he was on the island called Patmos. History records that he had been exiled there. John recorded that he was there for two primary reasons: (1) the Word of God—indicating that he had boldly bore witness to the truth, and (2) in testifying about Jesus. He said earlier that he "bore witness to the word of God and to the testimony of Jesus Christ, even to all that he saw" (Revelation 1:2).

Preaching Jesus came with considerable risk. Jesus had warned the disciples early on that they would be persecuted (Matthew 10:16-18) and hated (Matthew 10:22) because of Him. John had witnessed this hatred firsthand when his brother James was brutally killed with a sword (Acts 12:2).

It was John, however, that Jesus chose to give the last word. Jesus showed him things that were amazing and incredible, then commanded him to "write what you see in a book" (Revelation 1:11).

This "last word" that Jesus gave us through John was an invitation to "come." Come to Jesus if you wish to drink of the water of life without cost (Revelation 22:17).

Today, I will...think about that invitation and make sure I am ready.

WEEK #40

Philip

CHRIS MILLER

Prepared for the Task at Hand

Today's Scripture: Acts 6:1-5

It is one thing to go through intensive training in order to prepare for something. It is another thing to live in such a way that others look to you as one who is living prepared for whatever task comes up. Philip, the evangelist, was looked to by those around him as one of seven Christians who could handle a task which would keep the church unified.

When the church grows, satan intensifies his efforts to split the body of Christ. The church in Jerusalem faced an early moment of potential crisis in Acts 6 when the Hellenists complained that their widows were being neglected in the daily distribution. Instead of the apostles themselves designating certain people to make sure this problem was resolved, they exhorted the multitude of disciples to make the determination themselves as to which men would be qualified to make sure the need was taken care of. That's an important point. In our own congregations, we likely know our own members better than anyone else. We know their good qualities, and we know many of their scars. We know their talents, much of their daily walk, the knowledge and wisdom in the Word which they possess or lack, and their spirit of readiness or lack of enthusiasm. The apostles looked to the multitude because there were already Christians who were qualified and ready for the task at hand. They were to be "of good repute, full of the Spirit and of wisdom" (Acts 6:3). Philip, being one of the seven chosen, had been living prepared for a task before the need had even arisen.

The Lord needs people who live prepared for a work and are qualified spiritually that even one's own church family would quickly look to as being the kind of person who could accomplish the task. The apostles couldn't do everything; others had to step up and fill roles. No one can do everything, but everyone can do something. It is about being prepared before the need even comes up.

Today, I will...examine my spiritual walk, set specific goals, and work diligently to be the kind of person the congregation I worship with will always know is ready to do whatever is needed.

TUESDAY

No Small Task

Today's Scripture: Acts 6:5-7

Within minutes of digging in the dirt, a tender spot began to develop in the palm of my hand. It wasn't long before the blister appeared. Now, several weeks later, that place is completely healed the skin there is noticeably tougher, and there is a callous in that place. Physically speaking, callouses on our hands are often a sign of physical labor. Spiritually speaking, our goal in life as Christians should be to have lived in such a way that when we stand before our Savior we do so with "calloused hands" having joyfully been diligent in His work.

Philip was known for being about the work of the Lord. When sent somewhere, he gladly went. When presented with a specific work or goal to accomplish, he put forth the effort to see it through. It seems likely that the issue which had come up concerning the widows and the daily distribution in the early Jerusalem church had been resolved. Later in Acts 8:5, it says that "Philip went down to the city of Samaria and proclaimed to them the Christ." It is doubtful that he would have left had there not been a plan in place to make sure the earlier task he was selected for in Acts 6 was being carried out.

It was a noble work; it involved some precious people in the church, the widows. "Religion that is pure and undefiled before God the Father is this: to visit orphans and widows in their affliction, and to keep oneself unstained from the world" (James 1:27). Making sure each of the widows received food may not seem like all that difficult a task, yet it was crucial. Zechariah 4:10 reminds us there are no "small things" when it comes to God's work; each effort put forth in His name is precious, needful, and honorable. Let it never be that we serve with a mind clouded by comparisons, but let us focus on whatever the work is that is put before us.

Today, I will... give my absolute best in what I am doing to serve my Lord, realizing that every member of His body has a function and that my role is needed.

The Gospel Is for All

Today's Scripture: Acts 8:12

Often times, some Scriptures which seem to simply make a general statement, in actuality, carry some of the most challenging and deepest realities. Such is the case with Acts 8:5 when "Philip went down to the city of Samaria and proclaimed to them the Christ." The gospel going beyond Jerusalem meant that there had to be people who could see past the cultural divides of society. Samaritans were seen as outcasts by the Jews. But someone had to go, because the cross of Christ, the gospel, was and continues to be for all.

What kind of person does it take to go to Samaria? What challenges does that person face? What's their attitude like? What's their passion in life? How do they see people and how great is their love for those people? What will it take for us to cross the boundaries that society has put up, yet God never intended for us to be limited by? Who are the "Samaritans" in your life? Will you face ridicule by your own circle of people if you go to "Samaria"? Philip was focused on the Great Commission. We are told the results of his going there. "But when they believed Philip as he preached good news about the kingdom of God and the name of Jesus Christ, they were baptized, both men and women" (Acts 8:12).

Philip followed the example set by Jesus in John 4. Jesus "had to pass through Samaria" (John 4:4). That's where He met the woman at Jacob's well and had the conversation with her about being the Messiah. He crossed cultural boundaries to do so. She was shocked. His disciples would marvel. The message was delivered because Jesus saw a person with a soul who needed to know. Philip went to Samaria because he knew the value of the gospel, and the value of souls, no matter where they were from.

Today, I will... view each person I encounter as someone who has a soul and needs to hear the truth of the gospel.

THURSDAY

Time Worth Invested

Today's Scripture: Acts 8:26-29

Time is a valuable resource. Time that is "spent" is time wasted. Time that is "invested" sees a return on that investment. Our Lord knew and recognized the value of time and sense of urgency when He made the statement, "We must work the works of him who sent me while it is day; night is coming, when no one can work" (John 9:4). As the gospel was moving forward among the people of Samaria in Acts 8, an angel of the Lord spoke to Philip and instructed him to go to the desert to find one soul. Time is a resource. Time is valuable. Time should be invested instead of being spent. Philip's leaving the masses of Samaria to go to one person in the desert was time invested. It counted for something. That time carried with it a return on the investment.

We do not know how much time Philip spent with the Ethiopian. As Philip ran up to the chariot which the Ethiopian was riding in, he found a man who had been searching in the Scriptures. Specifically, he was reading from Isaiah 53 about the Messiah. He did not know who he was reading about. Philip invested his time. He took time to be with this person at the most important moment in this man's life. Taking time for the gospel is always time invested. "Then Philip opened his mouth, and beginning with this Scripture he told him the good news about Jesus" (Acts 8:35). There's no doubt that Philip could have had many other things he could have been spending his time doing. Philip, however, was someone who was intentional with how time was invested. He was in the desert, of all places. Imagine the chariot, the horses, the sights and smells, the scroll. Imagine their eyes meeting, the facial expressions of curiosity. Imagine hearing the Ethiopian's voice when he confessed that he believed Jesus was the Son of God. Imagine the water, his baptism, seeing his joy. Time invested.

Today, I will... think seriously about what I am doing with my time. I recognize and have decided that I will manage my time in such a way that my focus will be on time invested.

FRIDAY
Known by His Pursuit

Today's Scripture: Acts 21:8

We are known by what we pursue, what we talk about most, and by what others see us practicing. John was "John the Baptist" because he was a baptizer of people. Simon was "Simon the Tanner" because he was a tanner of animal skins. Philip was specifically known by his own pursuit in life. That which others knew him for. That which the Holy Spirit recognized him as. He is "Philip the evangelist." In Acts 21:8, we are told that "On the next day we departed and came to Caesarea, and we entered the house of Philip the evangelist, who was one of the seven, and stayed with him." While we know there have been many people who could be described as evangelists because of their pursuit, Philip is the only one in the New Testament specifically referred to in this manner of identification, as "the evangelist."

If you were to be identified by your pursuit in life, what would it be? Following the Ethiopian's conversion in Acts 8, the inspired writer says that in the route Philip traveled he "preached the gospel to all the towns until he came to Caesarea" (Acts 8:40). Years following that event, Luke found Philip and stayed at his house in Caesarea. A number of years defined how Philip will forever be remembered. He focused on becoming like Jesus by preaching, evangelizing, and winning souls. Jesus never lost sight of why He came. He was constantly seeking and saving the lost. It was His life's purpose and His life's pursuit. Philip will always be "Philip the evangelist" because that is who he was and what he did.

Right now there are approximately 8 billion people on the planet. It is estimated in 30 years the world population will be approximately 10.9 billion. The Lord needs people who will make their life's pursuit to be evangelists. "Do the work of an evangelist, fulfill your ministry" (2 Timothy 4:5).

Today, I will... be honest with myself if assessing what I am known for in life. I will set my daily goal to be a soul winner. I want to be more like Jesus.

WEEK #41

Matthew

MATTHEW SOKOLOSKI

What Do We Know about Matthew?

Today's Scripture: Matthew 9:9-13

I must be honest; I am biased in favor of the name Matthew. My mother thought it was a good Bible name and liked it first! And it is possible that in one or two smart-alecky moments, I may have reminded my parents that it does mean "Gift of God." So, although I am rarely called by my full first name, "Matt" or "Soko" being the usual, I still tend to use Matthew in writing and am rather attached. Yet, while I feel some sort of connection to the gospel writer, we actually know very little about Matthew.

Matthew writes in Matthew 9:9 "As Jesus passed on from there, he saw a man called Matthew sitting at the tax booth, and he said to him, 'Follow me.' And he rose and followed him." We get the same account in Mark 2:14 and Luke 5:27, except that he is referred to as Levi (Mark adds "son of Alphaeus"). Similar to Simon/Peter and Saul/Paul, there are two names referring to the same person, likely due to different languages. The only other time Matthew mentions himself is in the list of the twelve apostles in Matthew 10:3, when he lists himself as "Matthew the tax collector."

While Matthew 9:10 and Mark 2:15 both mention a dinner with "many tax collectors and sinners" just after the calling of Matthew, it is Luke who makes it clear that it was Matthew/Levi who "made him a great feast in his house" (Luke 5:29). Besides being listed as an apostle in Mark 3:18, Luke 6:15, and Acts 1:13, these are all the places in the New Testament where he is mentioned by name. Tradition suggests that he ministered in Judea and in other countries, perhaps Ethiopia, before dying a martyr, but there is little in the way of reliable record. As we focus on the Biblical text, our next question is to ask what we can infer about Matthew based on what we know.

Today, I will...answer when Christ calls me to follow Him.

What Can We Infer about Matthew?

Today's Scripture: Mark 2:13-17

When we encounter Matthew, we know that he is a tax collector. If you have grown up around Bible classes, you know that tax collectors were lumped in with sinners. Any brief research into tax collectors in the first century will tell you that they were despised. Tax collectors were seen as traitors for serving the Roman government, unclean because of their regular interaction with Gentiles, and unscrupulous because they could gather taxes over the necessary amount to pad their own pockets. It seems safe to assume that Matthew was despised by his fellow Jews. What led Matthew to take on this profession, we have no idea.

What we do know is that when Jesus said to him "Follow me," he left everything and followed Jesus. It seems reasonable to assume that Matthew had already heard about Jesus, since just before the "Follow me" encounter we have the account of the healing of the paralytic who was lowered down by his friends from the roof in Capernaum (Mark 2:1-5). As Jesus was heading back out beside the sea with a crowd in tow, He passed Matthew and told him to follow. Capernaum is said to perhaps have had a population of around 1,500 people at that time. By this point Jesus had already been teaching and healing throughout Galilee, "so his fame spread throughout all Syria" with great crowds following Him (Matthew 4:23-25). Whatever the specific circumstances, Matthew was convicted to drop everything and follow!

Not only does Matthew follow Jesus, but he throws a great feast for Jesus at his house. I don't know about you, but when I have a party at my house it is with friends rather than strangers. Assuming that held true for Matthew, he called all of his friends together—a large company of tax collectors and sinners (which perhaps included prostitutes per Matthew 21:31-32). Whatever change was happening in Matthew, we know that he wanted to share it—and Jesus—with others. While we don't know much about Matthew, we do know that a transformation was occurring.

Today, I will...put everything else aside and follow Jesus in what He asks me to do in service to Him.

What Can We Learn from Matthew?

Today's Scripture: Mark 4:13-20

Knowing so little about Matthew specifically, what practical lessons can be made to our own lives? We know that Jesus saw Matthew and said "Follow me"— and Matthew did just that! I wish we knew more of the circumstances. Was Matthew satisfied with his chosen job and the material success that came with it? Or was Matthew miserable in his job anyways, tired of the rejection, and looking for a way out? We can try to infer from the Biblical record, but we simply do not know.

Given Matthew's extensive quoting and allusion to the Old Testament in his gospel account, it appears that Matthew was very familiar with the Hebrew scriptures. Even if he was despised as a tax collector by his people, did he deep down cherish his Jewish background? Was he himself, awaiting the Messiah? Again, we do not know the internal disposition of Matthew, but we do see the outward effects of whatever was going on when Jesus told him to follow. Matthew was willing to leave everything and follow Jesus. Typically, when you walk out on a job, you are not invited back! Matthew likely had a lucrative career, yet he dropped it in a moment to follow Jesus.

And that seems to be one practical lesson to take from Matthew—we must be willing to leave behind whatever it is that prevents us from following Jesus. As you reflect on your own Christian walk, what changes did you make and what former idols did you cast off to follow Jesus? Or perhaps, you are still of two minds and need to make the decision and the commitment to change, to drop whatever it is that is holding you back, and to follow Jesus. The thorns of the world— "the cares of the world and the deceitfulness of riches and the desires for other things"—can choke out the word and our desire to follow Jesus (Mark 4:19). We must cast off the counterfeits and instead follow Jesus, the One who is the answer to our deepest needs.

Today, I will...not let anyone or anything get between me and a chance to follow and serve the Lord.

What Can We Learn from Matthew?

Today's Scripture: Luke 5:27-32

What is your purpose in life? Where do you find fulfillment? What will your legacy be? In our individualistic and self-focused culture, we tend to think of the legacy we want to leave for ourselves—how we will be remembered, or what we will leave behind that will outlast us. Matthew provides us another opportunity to think about legacy, but not in the way the world usually thinks about it. We see in Matthew, an apostle and gospel writer, that his concern was not about being remembered or making himself look good, but instead making Jesus known. We don't know much about Matthew, but we know much about Jesus because of Matthew. And that is a valuable lesson to take from Matthew. Our legacy is not to be known, but to make Jesus known!

For most of us, our names are quickly forgotten, even by our descendants over a few generations. Perhaps if you are "lucky" you will be a footnote in a history book somewhere. But for most of us, we will be forgotten by the world. However, the most important thing is that we will be remembered by God—that God knows us because of the reconciliation offered through His son! Even the greatest legacies by human standards can be forgotten, so why strive for something that is most likely to fade away? Instead, we play an important role in continuing the love and teaching of Jesus to the next generation. We can be part of a chain that begins with Jesus and lasts until He comes again! Our legacy is His legacy, and one of the best things we can do is invite others to become part of Jesus' legacy. We can invite others to know God and be known by God. That is the kind of legacy that Matthew leaves, by pointing us to Jesus the Messiah. What are we doing to make Jesus known to others, both as an individual and as part of His body, the church?

Today, I will...strive to make my legacy telling others about Jesus through my words and deeds.

How Does Matthew Relate to Christ?

Today's Scripture: Matthew 28:19-20

As we close out this series of devotional thoughts on Matthew, let's recap where we have been. First, we know very little about Matthew. Matthew was a tax collector who suddenly left his post to follow Jesus. Immediately after Matthew's calling, we see him hosting a great feast for Jesus with other tax collectors and sinners. Matthew was willing to leave behind his old profession, his old life, and follow Jesus. What a radical transformation from tax collector to disciple! Just as Matthew was willing to cast off his old life for the new way of Jesus, so must we be willing to cast off the idols that call for our attention. Not only that, Matthew's life and legacy was changed. But his legacy was not to glorify himself, but to glorify Christ! Because of Matthew, we know more about Jesus.

So how does Matthew relate to Jesus Christ? Not only does he choose to follow Jesus, but he invites others to follow Him too. He invited other tax collectors and sinners to know Jesus. Jews, who would have despised him as a tax collector, became the audience to whom he appealed so that they too might know Jesus. Matthew's intended audience was primarily Jewish because of the ways in which he appealed to the Old Testament and the clear connections he made between Jesus and Messianic prophecies. What may seem like merely a list of names in the beginning of his gospel account serves the vital purpose of showing how Jesus is indeed the son of David, not just a son of David, but the King of Kings, the awaited Messiah! Matthew pointed the way to Christ, by showing how Jesus was indeed the Christ, and he invited his people to repent and see the kingdom of heaven is at hand!

Matthew's legacy lives on through his gospel account that invites you and me to also know that Jesus is the Christ. Not only that, but he records the commission that Jesus gave his disciples, that still applies to us today—to go and make disciples of all nations!

Today, I will...go, and spread the gospel of Jesus to the world.

WEEK #42

Mark

TRAVIS BOOKOUT

Incredible Opportunity

Today's Scripture: Acts 12:6-19, 25

The book of Acts introduces us to a man named John, who was also called Mark or John Mark (Acts 12:12). In this study, we'll just call him Mark. His mother's name was Mary. Their home in Jerusalem seemed to have been a haven for early Christians in times of persecution.

In the story that introduces Mark, his mother's home was the first place Peter arrived after escaping from jail. God miraculously delivered Peter from chains, soldiers, and locked gates. Once Peter was free, he immediately went to Mary's house. At their house, "many were gathered together and were praying" (Acts 12:12).

Think about that evening. Mark was surrounded by Christians in his house. They each could be arrested. An outbreak of terrible persecution had just begun. James, the brother of John, had been killed, and Peter was thrown in prison. Mary, Mark's mother, demonstrated incredible bravery by not only remaining faithful to the Lord, but inviting Christians into her home for prayer. It's no surprise that this was the first place Peter, fresh out of jail, knew to go.

Mark had some pretty incredible Christian examples in his family. His mother's faith was truly something to behold. But he also had a relative named Joseph—we usually call him Barnabas—who was well known in the early church (Acts 4:36-37). His generosity and encouragement earned him the nickname "Son of Encouragement." He and Paul were also faithful missionaries and teachers of the Word of God.

When they began their missionary journeys, Mark left his mother's house and went with them (Acts 12:24-25). I can't imagine the excitement and fear he must have been experiencing. He assisted and ministered to them while they proclaimed God's Word (Acts 13:5). What an incredible opportunity to follow the example of faithfulness seen in his mother, join Barnabas and Paul on a world-transforming mission, and serve the kingdom of heaven!

Today, I will...learn from the faith and courage of those around me and take chances for the kingdom's sake.

Fear and Failure

Today's Scripture: Acts 13:4-5, 13-14

Paul, Barnabas, and Mark began their missionary journey in Acts 13. They left Antioch, being sent out by the Holy Spirit, and eventually arrived at Salamis. Paul and Barnabas preached in the synagogues while Mark assisted them (Acts 13:5). We are not told exactly what this assistance was, but he was actively involved in helping serve their ministry. Journeying through the land they reached Paphos, where they met a magician. He was a Jewish false prophet and stood in opposition to the kingdom work taking place.

Mark had seen opposition and persecution in Jerusalem. But away from his mother, home, and so many loved ones, he saw a tense moment when the magician stood up against Paul and Barnabas. Paul rebuked the man harshly, and the Holy Spirit struck him with blindness in the presence of all. This had a stunning impact on Sergius Paulus, the proconsul, who then came to believe the teaching of the Lord. It seems that this was all a little too much for Mark. The very next verse (Acts 13:13) states that Mark decided not to travel any further with Paul and Barnabas. He returned home to Jerusalem.

That sounds innocent enough. We were not told his exact plans at the beginning of the journey. We might think he only planned on traveling this far and helping as much as he could before returning home, but that's not how Paul took it. Paul saw this as a desertion. Mark abandoned them in Paul's eyes. Later, as we'll see, this became the subject of an intense argument between Paul and Barnabas.

It appears that the first sign of opposition led to fear and doubt, and Mark, who thought he was ready, realized he was not prepared for what lay ahead, and he turned back.

Today, I will...not let fear hold me back from service to Jesus.

WEDNESDAY
Second Chances
Today's Scripture: Acts 15:36-41

Paul and Barnabas did not let that setback stop their mission. Throughout Acts 13 and 14, they continued to travel, preach, and suffer. They were rejected, hated, and attacked. This persecution culminated in Paul being stoned in Lystra and left for dead (Acts 14:19). But they continued through pain and tribulation, preaching the Word of God, establishing churches, and even revisiting those dangerous cities to strengthen the churches.

In Acts 15, after a major theological debate in Jerusalem, Paul decided to go on another missionary journey with Barnabas (Acts 15:36). Barnabas agreed, and like last time, he wanted to bring Mark with them (Acts 15:37). Paul felt strongly that Mark should not come. Barnabas wanted to give him a second chance, and Paul did not.

We don't know the content of this disagreement. Perhaps Barnabas was sympathetic to Mark's struggles when he left the first time. Maybe Barnabas was as hurt as Paul but more forgiving. Maybe this was their chance to minister to Mark.

Paul might have still been angry or embittered with Mark. Paul might have accused Barnabas of nepotism (Colossians 4:10). Maybe Paul loved Mark dearly, but after being stoned and left for dead, was concerned that as much as Mark was a good and godly man, traveling into dangerous cities and risking his neck was not his gift or calling. Either way, Mark's fate in ministry hung the balance.

Mark made a mistake. He left his ministry post, hurting feelings and probably hindering the work of others. He also wanted to try to do better as the years went by. He wanted that second chance, and while Barnabas was willing to give it, Paul was not.

In the church, you may find more forgiveness among some than others. Some may hold your faults against you for years. But that is no reason to give up. Mark did go on another missionary journey. Barnabas put his reputation on the line for Mark, and Mark made things right.

Today, I will...offer forgiveness, accept forgiveness, and not let the criticism of others keep me from serving God.

THURSDAY
Making Things Right
Today's Scripture: 2 Timothy 4:11

I'm not a big fan of controversy, and I don't like to see people argue, especially if it's about me. How uncomfortable this "sharp disagreement" (Acts 15:39) must have been for Mark. Luke is writing a public report. Mark knew full well how Paul felt. He knew why Barnabas and Paul split up. He knew why the team wasn't together any longer.

It's hard not to take things like that personally. Mark could have felt so worthless that he gave up his ministry dreams. Or, what people often do, Mark could have lashed out in anger. He could have started mentioning all of Paul's failures and weaknesses.

We don't know how Mark handled it. We don't know if he cried, got angry, or was just so overwhelmed by gratitude for Barnabas that he didn't think much about Paul. But we do know that he sailed on serving the Lord. This is the last time we meet Mark and Barnabas in Acts, but it is not the last time we meet them in Scripture.

It's sometimes hard to know whether a person named in Paul's letters is the same person in Acts or the Gospels. Just like today, two different people can have the same name. But there are four likely references to Mark made in the rest of the Bible. Three are from the letters of Paul (Colossians 4:10; Philemon 1:24; 2 Timothy 4:11), and one is from Peter (1 Peter 5:13).

I particularly want to note 2 Timothy 4:11. In some of Paul's final words, as he prepared for his death, he desired for Mark to be with him. He wrote to Timothy, "Get Mark and bring him with you, for he is very useful to me for ministry." How good those words must have been to hear. The one who once abandoned Paul (think about Demas in the preceding verse) was later called to be present with him. Mark was useful. Mark has made things right with a lifetime of service to God.

Today, I will...faithfully live out my calling and see what reconciliation with God brings.

FRIDAY

Telling the Story of Jesus

Today's Scripture: 1 Peter 5:13

On the first missionary journey, Paul and Barnabas proclaimed the Word of God while Mark assisted them (Acts 13:5). Maybe he helped to carry scrolls and writing utensils, procure the crowds, or get them water. We know very little about Mark as a preacher. He helped others in their preaching and teaching. Paul's concluding compliment was that Mark is "very useful to me for ministry" (2 Timothy 4:11).

Near the end of 1 Peter, Peter wrote, "She who is at Babylon, who is likewise chosen, sends you greetings, and so does Mark, my son" (1 Peter 5:13). Early church tradition holds that this Mark, who was with Peter, was the same Mark we have been talking about in these lessons. He eventually ended up in Rome assisting Peter in ministry.

Based on even earlier reports, second-century Christian leader Papias of Heirapolis, said that Mark was a scribe for Peter, writing down stories about the Lord from Peter. Those stories were organized into a gospel that we all have in our Bibles. The gospel of Mark is the record of the life of Jesus by Mark, son of Mary, who grew up in Jerusalem, traveled with Paul, traveled with Barnabas, and traveled with Peter. He collected stories, aided in the ministry of others, and wrote one of the most compelling, exciting, beautiful, convicting, and transforming stories about Jesus ever written. Some even speculate that he makes a brief, mysterious appearance in this gospel (Mark 14:51-52).

Mark was not a Christian because of Paul, Peter, or even Barnabas. He was a dedicated follower of Jesus because of Jesus. And it shows in his writings. If he were primarily devoted to Paul, his faith would never have survived. Even Barnabas and Peter were severely flawed humans who could lead one astray (Galatians 2:11-14). Only his love and commitment to Jesus could have produced a writing that has changed the world like the gospel of Mark.

Today, I will...put my faith in Christ rather than men.

WEEK #43

Judas

ANTHONY WARNES

What Is Your Price?

Today's Scripture: Matthew 26:14-16

What price would you need to walk away from the Lord? $100,000? $500,000? $1,000,000? This seems like an absurd question, doesn't it? We know what Jesus said about this, "for what does it profit a man to gain the whole world and forfeit his soul" (Mark 8:36). Why would anyone leave the Lord for money? We know that we cannot take it with us into the next life, for it will not profit us there. Why would we leave our Lord who left the Father's side for us? How could any amount of money give us what Jesus gave us on the cross? How could we betray the One who loves us so?

Sadly, Judas had a price. Thirty pieces of silver. According to Sellers Crain (*Truth for Today Commentary*), "Under the Law, the amount offered to Judas was the price to be paid for a slave who had been killed by an animal (Exodus 21:32)." Judas received for Jesus' betrayal the price of a slave.

Back to the original question: What price would you need to walk away from the Lord? Our initial thought would be "there is no amount of money that I would ever take." So, let's ask it in another way. What is the price you need to stay with the Lord?

Is your happiness the price that you need to stay with the Lord? If your livelihood was taken away, if your health was taken away, if your children or spouse suddenly passed from this life...would you walk away from Him? Job's wife had a price to stay with the Lord: all of the things mentioned above. When her husband's livelihood was destroyed, when her children were killed, when her husband lost his health, her response was "Curse God and die" (Job 2:9). Her price had been paid and she could not stay.

Today, I will...look at my life and ask, "Do I have something in my life that I am valuing more than I value Jesus?" If I find something, I will re-evaluate my priorities.

TUESDAY
A Seared Conscience
Today's Scripture: Matthew 26:20-26

Paul talks about men whose "consciences are seared" (1 Timothy 4:2). The NASB 1995 says they were seared "as with a branding iron." Can you imagine taking a red-hot branding iron, and pushing it onto your skin? It would immediately start harming your skin. If it is pushed too hard and too long, it would permanently damage your nerves, leaving you with little feeling in that area.

If we are not careful, we can do this with our lives when it comes to sin. Sin can hurt at first because our conscience is pricked. Yet, if we continue to sin and ignore that pain, eventually it might become a long-lasting brand that is even more destructive to the conscience. They say that human branding is a permanent mark on the body. A seared conscience can also become a permanent problem.

Judas was in the process of searing his conscience. He had already made the decision to betray his Lord, and he had already accepted the money. So, when Jesus told His group of apostles (with Judas present), "Truly, I say to you, one of you will betray me" (Matthew 26:21), Judas had to think quickly of what to do. As he witnessed each one of them go around the room saying, "Is it I, Lord?" (Matthew 26:22), Judas had to have felt the stinging pain of guilt. He then thought he would try to cover it up as he too asked "Is it I, Rabbi?" To which Jesus responded, "You have said so" (Matthew 26:25). How hard did Judas have to push down on the branding iron to stop his conscience from hurting as he got up from the table? Judas seared his conscience. Do we ever do this?

Today, I will...stop and contemplate my situation and actions when my conscience is stinging. I will not just push my conscience away; rather I will evaluate my feelings with biblical truth and act properly.

The Remorse of Judas

Today's Scripture: Matthew 27:3-5

Every one of us has done things that we regret. Paul said, "for all have sinned and fall short of the glory of God" (Romans 3:23). This is why Jesus had to come and die, to pay a ransom for our sins. The question is, what do we do with our guilt and remorse of sin when we have come to the realization that we have done something unpleasing to the Lord?

Judas had deep remorse for his betrayal of Jesus. Maybe he had assumed that Jesus would eventually free Himself. When he came to his senses and realized that Jesus was not going to get out of this alive, "he changed his mind and brought back the thirty pieces of silver to the chief priests and the elders" (Matthew 27:3). The wave of remorse that went across him had to have been overwhelming. Yet there was a huge problem: his change of mind was too late. Jesus was already in the hands of evil men, and there was nothing he could do to change the consequences of his actions upon Jesus.

So how did Judas cope with his deep remorse? Judas hung himself (Matthew 27:5). He felt as if there was nothing that could ever get him back into the good graces of the Lord. He completely lost all hope for himself.

There is another man who had remorse for the things he did—Saul. He "approved" of the execution of Stephen (Acts 8:1). He was "ravaging the church" (Acts 8:3). When Jesus met him on the road to Damascus, I would imagine that the remorse was unbelievable. Yet, instead of killing himself, he found hope in the Lord and allowed the Lord to turn him into the man we know as Paul.

Today, I will...remember that the Lord died to save me from my sins. I will remember that there is nothing that I have done that the Lord cannot forgive. I will remember the hope I have in Him and His blood.

satan Used Judas

Today's Scripture: Luke 22:3-6; Luke 4:13

satan is very crafty and observant. As he was looking for a way to get to Jesus, he found Judas.

The priests and scribes were constantly trying to find ways to get Jesus and "put him to death" (Luke 22:2). So how happy must they have been to have Judas seek them out to negotiate the terms of Jesus' betrayal? Luke 22:3 shows that this meeting happened after Satan "entered into Judas."

Did Judas have a choice in the matter? Of course, he did. Paul saic, "No temptation has overtaken you that is not common to man. God is faithful, and he will not let you be tempted beyond your ability, but with the temptation hc will also provide the way of escape, that you may be able to endure it" (1 Corinthians 10:13). Judas could have turned to the Lord, instead of allowing satan in, yet he chose poorly.

Because satan found Judas, and Judas accepted satan, Judas started acting like satan. Notice what Judas did in Luke 22:6, "So he consented and sought an OPPORTUNITY" (emphases added). Interestingly, this is exactly what satan had been doing ever since the temptations of Jesus. Luke 4:13 says "And when the devil had ended every temptation, he departed from him until an OPPORTUNE time" (emphasis added).

Earlier in Jesus' ministry, He was talking to people who at one point believed in Him. These had changed their minds on Him. So, Jesus told them, "Why do you not understand what I say? It is because you cannot bear to hear My word. You are of your father the devil, and your will is to do your father's desires" (John 8:43-44). They (like Judas) did not have to have satan as their father, yet they chose to. And by choosing satan, he would use them. satan has NO power over us, unless we choose to let him.

Today, I will...thank God for being my Father, and then make sure that I am doing His deeds, and not satan's.

Jesus Loved Judas Too

Today's Scripture: Luke 6:12-16; John 13:5-11

How could anyone love the vile of this world? How could anyone serve the murderers around them? Jesus did. Jesus prayed for and served Judas Iscariot (the one that would eventually betray Him).

Jesus prayed for Judas. In Luke 6:12, we see Jesus praying all night to the Lord. What was He praying about? We see that on the next morning, He found His disciples and hand selected twelve of them to be his apostles (6:13). What was He praying about all night? It is my assumption that He was praying about His selection. Praying for the men that would follow Him over the next few years. I would imagine that He even prayed about the one who would betray Him. Do I pray for those that hurt me? Jesus said, "pray for those who persecute you" (Matthew 5:44). Jesus showed us how we can pray for the evil and live our lives for them. Nowhere in the Gospels do we see Him treating Judas poorly. Rather, we see Him praying for him as, Jesus chose him.

Jesus also served Judas. In John 13:5-11, we have the account of Jesus washing the apostles' feet. I would imagine that coming up to Peter (even with his many objections), that serving Peter, and John, and the majority of the apostles was a great joy to the Savior. What kind of emotions would have gone through Jesus' mind as He served Judas? I would imagine that sadness prevailed as He knew what was ready to transpire over the next few hours. That Judas would leave the upper room and go to meet up with Jesus' enemies. But He still washed Judas' feet.

If it was any of us in Jesus' place, would hatred win out? Would we really pray for Judas (or choose him, for that matter)? Would we really serve him? Or would we want to ignore him? Tell everyone all of the awful things about him?

Today, I will...look for the "unlovable" people and love them too.

WEEK #44

Lazarus, Mary, and Martha

BART WARREN

When Jesus Doesn't Come
Today's Scripture: John 11:21, 32

At separate times, both Martha and Mary said to Jesus, "Lord, if you had been here, my brother would not have died."

There are a few ways to understand these grief-stricken words.

First, it is likely these were often repeated words around the home: "If only Jesus was here." It was a common sentiment in that household that life was better when Jesus was around.

Second, there is an acknowledgment that Jesus has the special power and ability to accomplish feats that others cannot.

Third, it seems likely that there was also regret and confusion in these words. When Jesus was so greatly needed, He was not there. Why not? Didn't He know they needed Him? Did He care? Yet, because they were so confident that He loved them, they struggled to understand why He did not do anything about the situation. Why didn't He prevent the tragedy from occurring?

We have probably found ourselves in similar situations. We all hurt and suffer. It is natural for believers to ask God where He is and why He allows such painful events to transpire (Psalms 13:1; 42:9; 43:2; etc.).

The response of Jesus to these sisters, particularly His response to Martha, is instructive (John 11:23-26). Their greatest need was not to have their brother back. Their greatest need was to trust Jesus. They needed to trust that, as the Lord of life, Jesus would provide for them in ways they did not yet see or understand. He was always there. He always knew.

The same is true for us—we must trust Jesus through the pain. We must acknowledge that He is matchlessly powerful and that life is better when He is involved. But we must also admit that He is always "here" (Matthew 28:20; Hebrews 13:5-6; Psalm 139:1-16). He blesses and restores in ways that bring Him glory and are often surprising to us.

Today, I will...acknowledge that, in spite of any suffering I may be experiencing, my greatest need is to trust my Lord Jesus who is "here" even now.

Martha: Preoccupied

Today's Scripture: Luke 10:38-42

Unfortunately, Martha is known for being preoccupied with the wrong things. On the positive side, it seems Martha was hospitable, a hard worker, and willing to be a humble servant. These are good things!

However, even acts of service can turn out to be hollow and vain if they are not motivated by love (1 Corinthians 13:3).

We all know what it is like to get busy and to be pulled in many different directions. Work, ballgames, meetings, projects, vacations, illnesses, etc.— the list goes on and on! We can identify with getting "choked by the cares and riches and pleasures of life" (Luke 8:14).

Jesus told Martha that she was "anxious and troubled about many things" (Luke 10:41). He was telling her that she had made the wrong choice. Her heart was preoccupied with the wrong things.
- Are we like this?
- Do we have so many activities going on (many of them likely very important) that we are no longer taking the time to pray? Have we stopped making the time to read and reflect on Scripture?
- Do we have so many commitments and obligations that we no longer make the assembly with the saints the priority we once made it?

Martha was worried about other people, not her own relationship with Jesus. She said, "Tell [Mary] then to help me!" (Luke 10:40).
- This is an easy trap into which many of us fall.
- Are we more worried about and preoccupied with other people— what they are doing or not doing—than we are about our own relationship with the Lord? (cf. Luke 12:13)

Today, I will...take the time to focus on Jesus and my relationship with Him. I will make a real effort to be quiet and distance myself from the distractions and the inconsequential cares of the world that are pulling me in the wrong direction.

Lazarus: Feasting

Today's Scripture: John 12:2

Six days before the Passover, Jesus therefore came to Bethany, where Lazarus was, whom Jesus had raised from the dead. So they gave a dinner for him there. Martha served, and Lazarus was one of those reclining with him at table. (John 12:1-2)

We know precious little about this particular man called Lazarus.

We know that he had a special relationship with Jesus—he was called "he whom you love" and when he became ill, his sisters sent word to Jesus to inform Him about the situation.

Strangely, Jesus lingered and delayed on purpose. Eventually, after Lazarus passed away, Jesus made His way to Bethany. At what amounts to a funeral visitation service, Jesus called Lazarus out of his tomb. Jesus raised him from the dead!

After Lazarus was raised from the dead, we find him feasting with Jesus.

This makes sense. If Jesus had raised you from the dead, I imagine you would be devoted to Him! You would want to spend time with Him in close fellowship. You would want to stay close to the One who had such power. This is exactly what we find Lazarus doing—feasting with Jesus.

Consider this: If you have been washed in the blood of Jesus (Revelation 7:14), meaning you have been baptized for the forgiveness of your sins (Acts 2:38; 22:16), then Jesus has in fact raised you from the dead!

We who were dead in our trespasses and sins, God made us alive together with Jesus! (Ephesians 2:5; Colossians 2:12). Therefore, we should be devoted to Jesus. We should be feasting with Him, staying close to Him and His people.

Today, I will...make sure that I have been raised to new life with Jesus (Romans 6:3-5). If I have been so blessed, I will give thanks for this new life. I will show Jesus my devotion by cheerfully praising Him for His goodness and His power.

Mary: At the Master's Feet

Today's Scripture: Luke 10:38-42

While her sister Martha was gently chastised by Jesus for being focused on the wrong things, Mary was praised for having chosen to sit quietly and peacefully with Him.

The text indicates that Mary was sitting at the Lord's feet. This is a position of humility where the inferior looks up to the superior. Several times Scripture records Mary being at the feet of Jesus.

What happens at the Master's feet?

(1) We learn. This is what Mary was doing in Luke 10:39—*listening to the teaching of Jesus.* In a world with so many competing philosophies and ideas (Colossians 2:8), it is imperative that we know and submit to the objective truth. It is Jesus who speaks (John 8:45-46) and is the truth (John 14:6).

(2) We cry. This is what Mary was doing in John 11:32-33—*weeping and expressing grief.* When we are distraught and hurting, where should we go but to the Lord? Jesus cares for us (1 Peter 5:7), and He is infinite in power, so He is well able to overcome our challenges.

(3) We worship. This is what Mary was doing in John 12:3—*offering a sacrificial gift to the One who had given her so much.* At the feet of Jesus, we offer Him praise for His forgiveness and we adore Him for His power, goodness, and mercy. Mary's worship helped to prepare Him for His burial (Matthew 26:9-13). Our worship helps to prepare the world for His return (1 Corinthians 11:26).

Today, I will...make sure that I am found at the Master's feet. I will make a concerted effort to spend time with Jesus, either learning, grieving, or praising Him. May it be said of us that we are focused on the Lord—learning from Him, crying with Him, and showing Him our appreciation by praising Him.

Jesus Loved Martha and Mary and Lazarus

Today's Scripture: John 11:5

How did Jesus demonstrate His love for this family? How did He display His special connection to them?

(1) He placed Himself in harm's way for their benefit. Jesus had angered powerful people and they wanted to harm Him (John 5:18; 7:1; 10:39). Thomas was under the impression it would be dangerous to go back to Bethany (John 11:16). This is what Jesus does for those He loves—He sacrifices His own well-being for the betterment of others (John 10:11-18; Romans 5:8).

(2) He wept with them. The shortest verse in the English Bible is also one of the most powerful and moving: "Jesus wept" (John 11:35). There are many possible reasons why Jesus was so deeply moved and wept on this occasion. One reason to weep would be the ugliness, brutality, and catastrophe of sin which would lead to His death, as well as the death of all others (Hebrews 9:27). Jesus was deeply moved when He saw Mary and her friends crying. In turn, He began to openly weep, causing some of the onlookers to say, "See how he loved him!" (John 11:36). Jesus walks with us through dark valleys and weeps with us.

(3) He taught the truth. As hard as it might have been to hear, Jesus told them that those who believe in Him would never die. Because Jesus loves us, He tells us the truth that we need to hear to live.

(4) He gave life. Jesus cried out with a loud voice and called the one He loved back into the land of the living (John 11:43). Just like Jesus gave Lazarus new life, He gives eternal life to those who love and obey Him (Ephesians 2:5).

Today, I will...acknowledge the love Jesus has for me and reciprocate that love (1 John 4:19).

WEEK #45

Mary Magdalene

JOEY SPARKS

Transferred

Today's Scripture: Colossians 1:13-14

In college, I went with some friends to watch the Harlem Globetrotters at the Pyramid in Memphis. On the map, our seats were in the last row of the lower bowl, but when we went to sit down, that row did not exist. They had sold us seats that were reserved for people who needed wheelchair access. To make up for the confusion, the staff transferred us from having no seats into a box suite full of sodas and snacks. I remember very little about the game itself, but I fondly remember the excitement and enthusiasm in our new place of luxury. We were transferred from being "left out" into a place of prominence.

Although Mary Magdalene is a key figure in the ministry, death, and resurrection of Jesus, the information in Luke 8:1-3 is all that we know about her life prior to meeting Jesus. She had been possessed by seven demons and Jesus cast them out of her. Demon possession was terrifying for those possessed and for their companions. They were afflicted physically and emotionally and were often cut off and kept away from daily public life. Mary was possessed by seven demons, meaning she likely endured even more terrifying experiences than the "typical" possession (whatever they might mean).

There is no legitimate argument for Mary's identification with the sinful woman in Simon's house in the previous chapter. She does, however, represent the principle Jesus highlights with that woman in Luke 7. Those who know they've been forgiven of much love much (Luke 7:47). Jesus delivered her from much terror and she loved Him much.

Christians have been transferred from the realm of evil into the love, compassion, and acceptance of Jesus Christ. We are no longer identified by the masters in our pasts, but live in redemption and freedom (Colossians 1:13-14). We have been freed of much, and we love Jesus deeply.

Today, I will...list 2-3 aspects of my old life from which Christ has delivered me, then list 2-3 blessings He has brought me into in Him.

TUESDAY
Transformed
Today's Scripture: Luke 8:1-3

At around the same time Augustus Caesar began his rule over the empire, Rome discovered great mines of marble. Quickly, he used this marble for extensive building and beautification projects, statues of pagan deities, and busts of prominent leaders. According to Seutonius, Augustus said at the end of his reign, "I found Rome built of brick and left her clothed in marble." Exaggerated or not, if a Caesar can "change brick to marble," how much greater is the transformation made by God!

The emphasis of this text in Luke 8 is Mary Magdalene's faithfulness to Jesus during His earthly ministry. In addition to the twelve apostles, many women followed Jesus as He went about preaching the gospel of the kingdom. Mary Magdalene is listed first of three specific women mentioned by name.

It is significant that women are highlighted by name. Any time that Jesus interacted with women, He elevated them higher than their time and culture did (the Samaritan woman recognized Jesus' difference in this in John 4:9). From time beginning, when men have followed their fleshly instincts, they wrongly use strength and leadership to intimidate and manipulate women. Jesus treated Mary with greater values than these. Neither did Jesus simply tell Mary and the other women who followed Him, "You can do anything a man can do." Instead, He released them from the evil forces that were enslaving them.

Additionally, it is significant that Jesus gave these women an important role among His followers. We're not told how they did this or from where their funds originated, but we do know that they "provided for them out of their means." Jesus' preaching and ministry needed the influence of these generous women. The preaching and ministry of the early church needed the influence of generous women like Dorcas, Mary the mother of James, Lydia, and Priscilla. The twenty-first century church where you live grows more into the likeness of Jesus Christ through the godly influence of generous, selfless, courageous women.

Today, I will...encourage a woman of a different generation from my own because of her faithfulness, service, and generosity.

WEDNESDAY
Together
Today's Scripture: Mark 15:40-41; John 19:25

In August 2022, Brazilian authorities found the body of a man thought to be the last surviving member of an indigenous rainforest tribe. He was known only as "Man of the Hole" due to his system of holes for hiding and hunting. Details are few, but they believe he died alone in his hammock after living the past 26 years—some 9,500 days—without meaningful human contact.[1] We can try to live alone, but we're not intended to live alone.

Mary Magdalene followed Jesus during His earthly ministry, but she also found herself witnessing the carnage of His crucifixion. She saw His wounded back and scalp. She witnessed His belabored efforts to carry His cross. She heard the clang of mallet on spikes. She felt the thud of the cross falling into place. She heard the mocking and the jeering. She heard her Master's familiar, compassionate voice during His hours of suffering.

But she was not alone. Just as she had followed Jesus alongside other women, so too she was with them when He went to the cross. Other disciples had fled (Matthew 26:56; Mark 14:50). But these ladies were watching from a distance. They had heard Him teach about this moment, but they had not fully understood it. They were seeing the opposition of the Jews turn to pure evil through the inhumanity of the Roman executioners.

Mary Magdalene didn't run in despair when Jesus was arrested and crucified. She resisted the urge to isolate herself in her moments of grief. "[She] who separates [herself] seeks [her] own desire" (Proverbs 18:1, LSB). She and these other ladies are wise examples of walking together in faith. "[She] who walks with the wise will be wise" (Proverbs 13:20, LSB).

Today, I will...pray for my closest group of friends in the Lord, plan a time to get together with them, and reach out to someone else who needs friends in Christ.

[1] https://www.sciencealert.com/the-last-member-of-an-isolated-amazon-tribe-dies-alone

THURSDAY
Tomb

Today's Scripture: Mark 15:45-16:4; John 20:1-2

When President Kennedy stood before congress in May 1961 declaring the ambition of the United States to put a man on the moon and bring him home safely before 1970, Neil Armstrong was not an astronaut yet. Even though the President's declaration was met with skepticism and misunderstandings, a team of thousands worked to make the landing possible. Armstrong joined their ranks in 1962. When the time came for NASA to decide who would be the first to walk on the moon, NASA officials admitted Armstrong was a clear choice because of his lack of a dominant ego. When thirty-eight-year old Armstrong finally walked on the moon's surface in July 1969, he became one of history's heroes.[1]

Mary Magdalene's steps on the Sunday following Jesus' death made her witness to one of the few historical moments greater than the moon landing. Early that Sunday morning, Mary Magdalene and the other women went to the tomb to finish preparing Jesus' body for burial. Any Friday ambitions for preparation were paused at sundown for Sabbath. Just as Mary Magdalene followed Jesus during His preaching ministry and supported His efforts financially, she came to the tomb to serve His body with generosity. When John records the events of that morning, she is the only one listed by name. She left quickly to tell Peter and John. (The other gospel accounts reveal the ladies heard from the angels about Jesus' resurrection). She then returned, and her weeping was interrupted by Jesus' appearance and words of good news. He is alive.

Jesus treated women with the utmost respect and gentleness during His time on earth. The most significant event in history was first discovered by a group of women. The first person Jesus told directly was a woman. Mary Magdalene was one of the first to "know Him and the power of His resurrection" (Philippians 3:10, LSB). Mary Magdalene's gratitude toward Jesus compelled her and her generosity defined her.

Today, I will...re-read one of the resurrection accounts (Matthew 28:1-15; Mark 16:1-13; Luke 24:1-12; John 20:1-18) through the perspective of the men and women at the tomb.

[1] https://en.wikipedia.org/wiki/Neil_Armstrong

FRIDAY

Tell

Today's Scripture: John 20:17-18; Matthew 28:19-20

After the World Trade Center South Tower was struck on 09/11, Stairway A was the only functional stairway near the zone of the crash. The 09/11 Commission Report acknowledged one person—later identified as Welles Crowther—went around screaming to others to follow him down Stairway A to safety.

Mary Magdalene proved to be a vital messenger about the details of Jesus' resurrection. She was the first messenger about the location of the tomb, telling the disciples where He'd been laid (Mark 15:45-47). Because its location was public knowledge, even skeptics could not deny the tomb was empty.

The Sunday morning of the resurrection began with fear, confusion, and continued heartache. When Mary Magdalene ran to tell Peter and John that Jesus' body was missing, she missed out on the angels' message to the other women about Jesus' resurrection. The angels said, "Do not be afraid." They were comforting the women's confusion over an empty tomb and their fright over the angels' appearance. But the angels' message also instructed them to tell the disciples that Jesus had risen. "Do not be afraid, go and tell."

Because Mary Magdalene ran to Peter and John, when she arrived back at the tomb, she was the first to hear directly from Jesus the message that He had risen. After her comforting interaction with Jesus at the tomb, "Mary Magdalene came, announcing to the disciples, 'I have seen the Lord,' and that He had said these things to her" (John 20:18, LSB).

"Do not be afraid, go and tell" was the message on that Sunday morning, and that has been the message to Christ's followers ever since. Before returning to heaven, Jesus would remind the disciples in these familiar words, "Go therefore and make disciples of all the nations, baptizing them in the name of the Father and the Son and the Holy Spirit, teaching them to keep all that I commanded you; and behold, I am with you always, even to the end of the age" (Matthew 28:19-20, LSB). Go and tell; do not be afraid.

Today, I will...list 2-3 people I can tell about the risen Savior and invite them to worship this Sunday. I will pray to God for help to overcome fear, then tell them about Jesus.

WEEK #46

Luke

DAVID SALISBURY

Christian—Noun or Adjective?

Today's Scripture: Colossians 4:14

As Paul concluded his letter to the Colossian Christians, he said "Luke the beloved physician greets you, as does Demas" (4:14). It is the only reference in Scripture to Luke's occupation as a doctor. While the training for a doctor in Paul's day was different from modern medical school, Luke had certainly received an education and would have had some type of medical practice before he became a Christian. He might well have continued to practice medicine while following Jesus, too.

For some followers (including the apostles), becoming a Christian meant leaving behind their old way of life. That included their occupation. Peter told Jesus, "We have left everything and followed you" (Matthew 19:27). Matthew walked away from his tax collection booth and apparently never went back (Matthew 9:9). But others continued to work after becoming a Christian. Paul, Priscilla, and Aquila all continued to make tents. They simply became Christian tent makers. Luke may have been one of the first Christian doctors.

That brings up an interesting question of grammar. Do we use the word *Christian* as a noun or an adjective? When I say "I am a Christian," I am using it as a noun. My identity is bound up in Jesus Christ and what He did for me on the cross. But I also know farmers, teachers, business leaders, and others who would say the word *Christian* describes how they do their work. They take Paul's words in Colossians 3:23-24 seriously, "Whatever you do, work heartily, as for the Lord and not for men... You are serving the Lord Christ."

Luke is a great reminder that our influence as Christians includes the good that we can do in the workplace. May the change Christ has brought about in us be so evident to everyone we work with that they can see our good works and glorify our Father in Heaven.

Today, I will...pray specifically that God would help me to let my faith shine at work. I will pray for my coworkers to come to faith as well.

TUESDAY

Taking Attendance

Today's Scripture: Luke 1:3-4

My home congregation had about 600 people. I know this because we had a board in the lobby with the attendance numbers. The first congregation I preached for averaged about 40 members. We had the same board, but it was at the front of the auditorium. Tracking attendance is nothing new. Even on the day of Pentecost, somebody stopped and estimated the count at "about three thousand" (Acts 2:41).

Luke was a numbers guy and regularly told us how many people were at different events. But numbers are facts and can't tell a story. If we have a youth event and 100 kids show up, that's a fact. But if we planned on 175, we would be discouraged. On the other hand, if we expected 50 kids, we would be delighted. Accurate numbers tell one fact but can never tell an entire story. The movement of the kingdom of God among men is a story, and our lives serving Him are part of that story.

While Luke gave us rough counts of how many people were fed by the loaves and the fishes or heard Peter's sermon on Pentecost, the number one stands out in Luke's writing. As much as Luke cared about the crowds of people, he wrote both volumes of his work for one person—Theophilus. The one person Luke cared about most was you, the reader! Luke said in Luke 1:3-4, "it seemed good to me ... to write an orderly account for you, most excellent Theophilus, that you may have certainty concerning the things you have been taught." Luke wanted you to be sure of the truth about Jesus!

I hope we keep taking attendance because every person we count is a soul that matters to God. But of all the people we count, we always want one more person to respond to the truth about Jesus. You matter to God, and He inspired His Word for you!

Today, I will...think about one person I can encourage with the gospel.

Research and Inspiration

Today's Scripture: Luke 1:1-4

Between the gospel of Luke and the book of Acts, Luke wrote 27.5% of the words of our New Testament—more than any other author. Luke was inspired by God through the Holy Spirit (2 Peter 1:21) to write what he did. But inspiration didn't mean Luke turned his brain off to write to us. He tells Theophilus in Luke 1 that many people had set out to create an accurate account of the ministry of Jesus. But in verses 3-4, he says, "It seemed good to me also, having followed all things closely for some time past, to write an orderly account for you, most excellent Theophilus, that you may have certainty concerning the things you have been taught." Luke did research to produce his two-volume set on the history of Jesus and the church.

I'm reminded that part of serving God means loving Him with all our minds (Matthew 22:37). It was Peter who advised Christians to be "preparing your minds for action" (1 Peter 1:13). Faith has never required us to check our brains at the door! Trusting God does not mean denying facts, but instead embracing the great truths of the universe. It makes sense to believe in God. And if I believe in God, then it makes sense to trust Him to know everything about this life and the next one. Luke did research for what he wrote because he knew that the gospel could and would stand up to intellectual scrutiny. When Peter and John are asked to testify before the Sanhedrin in Acts 4, they defend their teaching by saying, "We cannot but speak of what we have seen and heard" (v. 20). The faith they preached was not a new philosophy but the facts about Jesus Christ.

When we share the gospel today, we can logically appeal to thinking men and women to accept Jesus as Lord and Savior and obey His gospel.

Today, I will...glorify God for His power and wisdom evident in creation and the Bible.

One Friend

Today's Scripture: 2 Timothy 4:11

It's been said that "I'm sorry" and "I apologize" mean the same thing—unless you're talking to someone about their dog being run over. There are many situations where we don't know what to say. Sometimes we are so afraid of saying the wrong thing that we decide it's better to say nothing at all. When a child or a spouse dies or a pregnancy is lost, even good brethren may pull back because they don't have the right words. But saying nothing and not caring about someone's pain can feel the same to the grieving person. Our silence and absence can leave them feeling very alone during a very dark time.

There are lots of great ways you could describe Luke. He was a doctor and an inspired author of one of the gospel accounts. He was instrumental in helping the early church spread the gospel. But of all the ways you could describe Luke, Paul called him "beloved" in Colossians 4:14. Luke was Paul's friend—and sometimes those were in short supply! As Paul wrote from prison to Timothy, he told Timothy how some friends have deserted him, and others are away on kingdom business. He said in 2 Timothy 4:11, "Luke alone is with me."

Sometimes the greatest act of friendship we can show is just showing up. While Job's four friends did many things wrong once they started talking to him, the best thing they did was to come to him during his time of suffering. As Paul faced the uncertainty of his future in a prison cell, Luke remained with him. Luke wasn't a prisoner but stayed with Paul to comfort him. Even when you don't know the words to say, you can let a suffering brother or sister know that you love them.

Today, I will...find someone I can sit with at church or a shut-in I can visit. They will remember the time I spend with them more than any words that I can say!

FRIDAY

Tell Me the Story of Jesus

Today's Scripture: Luke 1:1-4; 24:25-27

The gospels are powerful accounts of the life and ministry of Jesus told by eyewitnesses. The story of who Jesus was and what He did in His life, death, and resurrection is life-changing for anyone who reads it. Matthew and John were both apostles of Jesus, and tradition says that Mark was a close companion of Peter, so those three accounts all come directly from people who saw and heard the events they told us about.

Luke was different. First, Luke was a Gentile. The other three writers were Jewish and grew up knowing about God and His will as expressed through the Hebrew Scriptures. They knew they were the people of God and were expecting the Messiah. But Luke didn't have any of that background. His first exposure to the God of Abraham, Isaac, and Jacob would have been hearing about Jesus. Second, Luke didn't appear to have met Jesus. He heard about Jesus from those who had seen Him. Luke came to faith because of the record others told him about Jesus as the Son of God. Luke believed the witnesses were reliable and that the story of Jesus was truthful. He eventually staked his life and eternity on the truthfulness of the story of a man he never saw personally.

In those two ways, Luke is a lot like us. Most of us grew up in a world where our first exposure to God's Word came through the New Testament and the story of Jesus. When we study the Old Testament, it is through Christian eyes, not Jewish ones. And all of us came to faith because we believed the testimony of those who saw Him firsthand. That may explain why Luke's gospel is so easy to relate to! Luke told us the story of Jesus so we can come to faith just like he did.

Today, I will...think about the people who taught me the gospel and be reminded of the faithful people through the ages that made it possible for me to know the truth.

WEEK #47

Paul

JIM GARDNER

Young Paul: Devout and Wrong

Today's Scripture: Acts 22:3-5

The apostle Paul began life as the child of Jewish parents in Tarsus, the capital city of the Roman province of Cilicia in what is now southeastern Turkey. He was named Saul at birth, presumably after King Saul, the most prominent historical figure in the tribe of Benjamin to which he belonged. Paul's parents were apparently wealthy. They were Roman citizens at the time of Paul's birth, when Roman citizenship was not yet widely extended in the empire outside of Italy. Although Tarsus was an important educational center itself, Paul described himself as having been "brought up" in Jerusalem and "educated at the feet of Gamaliel" (Acts 22:3), arguably the leading Jewish teacher in their world. We do not know whether his family moved to Jerusalem for the purpose of his education or if he was sent away to go to school there. His birth date is entirely unknown and could have been as early as perhaps 5 BC or as late as around 5 AD. He never mentioned any personal knowledge of the earthly ministry of Jesus, so it seems probable that he had returned to his native city after his education was completed, and only later came back to Jerusalem as an adult. He described himself as a young man as "advancing in Judaism beyond many of my own age among my people, so extremely zealous was I for the traditions of my fathers" (Galatians 1:14).

Saul not only approved of attempts to stamp out by violence what he regarded as the heresy of Christians, but also volunteered to extend those efforts to Damascus with official authority from the high priest in Jerusalem (Acts 9:1-2). That he was granted such authority suggests his status as a recognized leader.

Intelligent, bold, devoted, admired, and terribly wrong—the young man who would become the apostle Paul stands as a warning that great gifts and mistaken faith can do terrible things, but also as a promise that grace can forgive and transform. As he would say himself, "Christ Jesus came into the world to save sinners, of whom I am the foremost" (1 Timothy 1:15).

Today, I will...thank God for the grace that He extends to each of us, and for sending His Son to save a sinner like me.

Paul, the Witness

Today's Scripture: Acts 9:1-19

The conversion of Saul of Tarsus into Paul the apostle is one of the most striking evidences for the truth of the Christian religion. History contains no record of any similar event in which a leading figure on one side of a bitter controversy suddenly changes sides, offering as explanation his actual experience of divine rebuke.

The conversion story is recorded three times in Acts 9, 22, and 26. All three accounts emphasize the objective, factual basis on which the persecutor decided to become a believer and an apostle.

On the road to Damascus, there is no indication that Saul was troubled by feelings of guilt. He was doing what he thought was right on his own initiative, going beyond any duty others would have imposed on him. As he would many years later say to the Sanhedrin, "I have lived my life before God in all good conscience up to this day" (Acts 23:1). He did not change his mind about Christ because he felt guilty. He recognized his guilt only when he recognized that Christ was speaking to him from heaven. Thus it was Christ the Lord who he had persecuted.

Similarly, just as emotion did not cause but resulted from Saul's changed convictions, so sophisticated theological reasoning has no role to play in explaining the direct evidence of Saul's senses in Christ appearing and speaking to him. As with the other apostles, at the core of Paul's apostleship is his role as witness. He could have truly said with the apostle John, "that which we have seen and heard we proclaim also to you" (1 John 1:3). Many in the religious world think of Paul primarily as a theologian, even credit him with helping determine the nature of Christian faith. Nothing could be more wrong. Paul would have regarded the idea of a "Pauline theology" as an insult and accusation. As he wrote to the Corinthians, he could have chosen "lofty speech or wisdom," but determined "to know nothing among you except Jesus Christ and him crucified" (1 Corinthians 2:1-2).

Today, I will...focus on nothing, but "Jesus Christ and him crucified."

Paul, the Missionary

Today's Scripture: Acts 9

The narrative in Acts and Paul's comments in Galatians 1 make clear that immediately after his conversion, Paul began preaching the gospel he had so violently opposed. Paul's special credibility as a witness would have been as obvious then as it is today. He would persuade many to believe but enrage those who hated his beliefs. For many years, Paul's ministry and movements would be carried out under threat of violence.

Luke described Paul as being sent to Tarsus by the Jerusalem Christians in response to a plot to kill him (Acts 9:28-30). When Christianity began to prosper among Greek speakers in Antioch, Barnabas made the long journey to Tarsus to bring Paul to Antioch. Barnabas obviously felt Paul was uniquely qualified to reach the Greek-speaking world. Indeed, this marked a fulfillment of God's purpose for Paul that he had explained to Ananias even before Paul's baptism: "he is a chosen instrument of mine to carry my name before the Gentiles and kings and the children of Israel" (Acts 9:15). The church at Antioch would later send Paul and Barnabas on their missionary journeys (Acts 13:1-3).

Having found his true purpose, Paul stayed focused on that purpose throughout the rest of his life. He recognized that he "had been entrusted with the gospel to the uncircumcised" (Galatians 2:7), and that by being "entrusted with a stewardship" he was under the "necessity" of preaching (1 Corinthians 9:16-17). Yet, Paul wanted to do more than his duty. He preached "free of charge," but that is only one way in which he demonstrated the broader principle of doing not just what was expected of him, but whatever lay in his power, as a free will gift to God and to the lost, "that by all means I might save some" (1 Corinthians 9:18-23).

Today, I will...focus on the purpose that God has given to me. I will strive to not only do just what God expects, but to tackle anything that is in my path as a free will gift to God.

Paul, the Prisoner for the Lord

Today's Scripture: 1 Corinthians 7:17

Prison is the setting for a substantial portion of Paul's life as related in the New Testament. Of that portion of Acts that concerns Paul, almost half tells the story of Paul's brief imprisonment in Philippi and his long imprisonment in Jerusalem, Caesarea, and Rome. He wrote seven of his letters from prison. He almost certainly experienced imprisonments beyond those specifically mentioned in the Bible. Writing well before his arrest in Jerusalem, he described himself as having undergone "far more imprisonments" than those claiming to be apostles to the Corinthians (2 Corinthians 11:23). Ancient traditions exist of an imprisonment in Ephesus and a second imprisonment in Rome after the close of Acts.

All of us must serve God where we are, if we are to serve Him at all. Writing in the context of marriage and one's place in society, Paul set forth a general rule that applies in every aspect of life: "Only let each person lead the life that the Lord has assigned to him, and to which God has called him" (1 Corinthians 7:17). Paul lived what he preached. He used his freedom to serve the Lord; he used his imprisonment to serve the Lord. He described himself to the Ephesians as a "prisoner for the Lord" (Ephesians 4:1). This phrase recalls similar, more famous language in passages such as Romans 1:1 where Paul described himself as the "servant" of Christ, using a strong Greek word that meant a slave rather than a hired servant. Paul saw his duty to serve God as a constant truth, independent of circumstance, and harsh circumstances as the opportunity to demonstrate faith.

Writing from prison, he reassured the Philippians, "I want you to know brothers, that what has happened to me has really served to advance the gospel, so that it has become known throughout the whole imperial guard and to all the rest that my imprisonment is for Christ" (Philippians 1:12-13).

Today, I will...serve the Lord where I am.

Paul, the Sufferer with Christ

Today's Scripture: Philippians 3:7-8

Paul lived an unrelentingly intentional life. He compared himself to an athlete, entirely focused on winning the race, bringing every part of his life under subjection to achieve the goal (Philippians 3:12-14; 1 Corinthians 9:2-27). In this, he saw himself as following the example of Christ. When Paul exhorted the Corinthians, "Be imitators of me, as I am of Christ" (1 Corinthians 11:1), he did so in the context of teaching an unselfish willingness to give up one's own freedom and interests in the service of others. His rule was "Let no one seek his own good, but the good of his neighbor" (1 Corinthians 10:24).

Paul's rule for how to live was clearly based on Christ's example. "Have this mind among yourselves, which is yours in Christ Jesus, who, though he was in the form of God, did not count equality with God a thing to be grasped, but emptied himself, by taking the form of a servant" (Philippians 2:5-7).

By choosing to follow Christ, Paul gave up a safe and respected place in society for a life of hardship and peril. On an even more fundamental level, he gave up the right to view mistaken people merely as enemies to be justly punished, and assumed the burden of loving even enemies, whose salvation is worth any sacrifice.

God told Ananias before Paul's baptism that he would show Paul "how much he must suffer for the sake of my name" (Acts 9:16). Self-denial was always the only way that Paul could follow Christ, because it was the path Christ chose for Himself.

From his imprisonment in Rome, Paul summed up the meaning of his life: "But whatever gain I had, I counted as loss for the sake of Christ. Indeed, I count everything a loss because of the surpassing worth of knowing Christ Jesus my Lord. For his sake I have suffered the loss of all things and count them as rubbish that I may gain Christ" (Philippians 3:7-8).

Today, I will...identify how I suffer with Christ and thank God for his strength to endure.

WEEK #48

Timothy

LARRY ACUFF

MONDAY
Hope Is Full Assurance
Today's Scripture: 1 Timothy 1:1-2

In meeting God's people, the Bible says, "Paul, an apostle of Christ Jesus by command of God our Savior and of Christ Jesus our hope, To Timothy, my true child in the faith: Grace, mercy, and peace from God the Father and Christ Jesus our Lord" (1 Timothy 1:1-2). The writer is saying to Timothy, "...Christ Jesus our hope...." Hope is full assurance not uncertain desire. Looking at the above verses there are five things that makes the hope, of which Paul wrote to Timothy, full assurance.

God is the foundation of hope. The Psalmist wrote, "And now, O Lord, for what do I wait?

My hope is in you" (Psalm 39:7). Without God man has no hope. He is the foundation!

The Bible is the function of hope. "My soul longs for your salvation; I hope in your word" (Psalms 119:81). The Psalmist wrote, "Through your precepts I get understanding: therefore I hate every false way" (Psalm 119:104). When Paul wrote that Christ Jesus is our hope and God is the foundation of it, then it is conveyed unto us through His word.

Resurrection is the future of hope. Luke revealed to us, "Now when Paul perceived that one part were Sadducees and the other Pharisees, he cried out in the council,'"Brothers, I am a Pharisee, a son of Pharisees. It is with respect to the hope and the resurrection of the dead that I am on trial'" (Acts 23:6). I have hope because of the resurrection of Jesus Christ.

Weariness, however, is the failure of hope. Isaiah taught us, "You were wearied with the length of your way, but you did not say, 'It is hopeless'; you found new life for your strength, and so you were not faint" (Isaiah 57:10). Isaiah said, "you were wearied..." but you found new life in hope.

Today, I will...pray that my life will be strengthened because of the hope that is found in Christ Jesus.

TUESDAY
Prayer Sets the Pace
Today's Scripture: 1 Timothy 2:1-8

Paul called Timothy "my own son in the faith" (1 Timothy 1:2 KJV). In 1 Timothy 2, Paul gave him instruction in prayer. James told us, "The prayer of a righteous person has great power as it is working" (James 5:16). Paul wrote to the Thessalonians that we are to "pray without ceasing" (1 Thessalonians 5:17). In 1 Timothy 2:1-8, we are taught that prayer sets the pace.

The People of Prayer set the Pace. What kind of people are we? Verse 8 says, "I desire then that in every place the men should pray, lifting holy hands without anger or quarreling." My life is a reflection of Jesus. Is it a righteous life (1 Timothy 6:11)?

The Purpose of Prayer sets the Pace. Paul wrote the following: "Let us then with confidence draw near to the throne of grace, that we may receive mercy and find grace to help in time of need" (Hebrews 4:16). We pray for mercy! Our great example is Jesus Christ. When we examine His prayer in John 17, we find three specific things for which Jesus prayed: first, He prayed about His work (vv. 1-6); second, He prayed for His disciples (vv. 7-20); and finally, He prayed for all of us (vv. 20-26).

The Priority of Prayer sets the Pace. Paul urged "that supplications, prayers, intercessions, and thanksgivings be made for all people, for kings and all who are in high positions, that we may lead a peaceful and quiet life, godly and dignified in every way" (1 Timothy 2:1-2). Prayer must be a priority. Think about the words of the song, "Ere you left your room this morning, Did you think to pray?... Oh, how praying rests the weary! Prayer will change the night to day; So, when life gets dark and dreary, Don't forget to pray."

Today, I will...pray fervently, not only for my spiritual growth but for all men everywhere.

Be an Example

Today's Scripture: 1 Timothy 4:12

One of the great things about meeting God's people is the example that is set before us. There is probably no greater encouragement than that given by Paul to this young man Timothy. Here is what he wrote, "Let no one despise you for your youth, but set the believers an example in speech, in conduct, in love, in faith, in purity" (1 Timothy 4:12). It isn't hard to understand what Paul was writing to Timothy. Timothy is mentioned approximately twenty-eight times in the New Testament. Two of the New Testament books are addressed to him. Timothy was told to "set the believers an example."

Don't you love youth? Energetic, freshness in their approach to life, and often times very bold. There are also downsides, such as rashness and inexperience. Youth, many times, cannot see the result because of a lack of experience. However, Paul wrote to Timothy and instructed him to set the example in speech, in conduct, in love, in faith, and in purity.

We are an example in our speech. The holy Scriptures say, "Let the words of my mouth and the meditation of my heart be acceptable in your sight, O LORD, my rock and my redeemer" (Psalm 19:14). Also, we are told, "Let your speech always be gracious, seasoned with salt, so that you may know how you ought to answer each person" (Colossians 4:6).

We set the example in love. The writer of Corinthians reminded us that if we have not love, all our works are of no profit (1 Corinthians 13:3). Paul, in that thirteenth chapter, went on to describe for us the characteristics of love.

In Philippians 4:8, we are told to think about several things and one of them is purity.

Today, I will... pray that my life will be an example in speech, in love, and in purity.

THURSDAY
Finish Well

Today's Scripture: 2 Timothy 4:6-8

The apostle Paul's life is coming to an end. His second letter to Timothy was written sometime around AD 64-65 from a dark, damp Roman prison cell just before his death in AD 67. In the last chapter of 2 Timothy, this great apostle left some instruction about finishing well to his protégé. There are five tremendous truths in this chapter.

The first truth is to preach well! "Preach the word" (2 Timothy 4:2). Not everyone who is reading this is a preacher. However, everyone's life is a sermon. What sermon are we preaching?

The second truth is your life is a pattern shown. This is expressed in 2 Timothy 4:7 when Paul said, "I have fought the good fight, I have finished the race, I have kept the faith." What is the pattern of your life? I remember a gospel preacher who preached for a wonderful church for many years. Someone told me that you could set your clock in the mornings by observing the time that he came out of his house to go to his office. Every day at 8:00 a.m. he would come out of the door. Our lives are a pattern.

The third truth is that we are partners in the work of the Lord. Paul wrote, "Luke alone is with me. Get Mark and bring him with you, for he is very useful to me in the ministry" (2 Timothy 4:11). Paul to the Corinthians said, "Working together with him, then, we appeal to you not to receive the grace of God in vain" (2 Corinthians 6:1).

The fourth truth is that as Christians we have the presence of the Lord. Paul said, "But the Lord stood by me and strengthened me" (2 Timothy 4:17).

The fifth truth is that we praise God. Paul wrote, "To him be glory for ever and ever. Amen" (2 Timothy 4:18)

These five truths help us to finish well.

Today, I will...pray God will help to influence others and finish well.

Timothy's Life Relates to Christ

Today's Scripture: 2 Timothy 1:5

While Timothy was a faithful worker with the apostle Paul, he more so was a follower of the Lord Jesus Christ. Yes, he was Paul's son in the gospel, but above all, it was Christ Jesus that he sought to please. Timothy relates to Christ in three areas.

Timothy's life relates to Christ in submission, as Christ was submissive to the father. The Holy Scriptures record for us, "For I have come down from heaven, not to do my own will but the will of him who sent me" (John 6:38). In this way, Timothy related to Christ because he was submissive to the will of God. Timothy was a faithful servant as seen in Paul's writings. Paul wrote, "But as for you, continue in what you have learned and have firmly believed, knowing from whom you learned it" (2 Timothy 3:14).

Timothy's life relates to Christ in His service to the kingdom. Christ died for the church. The Bible tells us, "Husbands, love your wives, as Christ loved the church and gave himself up for her" (Ephesians 5:25). Christ not only died for the church, but He is the head of it (Colossians 1:18). Christ was a servant, "even as the Son of Man came not to be served but to serve, and to give his life as a ransom for many" (Matthew 20:28). Likewise, Timothy had a servant attitude as is seen in Paul's writing to the Philippians. He wrote, "But you know Timothy's proven worth, how as a son with a father he has served with me in the gospel" Philippians 2:22).

Timothy's life relates to Christ in His statements about Scripture. Jesus said, "You search the Scriptures because you think that in them you have eternal life; and it is they that bear witness about me" (John 5:39). Timothy had known the holy Scriptures from his youth up, as was recorded in the following passage, "and how from childhood you have been acquainted with the sacred writings, which are able to make you wise for salvation through faith in Christ Jesus" (2 Timothy 3:15).

Today, I will...pray that I may be like Jesus and like Timothy and be submissive to God and to His Scriptures.

WEEK #49

Titus

MIKE VESTAL

Singing Redemption's Song in Jerusalem

Today's Scripture: Galatians 2:1-5

Some people make a difficult situation even worse by being thoughtlessly guilty of spiritual arson, but not this man. He is mentioned by name only about twelve times in the New Testament. We should think of him as a troubleshooter, a bridge-builder, an individual with special gifts and abilities who had a unique talent to go to difficult places and circumstances and improve things by God's grace. While he was surely one of Paul's most trusted coworkers, his name never occurs in the book of Acts. His name was Titus.

We can read of Titus's value to Paul in a quartet of epithets from his pen. (1) He called him "my true son in our common faith" (Titus 1:4 NIV). (2) Paul referred to his restless spirit concerning the whereabouts of "my brother Titus" in 2 Corinthians 2:12-13 and to his subsequent joy in hearing from him. Finally in 2 Corinthians 8:23 he was called (3) "my partner" and (4) "fellow worker for your benefit." What amazing statements these were about Paul's feelings of closeness to this man and the bond they shared in Christ!

Titus first appeared in Galatians 2 in Jerusalem in a scene that must have been very heated. Paul would encounter individuals who had set out to distort the "freedom that we have in Christ Jesus, so that they might bring us into slavery" (v. 4). These teachers sought to add circumcision and various aspects of the law to God's conditions of salvation in Christ. As a result, Titus evidently became a test case or "Guinea pig" regarding the nature of the gospel and its spread among the Gentiles. Paul said, "But even Titus, who was with me, was not forced to be circumcised" (v. 3). Paul could not be more clear or forceful as he wrote, "to them we did not yield in submission even for a moment, so that the truth of the gospel might be preserved for you" (v. 5).

Today, I will...prayerfully meditate on the nature of the gospel and the preciousness of being family in Christ.

TUESDAY

Proclaiming Good News in Tough Places Like Corinth

Today's Scripture: 2 Corinthians 2:12-13; 7:5-15

One sees the name of Titus mentioned in 2 Corinthians more than any other book. Due to pride, immaturity, division, and quite serious doctrinal misunderstandings, the situation in the church at Corinth would have been extremely volatile. To make these matters worse, there was an element at Corinth who seemed to question Paul's credibility as an apostle and even his character.

Paul initially was unable to go to Corinth to address these and other matters personally; he instead sent Titus. To entrust such a task to Titus speaks volumes about him. Some otherwise seemingly reasonable Christians might have poured gasoline and lit a match on the circumstances at Corinth, but not Titus. He responded rather than reacted. He displayed godly character, mature judgment, and remarkable love for Jesus and His church. And the situation in the church at Corinth improved by God's grace!

According to 2 Corinthians 2:12-13 and 7:5, Paul was going through an exceptionally difficult time in his life and ministry. He was very concerned about how things were developing in Corinth and had not yet heard news from Titus. Paul stated, "But God, who comforts the downcast, comforted us by the coming of Titus" (7:6). Titus brought very encouraging news regarding the church (7:5-16). But it wasn't just the news Titus shared that made Paul greatly rejoice; it was the attitude he showed as he spoke of things! Paul wrote, "and not only by his coming but also by the comfort with which he was comforted by you, as he told us of your longing, your mourning, your zeal for me, so that I rejoiced still more" (v. 7). The good news Titus shared was enhanced by the spirit in which he shared it.

Today, I will...fervently pray for the ability to properly handle Scripture, to wisely evaluate circumstances, to ever display godly character and to respond rather than to react to what I observe. And may I always emphasize good news in Christ with joy!

Displaying Godliness and Integrity Throughout Macedonia

Today's Scripture: 2 Corinthians 8:16-24

Like many Christians today, Titus was a person on the go for Jesus. A collection was taken by churches throughout Macedonia (often predominately Gentile in nature) to help those in need throughout Judea (mainly Jewish in nature) who were experiencing a time of famine (Acts 11:27-29; Romans 15:25-27; 1 Corinthians 16:1-2). Churches throughout Macedonia, like Philippi, Thessalonica, Ephesus, and Corinth, all were involved in this effort. It would be crucial that those who received and delivered these contributions from Christians be men of unquestioned integrity and godliness. Paul knew that this matter would be one where Titus would particularly shine.

Paul described how Titus responded to this special need. He said I thank "God, who put into the heart of Titus the same earnest care I have for you. For he not only accepted our appeal, but being himself very earnest he is going to you of his own accord" (2 Corinthians 8:16-17). The apostle also added, "we carry out this act of grace that is being ministered by us, for the glory of the Lord himself and to show our good will. We take this course so that no one should blame us about this generous gift that is being administered by us, for we aim at what is honorable not only in the Lord's sight but also in the sight of man" (vv. 19-21).

It also is noteworthy how Paul related his closeness to Titus, "As for Titus, he is my partner and fellow worker for your benefit" (vs. 23). The apostle unhesitatingly gave his full endorsement to Titus as a man of godliness and integrity. One can only imagine the black eye given to the Lord's church if some of the men appointed to receive and deliver funds to those in need turned out to be unscrupulous or lacking in integrity!

Today, I will...seek to prayerfully apply an extra measure of godly character in all my financial interactions with others so that God be glorified and to show good will to all.

Setting Things in Order in Crete

Today's Scripture: Titus 1:5; 3:4-7

Titus 1:5 serves as a key passage to unlock the message of the book that Paul initially penned to this servant of God, "This is why I left you in Crete, so that you might put what remained into order, and appoint elders in every town as I directed you." To think of working at Crete as a "challenge" would have to be an incredible understatement! Every church has something that needs to be "put in order," even the best ones. But apparently, there was a massive load that needed to be "set in order" in the church at Crete.

Paul himself would state, "One of the Cretans, a prophet of their own, said, 'Cretans are always liars, evil beasts, lazy gluttons.'" Then he added, "This testimony is true" (Titus 1:12-13). All three chapters of the book stress the importance of truly living according to the gospel of Christ. For example, consider Titus 3:8 (NKJV), "This is a faithful saying, and these things I want you to affirm constantly, that those who have believed in God should be careful to maintain good works. These things are good and profitable to men." Elsewhere he wrote that Christians should "adorn the doctrine of God our Savior in all things" (Titus 2:10 NKJV).

Although the book is quite brief, it contains three rich but compact doctrinal statements. Titus 1:1-4 lifts up "the truth, which accords with godliness" and the "eternal life" it reveals in Christ through the proclamation of the gospel. What God has made possible in Jesus is part of a plan "promised before time began." Titus 2:11-14 speaks of how God's grace has appeared in the form of Jesus, but also that grace also "trains" or "instructs" about how to live properly. The grace that brings us to God helps instruct us after we come to Christ! Titus 3:4-7 speaks of God's grace coming from His love, mercy, and kindness.

Today, I will...seek to show God's love, kindness, and mercy to everyone I encounter.

Seeing Jesus in Titus

Today's Scripture: Titus 2:7-8, 11-14

C.H. Spurgeon said, "Our lives should be such as men may safely copy." This stunning thought certainly is true with Titus. If to see Jesus is to see the Father (John 14:8-9), then to see a Christian is to see something of Jesus (1 Peter 2:21-22)! How did Titus beautifully reflect the Lord?

Both Jesus and Titus were "Exhibit A" concerning the grace of God. Jesus is the reason the amazing grace of God is available to all men (Hebrews 2:9). Titus proved the grace of God was available to all men, including Gentiles, without submitting to circumcision and obedience to various aspects of the old law (Galatians 2:1-5). Both willingly accepted the controversy and sacrifice that came with making God's grace to others.

Both Jesus and Titus were troubleshooters and bridge builders who went to very difficult places and brought good news that transformed lives. Jesus left the glory of heaven, came to a sin-infested world, and brought salvation and hope (Matthew 1:21-25). Titus went to difficult places like Corinth and Crete and brought them salvation and greater hope in Christ.

Both Jesus and Titus were known for their compassion, godliness, and integrity in dealing with others. Jesus went about doing good (Acts 10:38). He truly cared for people (Matthew 9:36). Titus especially reflected these attributes when he went to the churches of Macedonia to help with the collection to help the needy of Judea (2 Corinthians 8:16-24).

Both Jesus and Titus were experts at setting things in order. Jesus made sinners right with God through the gospel (Romans 3:21-26). Titus encouraged churches and individual Christians to improve and mend areas that really needed attention (Titus 1:5). They both made places better for their having been there.

Today, I will...humbly pray "Let the Beauty of Jesus be Seen in Me."

WEEK #50

Dorcas

DAVID SPROULE

Thank God for Faithful, Christian Women

Today's Scripture: Acts 9:36

Take a moment and think through the Christian women mentioned by Luke in the book of Acts. While some may suggest that there are "not many" women mentioned in the book, the focus should not be on the quantity but on the quality of those included.

The text emphasizes that "women" were being equally converted to Christ as were the "men" (Acts 5:14; 8:12), including "leading women" in Thessalonica (Acts 17:4), "prominent women" in Berea (Acts 17:12), and "a woman named Damaris" in Athens (Acts 17:34). "Women" were also equally being persecuted for being Christians as were the "men" (Acts 8:3; 9:2; 22:4). Contrary to the opinion of some, women were given a prominent place in the record of the early church.

With the exception of Sapphira, who sinned against the Holy Spirit (Acts 5:1-11), the other Christian women named in the book of Acts are highlighted for their acts of service. Mary, the mother of John Mark, was hosting a church prayer meeting in her home (Acts 12:5-12). Immediately upon her conversion, Lydia from Thyatira opened her home in Philippi to Paul and Silas, in a display of Christian hospitality (Acts 16:14-15). Priscilla not only worked alongside her husband, Aquila, in their trade of tentmaking (Acts 18:2-3), but she also endeavored at his side in teaching and explaining "the way of God more accurately" (Acts 18:24-26). While they are not named, only one thing is stated about Philip's four virgin daughters—they "prophesied" (Acts 21:8-9).

Every time we read about a Christian woman in the book of Acts, she was either being persecuted for her faith or she was living out her faith in service to the Lord and His church. So it is with Dorcas, who is introduced as "a disciple" (Acts 9:36) and is presented as an active, faithful Christian woman, worthy of imitation by all Christians (men and women alike).

Today, I will...thank God for faithful, Christian women, whom I have known, and I will reach out to some of them to thank them and encourage them.

Fill 'Er Up

Today's Scripture: Acts 9:36

When it comes to Lydia and Priscilla, the text tells us the trade in which they were engaged. Lydia was "a seller of purple" (Acts 16:14) and Priscilla was a "tentmaker" (Acts 18:2-3). But when it comes to Dorcas, there is no mention of her trade (if she had one), but it focuses squarely on her activity as a Christian.

Dorcas was not just "a Sunday Christian." She did not merely "go to church on Sunday," then do her own thing the rest of the week. She was known and loved in the church because of what she did for others in the church. She had a reputation in the church...as a servant.

Luke told us that Dorcas "was full of good works and acts of charity" (Acts 9:36). There are several things of note in this statement. The expression "full of" denotes that she was "abounding in, wholly occupied with" doing good toward her brethren. One is reminded of the house of Stephanas, who had "addicted themselves to the ministry of the saints" (1 Corinthians 16:15, KJV).

The word used for "acts of charity" focused not just on "an act of kindness" (which it was) but also on the "attitude of compassion and mercy" behind the act. She was truly "tenderly affectioned" in her acts of love (Romans 12:10, ASV).

Finally, as we consider how "full of good works and charitable deeds" she was, the NASB helps us to recognize the tense of the verb at the end. Luke used the imperfect tense to emphasize that these were works that "she did habitually." Serving others was just her way of life. She was always doing good to and for her fellow Christians.

What an amazing example of a selfless servant, who filled her life continually with tenderly affectioned acts of service! In the annals of history, this is all we know about her.

Today, I will...examine myself and ask, "Am I known for what I do for others? Is my life continually 'full of' tender acts of service toward my brethren?"

WEDNESDAY

Pure Religion

Today's Scripture: Acts 9:39

It may be the case that when some Christians pass from this life, it is not noticed and they are not particularly missed. What a sad testimony that would be! Such was definitely not the case with Dorcas.

When Peter arrived in Joppa and was brought into the upper room, where they had laid this dear sister's body, the room was full. Luke told us that "All the widows stood beside him" (Acts 9:39). The use of the word *all* is interesting. Was this "all" of the widows in the church there, or "all" of the widows in the city, or simply "all" of the widows who were in the room? Whatever the case, the word *all* emphasizes a complete company of affected souls.

Luke informed us that "all" of these women were "weeping and showing tunics and other garments that Dorcas made." The verbs *weeping* and *showing* are both in the present tense, emphasizing an ongoing activity upon his arrival. Can you picture the intensity and emotion of this scene?

Who were these souls so affected by the death of Dorcas? Widows! They are mentioned in both verse 39 and verse 41. The "good works" and "charitable deeds" of which Dorcas had been "full" and was habitually doing were directed especially at one group of people in the church—the widows. Just as God Himself has a special place for the care of widows (Psalm 68:5), He calls upon His church to look out especially for widows.

Dorcas understood "pure religion," which God defines for us in James 1:27, "Religion that is pure and undefiled before God the Father is this: to visit orphans and widows in their affliction." To "visit" in this text is not merely dropping by to chat, but focuses on (1) going by to see what they need and (2) doing whatever they need done.

When we pass, will there be any widows who take notice and are deeply affected?

Today, I will...start a new habit to actively know the widows in the church and actively find ways to serve them.

THURSDAY
Even Death Can Be a Teacher

Today's Scripture: Acts 9:37-41

Such a precious Christian woman is endeared to us in the closing verses of Acts 9! One may be inclined to conclude that the most meaningful lessons we learn from Dorcas are from her life, which was "full" of loving, devoted service to some wonderful Christian widows. However, she also teaches us valuable lessons in her death.

The death of Dorcas illustrates clearly for us the distinction between a person's spirit and the body. Dorcas "died," so they "washed" the body and "laid" it in an upper room (9:37). Her body was there "with them," but when Peter arrived, the widows showed the many things that Dorcas made "while she was with them" (9:39). So, which was it? Was she with them or not with them? Her body was there, but she was not.

Like the beggar Lazarus in Luke 16, the body of Dorcas "died" but her spirit was "carried" away (Luke 16:22). The body is merely a "tent" (2 Corinthians 5:1, 4; 2 Peter 1:13-14)—a temporary dwelling place for the eternal spirit. When "the spirit" departs from the body, "the body...is dead" (James 2:26), but the spirit never dies (cf. Revelation 6:9-11). The body of Dorcas was with the people, but her spirit was with "God who gave it" (Ecclesiastes 12:7). Death is not the end—it is merely a transition.

One other lesson we learn from her death is the impact that our lives have, even after we are gone. Dorcas was remembered (and missed) for all of the things that she had done while she was alive, and through those widows, her influence continued to live. What was true moments after Dorcas died was true of Abel millennia after he died—"though he died, he still speaks" (Hebrews 11:4). Our "works" (1 John 3:12) live on after we are gone—the good and the bad.

Yes, there is much for us to learn, even in Dorcas' death.

Today, I will...examine myself, ensure that I am ready for my own death, and carefully consider the influence that I am leaving behind.

Dorcas and Jesus

Today's Scripture: Acts 9:36-42

As one reads the moving account of the life, death, and resurrection of Dorcas in Acts 9, it is difficult not to make so many connections between her and Jesus. As her spirit left her body at death, so it was with Jesus. As they carefully cared for her body, so it was with Jesus. As her resurrection led many to believe in the Lord, so it was with Jesus.

There are also many similarities in Peter raising Dorcas from the dead and Jesus raising Jairus' daughter from the dead (Mark 5:21-43; Luke 8:40-56). Peter imitated very closely the actions and words of Jesus from that occasion.

But the main connection to consider between Dorcas and Jesus is how much Dorcas looked like Jesus while she lived. The life of Dorcas is summarized in these words: "She was full of good works and acts of charity" (9:36). In the very next chapter, notice how Peter summarized the life of Jesus: He "went about doing good" (10:38). Dorcas had filled her life, no doubt, with good works because that was what she saw in her Savior.

It was regularly stated that Jesus was "had compassion" for them (Matthew 9:36; 14:14; 18:27; Mark 1:41). The original word indicates to "be moved with pity" and "with sympathy," even "to one's inwards." And what you notice every time that you read this in the life of Jesus is that He immediately acted on behalf of the person(s). His pity and compassion "moved" Him to "do good" to those in need.

We find the same in the life of Dorcas. She saw widows in need, and, like her Savior, it appears that she was "moved with compassion" to "do good" unto them, including the making of "tunics and garments" for them (9:39). This was not a random response. Surely Dorcas was seeking to emulate her Lord. What a lesson for us!

Today, I will...follow the example of Dorcas, who followed the example of Jesus, and train my eyes to see needs, my heart to feel pity, and my hands to move to help.

WEEK #51

Barnabas

VAN VANSANDT

MONDAY

Generosity

Today's Scripture: Acts 4:36-37

Acts 4:36-37 introduces us to Joseph, who was given the name, Barnabas, by the apostles. The name Barnabas means "son of encouragement." He was a Levite from Cyprus. He was a property owner, sold the land, and brought the money to the apostles.

For years I have made public remarks of hope, change, and growth, with the phrase: "When I grow up..." For today's purpose I will say, "When I grow up, I want to be like Barnabas." First, I would like to be a property owner willing to get rid of some of one's holdings, and "seemingly" feel no sting to let the profits go to benefit others.

Second, what a blessing to be able to allow those funds to be used without the need of guiding stipulations. Generosity is a trait of the Father, as well as His obedient Son. "For God so loved the world, that He gave ... "(John 3:16). Jesus would put it this way: "Greater love has no one than this, that someone lay down his life for his friends" (John 15:13).

When one sees this trait exemplified in the Father and the Son, it makes perfect sense for a follower to know this trait and make it part of their own way. Let me encourage all of us to find a way to have generosity and let it shine in us.

Today, I will...be encouraged by the example of Barnabas to pray for a heart of generosity and a willingness to seek out opportunity to be generous, and to follow through like he did.

Son of Encouragement

Today's Scripture: Acts 4:36-37

There is no doubt of the value of being an encourager. The Lord's church needs more encouragers today. It would be so easy to climb aboard the wagon of negativity. There are many things at this time that old devil would love to use to discourage us from God's plan and promises. One of those things is negativity.

Just listen ... "nobody works in the church like they used to ... young people do not even think about spiritual things anymore ... I know for a fact the preacher gets all his sermons off the internet ... " We could make a much longer list, but, I hope we see the point of the moment.

It would be so much better if one would take the road of Barnabas: "We just finished a great VBS, everyone was so busy and so helpful ... Our teens really stepped up this year ... Our preacher is really making an effort to deliver what we need to grow."

To be an encourager is a personal choice. "But you, beloved, building yourselves up in your most holy faith and praying in the Holy Spirit, keep yourselves in the love of God, waiting for the mercy of our Lord Jesus Christ that leads to eternal life" (Jude v. 20).

Today, I will...apply myself to an extra effort in being an encourager for the Lord.

An Advocate for Others

Today's Scripture: Acts 9:22-27

Saul of Tarsus has obeyed the gospel, increased in his spiritual strength, and was one who kept the unbelieving Jews, of Damascus, at bay while proving that Jesus was truly the Christ. Saul's life was in danger. Fellow believers helped Saul to escape Damascus.

Saul journeyed to Jerusalem, wanting to "join up" with the disciples. These fellow believers were afraid of him. They also did not believe that he was a "true" disciple. Acts 9:27 tells us that Barnabas stepped in with the third trait that is very dominant in his ways. Barnabas was an advocate for others.

Barnabas took Saul to the apostles. He told them of Saul's conversion. Saul had seen the Lord on the way to Damascus. Jesus had spoken to Saul, and Saul preached boldly, in the name of Jesus, while in that city. When one's life is being threatened, there may not be a better gift than an advocate—one who can step in and say for them what they cannot seem to say for themselves.

Maybe you know someone who needs just that from you. A go-between can be such a sweet gift. In our world today children need advocates. The elderly need advocates. Maybe you know a new convert who needs an advocate. Continuing in the Lord's church theme, let us make a list ... elders, deacons, elder's wives, deacon's wives, preachers, and ministers of every type could use an advocate now and then.

Today, I will...pray that I might be a better go-between for those I know who could use, or are in need of that kind of blessing.

Willing to Go Where He Was Sent

Today's Scripture: Acts 11

In Acts 11 our leading example of certain helpful traits receives an "order" to leave Jerusalem and go to Antioch. We are told that he went. Barnabas had a trait that was more than just "one" sided. As we study his movements, it seems that the more he did, the further down the depth chart he went.

While coaching high school ball a few years back, there was one young man who seemingly slid further and further down the bench as new players were added to the team and signs of certain skills seemed to shine brighter in the newer players. The young man went to the head coach and informed him of his view of things, and he told him he would be quitting. The young man was not real keen on the place he was asked to go." Therefore, he did not go.

It takes a certain kind of servant heart, team player mentality to just go where you are sent. Barnabas had this kind of heart. Someone has noted that early on it looked like it was Barnabas and Saul. As time went on, it became more and more, Paul and Barnabas. Being moved further down the bench did not seem to affect Barnabas as it did my young friend.

Being willing to go where you are sent, in the work of the church, may very well be viewed as a lesser position. Either as a lesser position you once held, or even a lesser position than someone else is holding. That old devil would love to take that and run with all of us.

Today, I will...pray to do a better job in going where I am sent and growing where I am planted, giving all glory to God the Father and Jesus Christ His Son.

Always Giving His Best
Today's Scripture: Hebrews 12:2

Our final lesson with Barnabas is one that would do well to be the ending of every series about God's people. This last trait is the one trait that may resemble the Lord the most. At every turn and with every opportunity, Barnabas gave his best. One might even say he gave his all.

Our Lord and Savior gave His very best, His utmost, yes even His all. When we ponder from whence our Lord came, when we think about the very plan of the Father, surely we all come to the same conclusion. Jesus gave everything—His best, His utmost, His very self.

Jesus' purpose in coming to this earth was to save mankind. To accomplish this great feat, according to the Father's plan, Jesus was going to have to give Himself. He would be called to go to the cross, carrying the sins of the world, dying for sins He did not commit, receiving judgment He did not deserve.

All claims against Him were false—they had no case. ·

In our short, quick look at Barnabas, we see a life lived, given, offered, and yes, sacrificed. Not for the whole world, but rather for the desire and will of the Father.

Today, I will...to be like Barnabas "when I grow up." In so doing I want to look more and more like Jesus. My prayer is to be more attentive to the Lord's will, rather than my own.

WEEK #52

Aquilla and Priscilla

KERRY WILLIAMS

Lifelong Kingdom Friendships

Today's Scripture: Acts 18:1-3

As citizens of the kingdom of God (i.e., members of the church), one of the sweetest rewards we enjoy in this life is fellowship with one another. Although Christianity can demand a great price for some converts, including estrangement from family and friends, Jesus promised His kingdom would provide us with unique relationships and a new family. In Matthew 19:29, Jesus told us, "And everyone who has left houses or brothers or sisters or father or mother or children or lands, for my name's sake, will receive a hundredfold and will inherit eternal life." One of these precious relationships for the apostle Paul was his friendship with Aquila and Priscilla.

Paul first met Aquila and Priscilla in Corinth (Acts 18:1-3) on his missionary journeys. The couple had been expelled from Rome by the decree of Emperor Claudius and had relocated to the Grecian city to ply their trade as tentmakers. Sharing the same faith, dedication, and profession with Paul, the three became lifelong friends, coworkers, and traveling companions. Paul frequently expressed his deep love for the couple, sending greetings to them in three of his letters, and expressing thanks for their loyal friendship, writing, "Greet [Priscilla] and Aquila, my fellow workers in Christ Jesus, who risked their necks for my life..." (Romans 16:3-4).

Paul's relationship with Aquila and Priscilla illustrates the relationships God intended for us to enjoy in His church. As strangers in this world, our Father knew we would need the support and encouragement of a spiritual family to survive and remain faithful. We must recognize how much we need one another in Christ rather than fussing over every minor annoyance. Solomon wisely observed, "Two are better than one, because they have a good reward for their toil. For if they fall, one will lift up his fellow" (Ecclesiastes 4:9-10).

Today, I will... express my love and appreciation for my brethren and thank God for the blessing of a spiritual family.

Approaching Disciples in Love

Today's Scripture: Acts 18:18-28

As believers, sharing the gospel is our divinely ordained responsibility as we "Go therefore and make disciples of all nations, baptizing them in the name of the Father and of the Son and of the Holy Spirit" (Matthew 28:19). This charge is never more difficult than when we must correct the doctrinal misunderstanding of a Christ-follower who, in sincerity, loves the Lord with all of their heart but is mistaken on crucial aspects of truth. How do we honor their faith and correct their misunderstandings without offending or turning them away?

Aquila and Priscilla perhaps provide the best Scripture example regarding this challenging question. In Acts 18, we read the story of Apollos, a sincere and bold advocate of Christ Jesus who had a limited understanding of conversion and salvation as he only knew of John's baptism and not the new birth through new-covenant baptism (Acts 18:25). They were impressed by his speaking and his zeal, and "explained to him the way of God more accurately" (Acts 18:26). We are not told of the details of their conversation. Still, from that point forward, Apollos was entirely accepted in the faith and works with Paul to build up the church in Corinth (1 Corinthians 3:6). Clearly, Apollos received their correction, was baptized, and subsequently taught the whole truth.

How were they able to convince Apollos? They approached him with love, gentleness, and respect. Although Apollos did not yet understand the whole truth, they honored the faith he had and lovingly built upon that foundation to correct his misunderstanding. While Apollos was not yet a Christian (he hadn't been born again), they recognized him as a "disciple" (follower). Paul did the same with the Ephesian believers in Acts 19, who knew only John's baptism, as the text names them "disciples" (Acts 19:1). This approach is respectful rather than combative, providing a model of how to approach religious people today.

Today, I will... determine to approach my religious friends respectfully as I strive to teach them the whole gospel.

309

WEDNESDAY
Women in the Kingdom
Today's Scripture: Romans 16:3-4

God has called all of His children to service in His kingdom. He created both man and woman in His image (Genesis 1:27), and has made no distinction between man and woman regarding our worth and importance to Him (Galatians 3:28). However, although we all have the same value, we do not all have the same roles. God has assigned men leadership roles in His church, thereby prohibiting women from such responsibilities as preachers and elders (1 Timothy 2:12). This truth is not well-received by our society. It has led some to conclude that God has excluded women from critical aspects of the faith, including our primary mission of evangelism. The example of Aquila and Priscilla shows that nothing could be further from the truth!

Aquila and Priscilla were prominent figures in the life of Paul, the "Great Apostle," who took the gospel of Christ to the Gentile world. He affectionately referenced them both as dear friends and coworkers in the kingdom, even thanking them for risking their lives for him (Romans 16:3). The couple was instrumental in the conversion of Apollos, who went on to be a great church-builder and evangelist (Acts 18:24-28). They are mentioned by name six times in the New Testament, and four of the six occurrences list Priscilla's name first before her husband. This detail does not, in any way, contradict the New Testament's teaching on leadership roles for men and women. It shows that both God and the apostle Paul held Priscilla in high esteem and greatly valued her work for the kingdom.

Today, I will... offer a prayer of thanksgiving for the godly women in my life and express my appreciation for their critical role in the kingdom.

Partnership in Ministry

Today's Scripture: Acts 18:2-3

The institution of marriage is like no other relationship available to us in this world. We love our children, brethren, and friends, but none of those connections compare to what God intended marriage to be. In Genesis 2:24, as Adam first looked upon Eve, he said, "A man shall leave his father and his mother and hold fast to his wife, and they shall become one flesh." These words describe a unique bond we can only share between a husband and wife. It is a lifelong connection as the two individuals grow together as one. In a single word, it is a lifelong "partnership."

Few marriages demonstrate the partnership God intends, especially in the service of the Lord, as we see in the biblical description of Aquila and Pricilla. The couple was instrumental in evangelism (Acts 18:24-28), coworkers and friends of the apostle Paul (Acts 18:2-3), traveling missionaries spreading the gospel wherever they sojourned (Acts 18:18), and people willing to risk their lives together for the gospel (Romans 16:3). They are mentioned together six times in the New Testament, but interestingly, not once is either of them mentioned individually. In the mind of the New Testaments writers, they were seen as one. Have you ever known such a couple—inseparable spouses who love being and working together and can't picture one without the other? Aquila and Priscilla show us what "becoming one flesh" can be and how beautiful such a relationship can be.

All of us who are married should strive to have the unity of purpose and commitment to one another demonstrated by Aquila and Priscilla. Those not yet married should search for a spouse with whom they can share a life of service to God.

Today, I will... thank God for my spouse and strive to involve them in my daily ministry, expressing my need for them to be all I can be for God.

Dedication to Christ's Passion

Today's Scripture: 1 Corinthians 9:16

This world places so much emphasis on things that, in the grand scheme of eternity, don't matter. As servants of God, it is imperative that we focus our priorities on those things that matter most to Him. To our God, one thing in this world is always at the top of His priority list—the souls of mankind! Father God sent Jesus to this world so that humankind might be saved (John 3:16). God desires that no person perish but come to Him and be cleansed (2 Peter 3:9). He gave the blood of Jesus as payment so that we could be washed in His righteousness (2 Corinthians 5:21).

We recognize God's great passion, as we have named the charge to go and preach "The Great Commission" (Matthew 28:18-20). Do we personally share our Lord's passion for the souls of mankind? Do we demonstrate that passion by practicing evangelism day by day? The apostle Paul exemplified God's passion for souls, saying, "For if I preach the gospel, that gives me no ground for boasting. For necessity is laid upon me. Woe to me if I do not preach the gospel!" (1 Corinthians 9:16). His desire to see men saved was so encompassing that he says that he would give up his soul to see Israel redeemed (Romans 9:3).

Aquila and Priscilla shared the Lord's great passion for souls. They were forced to leave their home in Rome because of their faith (Acts 18:1), yet still joined with Paul in evangelizing in Corinth, then traveled with him to do the same in Ephesus (Acts 18:18-19). They risked their lives to further the gospel (Romans 16:3) and hosted the church wherever they sojourned (1 Corinthians 16:19). They were "all in" for the cause of Christ Jesus. They devoted their entire lives to further His passion that humankind be saved. Is their passion our passion? Do we live it every day?

Today, I will... strive to be passionate for the souls of mankind and reach out to others with the gospel.

Additional TJI Titles Available

NEW!The Church Matters: A Book for Young Adults
NEW! Weekly Peace for Senior Saints
NEW! Reviving the Revival (Chad Ramsey)

The Living Word: Sermons of Jerry A. Jenkins
Before I Go: Notes from Older Preachers

Thoughts from the Mound (Jeff Jenkins)
More Thoughts from the Mound (Jeff Jenkins)

Beyond the Valley of Death (Jeff Jenkins)

All I Ever Wanted to Do Was Preach (Dale Jenkins)
I Hope You Have to Pinch Yourself (Dale Jenkins)

The Preacher as Counselor (Dale Jenkins and others)

Don't Quit on a Monday (Jeff & Dale Jenkins)
Don't Quit on a Tuesday (Jeff & Dale Jenkins)
Don't Quit on a Wednesday (Jeff & Dale Jenkins)
Don't Quit on a Thursday (Jeff & Dale Jenkins)
Don't Quit on a Friday (Jeff & Dale Jenkins)
Don't Quit on a Saturday (Jeff & Dale Jenkins)
Don't Quit on a Sunday (Jeff & Dale Jenkins)

Five Secrets and a Decision (Dale Jenkins)
Centered: Marking Your Map in a Muddled World
(Dale Jenkins)
On Moving Well: The Scoop-Meister's Thoughts on Ministry Transitions
(Dale Jenkins)
Praying Always: Prayers for Preachers (gift book)
(Jeff & Dale Jenkins)
You're Fired! Now What? (Dale Jenkins)

Keys to Effective Ministry (Jeff & Dale Jenkins)
A Minister's Heart (Jeff & Dale Jenkins)
A Youth Minister's Heart (Jeff & Dale Jenkins)

A Mother's Heart (Jeff & Dale Jenkins)
A Father's Heart (Jeff & Dale Jenkins)

Immerse: A Simple Look at Baptism (Dale Jenkins)
We Think You'll Love It Here (personalized for guests)

His Word (Daily devotionals from the New Testament)
His Life (Daily devotionals from Jesus' life & ministry)
My Life (Daily devotionals covering the Christian life)
His Family (Daily devotionals studying the church)
My Family (Daily devotionals studying the home)
Meeting God's People (Daily devotionals on Bible lives of faith)

Weekly Joy for Senior Saints

The Glory of Preaching (Jay Lockhart &
Clarence DeLoach)
Profiles of Faith & Courage: Interviews with Gospel Preachers
(Dennis Gulledge)
Me, You, and the People in the Pews (Tracy Moore)
From Mother's Day to Father's Day (Paul Shero)
Little Fish, Big Splash (Mark Neaves &
Shawn Weaver)
The Three Little Ministers (Philip Jenkins)
Choice Over Circumstance (Drake Jenkins)
Pocket Guide for Preachers: 1 Timothy
(Joey Sparks & Cole Wade)

Free Evangelism Resources by Jerry Jenkins:
God Speaks Today
Lovingly Leading Men to the Savior

To order, visit **thejenkinsinstitute.com/shop**

Made in the USA
Middletown, DE
13 May 2024

54275786R00186